WE CAN DO BETTER

WE CAN DO BETTER

How to Save America's Future—An Open Letter to President Clinton

Senator Paul Simon

National Press

B O O K S

Library of Congress Cataloging-in-Publication Data

Simon, Paul, 1928-
We can do better:
how to save America's future—an open letter to
President Clinton.
300 pp., 15 x 23 cm.
Includes bibliographical references and index.
ISBN 1-882605-14-4: $23.95
1. United States—Politics and government—1993-
2. Clinton, Bill, 1946-.
I. Title.

E885.S57   1994
973.929—dc20
94-32165
CIP

PRINTED IN THE UNITED STATES OF AMERICA

10 9 8 7 6 5 4 3 2 1

Dedication

To Ray Johnsen, my friend during our days at Dana College and a coworker since those days. His dedication and loyalty have meant much to me and the people we have served.

Acknowledgments

Like every author, I am grateful to more people than I can properly acknowledge, but among them are my wife, Jeanne, who has tolerated my isolation when I am writing a book, the mess I create in the process, and then serves as my critic; my brother, Rev. Arthur Simon, a helpful critic through the years; Joel Joseph, publisher of National Press Books, who suggested the idea for the book; Jackie Williams, who follows my manual typewriter inaccuracies and scribblings, and then types the final product; Christopher Ryan, who helped run down footnotes and missing data; and the following who read all or parts of my rough draft and made suggestions or helped contribute with information:

Heather Booth, David Carle, David Ellwood, Patricia Albjerg Graham, Peter Hadinger, Jayne Jerkins, Susan Kaplan, Jeremy Karpatkin, Peter J. Kelley, Brian Kennedy, Tom Lynch, Marc Mauer, Vicki Otten, Aaron Rappaport, Bob Shireman, Jonathan Stein, former Senator Paul Tsongas, Paul Volcker, Judy Wagner, Senator Paul Wellstone and Cheryl Young.

All of them helped in the final product, but the conclusions of the book are mine, not theirs.

I am grateful to Alan Sultan and Shawn Ortiz for promoting the book, and Debra Greinke and Jessica Weiss for their help in editing this book.

Most of all, I am grateful to you who read this book and share my concern about where our society is going.

Contents

Foreword

by Senator Paul Tsongas

$10,000 per second. That's how fast our national debt grows. By the time you finish reading this foreword, the national debt will rise by more than $1.2 million, far more than most people earn in a lifetime. The national debt, which currently totals over $4.6 trillion, is our running tab that our children and grandchildren will be left to pay. We are bankrupting future generations.

Confronted with the burdens of a monstrous national debt, skyrocketing tax rates, an aging population and runaway federal entitlement programs, tomorrow's Americans will live in a nation unable to compete in the world economy or adequately defend itself. Without action today, it is very likely this country will be embroiled in an ugly generational conflict early in the next century.

To ensure the survival of the American dream and avert a fiscal nightmare for our children, stopping the flow of red ink must become a priority in Washington. While some steps have been taken to repair our fiscal condition, much more is needed.

Fortunately, Senator Paul Simon understands the problem and is willing to fight for the benefit of future generations. If there is a central theme to these extraordinary letters to President Clinton, it is the sacred responsibility we have to preserve and protect our society for our future generations. Anyone who doubts his conviction need only look at his unwavering support for the balanced budget amendment.

Balancing the budget and restoring our fiscal foundation require that the nation make some tough choices. Too often in the past, politicians and citizens have practiced a "don't ask, don't tell" policy on the deficit. Elected leaders have been unwilling to discuss the true nature of the problem for fear talk of lower Social Security checks or higher taxes will mean defeat at the ballot box. Meanwhile, citizens have not accepted that entitlement programs like Social Security and Medicare that primarily benefit middle and upper income families are the principal cause of the deficit.

As a result of our hypocrisy we stand very close to the brink of economic catastrophe.

Representatives must be willing to educate their constituents about the choices we face and not always make decisions based on the short-term political benefit. Members of Congress should be concerned with the general interest, not special interests. Paul Simon provides an excellent example of that type of leadership for members of Congress.

Equally important, citizens must understand that balancing the budget cannot be done solely by eliminating waste and foreign aid. To balance the budget, entitlement programs such as Social Security, Medicare and farm subsidies must be reduced. Especially if the money is found to finance Simon's thoughtful initiatives for education, employment, crime reduction and other areas. In my work with the Concord Coalition, a bipartisan organization dedicated to reducing the federal deficit, I have found that most Americans are willing to accept reduced government benefits in exchange for a zero deficit and are willing to pay as they go for new programs that are really needed. The key to earning people's support is honestly discussing the issues.

Paul Simon recognizes that right now Washington is not participating in the debate on deficit elimination. It is therefore no surprise that many Americans remain extremely frustrated with their government.

Senator Simon has examined the choices and put forward his conclusions in an intelligent and compelling manner. Obviously, not everyone will agree with his ideas. Frankly, I have concerns about some of the proposals put forward in his book. However, I believe *We Can Do Better* makes a valuable and necessary contribution to the national debate and calls attention to the most pressing issue facing the country: our national debt. At the very least, his book will focus our leaders on the need to address this problem immediately.

Time is not on our side. We must act quickly. Paul Simon is right, we can do better. We *must* do better.

Paul Tsongas
Concord, Massachusetts

One

On Behalf of Chelsea, Reilly and CJ

Dear Mr. President:

This is the first in a series of letters written by someone who in the first year of your presidency ranked fourth from the top in percentage of Senate votes for your programs. I expect to be supporting your reelection effort enthusiastically in 1996. I applaud your efforts on everything from health care to reducing the deficit; from the earned income tax credit that helps our poorest workers to leadership in improving the way we will finance assistance to students in higher education.

I am in my nineteenth year in Congress. I saw this nation languish for twelve years, and now I am eager to make up for lost time, not only to help you do better than the two previous administrations, but also to improve what is taking place now in Congress and the executive branch under your leadership. These letters are one person's effort to step back, survey the scene, and speak frankly about where we should go as we near the middle of your first term as President, in a nation of huge needs and huge potential.

One of the dangers of being President or a member of the United States Senate is that we can become so caught up with the latest polls, or today's mail, or the pleadings of our staff on the issue of the moment that sometimes we fail to focus on the long term—where we are and where we must go.

There is a relatively simple test that each of us in public life can apply—a test that can help put our daily activities into perspective. You can look at your fourteen-year-old daughter Chelsea, and I can look at my four-year-old granddaughter Reilly and my infant granddaughter Corey Jeanne, now called CJ by my son and daughter-in-law. We should ask ourselves if what we are doing will build a better future for Chelsea and Reilly and CJ and all their counterparts in this nation and around the world.

Applying that test is not always simple, but it can help in decision making. As proposals cross your desk, asking the question, "How will this affect the future of my daughter and other children of this nation?" can provide guidance in a surprising number of cases. That question, for example, elevates education as a priority and reduces the importance of matters with short-term appeal but no long-term benefit. As you look at Chelsea's world and personalize your decision making, ask yourself too how well our democratic process is working, whether it is responding to the needs of her future and that of her classmates in the nation.

For example, Chelsea's grandfather, your father-in-law, died after a serious stroke. But what about those who, after a similar disability, have to stay in a nursing home for two years or longer? Because of your service as President, you would be able to afford a nursing home for a loved one, but even as Governor of Arkansas, with a salary of $30,000 a year, that would have been difficult. For many Americans it is impossible. Even your fine proposal for health care does not take care of that eventuality.

Overall your record as President is a good one, a solid one. I am proud of my support for your election. It is already clear that you will go down in history as a better-than-average President, a President who tackled key problems deferred by earlier administrations. But I would like to see the history books use the adjective "great" when describing your presidency, and there is the possibility that will happen. Whether that happens is, in large measure, not my decision nor that of those who will write history, but yours. Events that we cannot foresee will help history reach a verdict, but you play a role in shaping those events.

The path to greatness does not wend its way through polls and its direction may not always please the media. Remember, too, that as politicians, you and I like the applause of crowds, but the sound of applause dies quickly and will not resonate in history books. You will serve yourself and the nation well by asking not how a certain policy is playing in Connecticut or Illinois or Wyoming, but how it is affecting the future of Chelsea and any grandchildren she may have one day. If you ask that question frequently, the nation will be well served and you can move from a good presidency to a great presidency.

It is with that hope that I write these letters. As a nation, we can do better, Mr. President.

Sincerely,

Paul Simon

Two

Reforming Campaign Financing

Dear Mr. President:

The mixture we have of money and politics undercuts our democracy. This issue, Mr. President, is fundamental. Those with power and wealth use our democratic process to add to their power and wealth. And the public sees a distorted system that should address fundamental problems but doesn't. What aggravates the public and intensifies its cynicism is not the unpopular vote a Senator or House member casts—the public does not expect us to agree with them at all times—but there is the belief that many legislative decisions are made because of heavy campaign contributions. Prior to his conviction on several charges of fraud and embezzlement, when reporters asked Charles Keating, a generous donor to political campaigns, whether the hundreds of thousands of dollars he contributed to campaigns influenced the conduct of the recipients, he replied, "I certainly hope so." That's the way the system works.

In addition, people in politics spend too much time raising money. If it were only the fact that we waste the most precious resource we have, time, that would be bad enough, but the methods of financing campaigns pervert the democratic process and do not serve the nation's needs. You have had your share of experiences with this demeaning system.

The campaign finance reform bills passed by the Senate and House in 1993 offered slight improvements but gave us thin soup, when what we need is meat and potatoes—genuine reform. You need to press harder to make the public see the flaws in our present system and understand that it needs wholesale change, and soon.

Bought and Paid For

Over and over on the Senate floor, I see the process that should be serving the public being twisted to serve those who contribute to our campaigns. The public senses this. Their perception is of people donating money that buys votes in Congress or contracts and appointments from the executive branch. The practice usually is not that crude or direct, but too often the net effect is about the same. This is not a new phenomenon. In his *Decline and Fall of the Roman Empire,* Edward Gibbon wrote more than two centuries ago: "The wisdom and authority of the legislator are seldom victorious in a contest with the vigilant dexterity of private interest."[1] He wrote of ancient Rome, but he might well be speaking of modern America.

Here's an illustration from my recent experience: I voted with you on the North American Free Trade Agreement, widely known as NAFTA. I started the process uncertain as to how I would vote, reading all I could, finally coming to the conclusion that it would create jobs and serve the nation's interest. After going through the studies by various groups, I decided that it was not even a close call. For the cause of this nation's working men and women, for our economic future, and for the cause of better relations with our neighbors, I supported NAFTA. But my long-time friends in the labor movement were not happy, and one respected official told a small gathering that I had been the recipient of more than $600,000 in contributions from them in the last election. He implied clearly that I had been bought and paid for and that there was something unethical about my voting against those who had been so generous to my campaign. Another time, when I served in the state legislature, someone asked me how I could vote against his measure, involving some point of the law about monuments in cemeteries, when he had donated $200 to my campaign. I volunteered to write a check giving him his money back. He declined. Years later, someone who had raised money for me said that he felt I owed him a federal judgeship. He does not have the temperament to be a good federal judge, but if the call had been marginal, his comment to me, no matter what his qualifications, would have precluded me from recommending him for a judgeship.

This system affects all of us. I have never made a promise involving my official duties in return for a campaign contribution. But if I arrive home late at night or at a hotel in Chicago at midnight and there are twenty phone calls waiting, nineteen of them from people whose names I do not recognize, and the twentieth from someone who gave me a $1,000 campaign contribution, at midnight I will not make twenty phone calls, but I might make one. Which one will I make?

You know the answer. And that means that the financially articulate have an inordinate access to policymakers, including to those who are the most careful on how these matters are handled. But what about the unemployed person who needs access, who probably does not follow the intricacies of legislative maneuverings and certainly will not make a significant campaign contribution? That person is lost in the process. That is the reason I have so many town meetings in Illinois, so that access is there for everyone, but that is a weak substitute for fundamental reform. The present system causes what former Representative Henry Reuss of Wisconsin calls "a psychological mortgage on members."

Are there no pluses to the present system? There are some, but the liabilities far outweigh the assets. When people contribute, they feel more involved in a campaign and are more likely to take an active role. One of the ironies is that a free political rally for a candidate for the U.S. Senate, for example, usually draws a modest crowd. But if there is a charge of $100 a plate for a dinner, and a reasonably effective committee selling tickets, there will be a larger crowd, and those gathered tend to be opinion molders. That may be more a commentary on the nature of our political meetings than a tribute to fund-raising dinners.

The traditional political rally is designed to enthuse the party faithful and often fails to do even that. The usual "We're all good and they're all bad" speeches turn off independents, and the free (and usually noisy) beer-and-burgers events appeal to the physically hungry more than the politically hungry. And you and I both know that no one is more certain of his or her position on any number of issues than an uninformed citizen who has had six beers.

One of the positive things you did, Mr. President, during your campaign was to shift the significant dialogue away from the political rally and over to the television and radio talk shows. Not only did you reach much larger audiences, you partially bypassed the political reporters who tend to ask process questions rather than issue questions. The woman on the call-in program whose husband is dying of cancer asks questions about health care, and that reflects the concerns of the American public. The reporter who asks why you slipped four points in the latest poll is straining to find some new angle to a story because he or she has heard you give essentially the same speech for the twentieth time. My instinct is that if political rallies were more reflective of the talk show format, with genuine dialogue, there would be more interest and greater understanding of the issues. The danger with the nature of today's political rallies is that they encourage massive oversimplification of complex issues and are too easily abused by small-time demagogues.

Reforming Presidential Campaign Funding

The funding of presidential races offers an example of genuine reform—and also demonstrates the reality that reform is never a fully completed process, that reforms eventually must be reformed. In a presidential primary, matching funds are available to candidates who raise at least $100,000 in twenty states in individual contributions of $250 or less. That helps candidates of limited means and is good. But the rules under which the funds can be spent are unworkable, as the Federal Election Commission acknowledges.

The great problem—where additional reform is needed at the presidential level—is in the fall run-off after the conventions. In your race against former President George Bush in 1992, you both received a grant of $55.2 million from the check-off that citizens may use when filing their federal income tax forms. That is the amount a candidate should spend in the general election, and for several elections after its passage it worked that way. But soon "soft money" entered the picture, money given by corporations, labor unions (neither of which can give directly to federal candidates), and individuals, all of whom donate to the national and state political parties and to their offshoots. In 1992 the national parties received $67.8 million ($36.2 million for Republicans, $31.6 million for Democrats) in soft money, and 43 percent of this soft money came in contributions of $50,000 or more.

The rules for disclosure of "hard money," direct contributions to federal candidates, are good and strict, as they should be. The rules on disclosure for soft money are considerably weaker. The amounts given to state parties and their creations in 1992 still have not been totaled and may never be. The soft money hemorrhage has significantly weakened presidential finance reform and should be halted.

The congressional campaign reform legislation that passed the House and Senate in 1993, in differing versions, does offer slight improvement, but the emphasized word must be slight. To achieve significant improvement we should shift the focus.

There has been a preoccupation with the political action committees (PACs) as the great source of evil. I would vote tomorrow to get rid of PACs, but if the aim is reform, you can place that one far down the list of changes that would really make a difference. In other words, if the aim of campaign finance reform is to score 100, give two points to eliminating PACs, with ninety-eight to go.

There are even some good things about PACs. For one thing, they can be a means for small donors to contribute. Also, at least now, if the Jones Furniture Manufacturing Company, of which Robert Smith is the president (all names are fictional), gives a House or Senate member $1,000 from its PAC, that donation is listed and clear for all to see. But if the present funding system is not dramatically altered, and the Jones Furniture Manufacturing Company has a serious legislative interest, eliminating the PAC will not stop this company's efforts to buy access to lawmakers. If the PAC is eliminated, Robert Smith's wife, Nancy Smith can donate $1,000, listing her occupation as "housewife," and the public will know almost nothing about the source of funds. And with the current growing trend of women not changing their names at marriage, Nancy Smith may well be listed as Nancy Bartholomew, and the trail to the real source of funding for the campaign becomes even fainter.

The other side of the story, however, is that PACs contribute overwhelmingly to incumbents. Even those who manage to offend some of the major sources of funds are helped more by PACs. Let me immodestly use myself, again, as an example. Because I have voted for many cuts in defense spending, sponsored legislation to bring insurance companies under the antitrust laws, have not voted with the big oil companies, and have favored politics generally not supported by the American Medical Association and other big contributors, my percentage of contributions from PACs has been well below average for an incumbent: 17 percent of my campaign contributions came from PACs in my last race, compared to an average of 36 percent for my Senate colleagues, exempting Senator David Boren of Oklahoma and Senator John Kerry of Massachusetts, neither of whom accept PAC contributions. In my 1990 race against Representative Lynn Martin, who later became Secretary of Labor, she received $1,193,942, from political action committees compared to my $1,480,221, a far above-average amount for a challenger. This undoubtedly helping my funding: The polls showed me winning. PACs don't like to offend incumbents —and they love winners. Some of those who contributed heavily to my opponent early in the election assured me that after the election, they would contribute to me. And they did.

What we need is public funding of campaigns. Anything short of this may improve the system a little, but only a little. If this idea is properly planned and clearly presented, it will have overwhelming popular support. Political leaders are correct when they piously say, "Opinion polls show that when the public is asked if they favor using taxpayers' money to fund campaigns, they overwhelmingly reject the idea." And then these same political leaders say that they will stand with public opinion "even though I would benefit from a change in the system." What they do not say is that incumbents recognize that the current system is strongly tilted toward reelecting them. Plus there is the never expressed but clear thought on the part of many: "Whatever system got me elected must be pretty good." My experience at town meetings in Illinois is that when the idea of public campaign funding is explained, people are overwhelmingly for it. What is needed is leadership to educate the public about the significance of such a change for them. The public pays for elections now but in the worst possible way: through distorted priorities that reflect law-making for donors rather than law-making to meet the nation's needs.

Senator John Kerry of Massachusetts introduced an amendment that six of us co-sponsored, calling for a system of public financing of Senate and House races. He proposed a voluntary $5 donation that anyone filling out a federal income tax form could check off and contribute toward campaigns, with no private contributions permitted, except for limited donations in the event of a primary contest.

First, Senator Kerry explained the problem with two illustrations:

> The LTV Corporation and the Wheeling-Pittsburgh Steel Corporation both lobbied aggressively for legislation that facilitated their claim to $144 million in tax refunds, despite the fact that prohibitions against those refunds existed where a corporation had done what those very corporations had done, which is cut off the pension plan payments to retirees. So they spent $201,304 in very targeted campaign contributions, some of them directed to two key Senators on the very legislative committees pertaining to that legislation. And all of those companies that have revoked the pensions for over 100,000 retirees, were allowed to claim relief under the new law in a special provision put in for them

by the committee on which those two legislators sat.[2]

Now, whether or not those two legislators did it, the appearances of impropriety screamed out at everybody so much that newspapers and others made direct allegations of impropriety.

Another example:

> Northrop Corporation sent well over $250,000 in PAC money to Congress in 1988. And it did so literally at the very moment that the Tacit Rainbow project came up in the Senate. Several thousands [of] dollars were contributed directly to the campaign of a chairman of one of the committees of jurisdiction. And although the anti-radar project had failed four flight tests [and] it had accrued enormous cost overruns, $180 million was budgeted for its continued development and the conflict of interest at the level of appearance once again surfaced in the press.

Then Senator Kerry explained the logic of his amendment:

> Think of what it would mean in this country to have the general election campaigns of the U.S. Senators funded by $5 contributions from anonymous people. You do not know who gave you the money. People who care about liberating their Congress from the special interests are the ones who gave it. But whether they be Democrat, Republican or Independent, they have given it because they want us to end the charade of pretending we are trying to set up a system that will help challengers, when in fact the current system is so anti-challenger it is incredible.[3]

To no one's surprise, the amendment lost 60-35. All thirty-five Senators voting for the amendment were Democrats, unfortunately. This issue should transcend partisan politics. That thirty-five Democrats bucked the pressures and supported it signals that this is an important battle for the public interest that can be won. One article calling for public financing observed: "Neither Congress nor the President should be looked to as the engine of reform."[4] The authors suggest there really has to be a grassroots movement to bring about change. While I strongly favor any public support that can be generated, the reality is that this issue is complicated enough that there will not be any sizable grassroots call for change. However, more than one-third of the Senate is willing to support this needed reform. If you as President of the United States came aboard strongly on this—with one-tenth the effort that you and your staff put forward so effectively on NAFTA—the measure would pass the Senate and the House.

The Honor Roll of Senators who voted for the Kerry amendment:

Daniel Akaka	Hawaii
Joe Biden	Delaware
Jeff Bingaman	New Mexico
David Boren	Oklahoma
Barbara Boxer	California
Bill Bradley	New Jersey
Dale Bumpers	Arkansas
Robert Byrd	West Virginia
Kent Conrad	North Dakota
Tom Daschle	South Dakota
Dennis DeConcini	Arizona
Chris Dodd	Connecticut
Russ Feingold	Wisconsin
John Glenn	Ohio
Tom Harkin	Iowa
Daniel Inouye	Hawaii
Ted Kennedy	Massachusetts
John Kerry	Massachusetts
Frank Lautenberg	New Jersey

Pat Leahy	Vermont
Harlan Mathews	Tennessee
Howard Metzenbaum	Ohio
Barbara Mikulski	Maryland
George Mitchell	Maine
Carol Moseley-Braun	Ilinois
Daniel Patrick Moynihan	New York
Claiborne Pell	Rhode Island
David Pryor	Arkansas
Harry Reid	Nevada
Don Riegle	Michigan
Paul Sarbanes	Maryland
Jim Sasser	Tennessee
Paul Wellstone	Minnesota
Harris Wofford	Pennsylvania

It is not only the pandering to big contributors that is wrong, it is the huge amount of time wasted by candidates, including incumbents, on raising money, time that should be spent becoming more knowledgeable about the many complex issues. In my last race for the Senate, I raised $8.4 million. But on a per capita basis for the number of voters in the state, mine was one of the least expensive races. Here is the breakdown for the 1990 Senate races, with the amount winners and losers spent, divided by the total Senate vote for that state (with the opponent's expenditure in parentheses):

Winner Spending Per Vote (Opponent's Spending)

Joseph Biden, D., DE	$14.16	($1.34)
Ted Stevens, R., AK	8.52	(zero)
John D. Rockefeller IV,D., WV	6.56	(0.06)
Max Baucus, D., MT	6.54	(2.34)
Claiborne Pell, D., RI	6.49	(5.65)
Jesse Helms, R., NC	6.45	(3.77)
Larry Pressler, R., SD	6.43	(1.76)
Alan Simpson, R., WY	6.35	(0.04)
Mitch McConnell, R., KY	5.54	(3.20)
Tom Harkin, D., IA	5.36	(5.15)
Larry Craig, R., ID	5.23	(1.72)
Daniel Akaka, D., HI	5.04	(6.86)
Bill Bradley, D., NJ	4.93	(0.41)
Robert Smith, R., NH	4.87	(1.10)

Pete Domenici, R., NM	4.73	(0.09)
James Exon, D., NE	3.96	(2.45)
Hank Brown, R., CO	3.60	(1.90)
Bennett Johnston, D., LA	3.57	(1.87)
William Cohen, R., ME	3.02	(3.14)
Howell Heflin, D., AL	2.90	(1.56)
Carl Levin, D., MI	2.71	(0.94)
John Kerry, D., MA	2.69	(2.24)
Phil Gramm, R., TX	2.56	(0.44)
Strom Thurmond, R., SC	2.55	(0.01)
Daniel Coats, R., IN	2.47	(0.72)
Paul Simon, D., IL	2.36	(1.51)
Mark Hatfield, R., OR	2.15	(1.35)
Albert Gore Jr.,D.,TN	2.08	(0.01)
David Boren, D., OK	1.55	(0.16)
Paul Wellstone, D., MN	0.74	(3.44)
Nancy Kassebaum, R., KS	0.52	(0.02)

Here's another flaw: Four incumbents in 1990 had no opposition: David Pryor of Arkansas, Sam Nunn of Georgia, Thad Cochran of Mississippi, and John Warner of Virginia. All are good legislators, but it is reasonable to assume that if we had a system in which an opponent would have the same amount of money to spend as a sitting Senator, the incumbents would have been challenged and the process of democracy would have been aided. No-choice elections are not elections.

As you look at the figures for the 31 contested Senate races, the person with the greater campaign treasury won in all but three. In all but three cases also the sitting senator outspent (usually by a substantial margin) the nonincumbent. And in all but one case, the sitting senator won.

Time and Money

People ask, how do I raise $8.4 million for a Senate race in Illinois? Not easily. I spend time in my home state but I also travel to New York, Los Angeles, and other cities where I can pull together a handful of people to raise funds. Particularly in an election year (which is every other year in the

House), I'll spend an hour or two on the telephone almost every day, raising funds. Because it is illegal to do this from the Senate and House offices, that also means spending ten or fifteen minutes getting to and from a nearby nongovernmental office to make the calls. Each year, thousands of people who visit the Senate and House chambers when we are in session are appalled at the few members who are on the floor participating in debate. Part of that is because committee meetings are often going on at the same time. (In this one respect, state legislative bodies have better rules. When state legislative bodies meet, most members are present to hear the debate.) But the visitors in the gallery who are appalled at the small numbers on the floor of either the House or Senate would be even more appalled if they knew this reality: If they are visiting the chambers in an election year, in all probability there are more House and Senate members making phone calls to raise money at that point (except for the time we are casting votes) than are on the floor of either chamber. Would we be serving the public better by listening to and participating in debate rather than making phone calls to raise money? To ask the question is to answer it.

Authors Ellen Miller and the late Phil Stern exaggerate when they wrote: "Money has become the medium of political participation in America today."[5] But that is closer to the truth than it should be. And they make this valid point: "We would never allow competing litigants to pay jurors or judges. Similarly, self-interested private money has no place in our public legislature and elections."

It is not only the campaign contributions that a candidate receives that can influence votes in the Senate and House, it is also the awareness of the money that can be shifted to the opposition candidate and used against an incumbent. "What a great thirty-second commercial they can use against me on this vote" is a sentiment heard over and over when members cast votes they believe to be in the national interest, but politically imprudent.

One senator's chief of staff told me: "Most senators would much rather ignore the special interests, but under the present rules of financing campaigns, they cannot." All of us belong to some "special interests." Teachers, for example, should not be ignored because they are a special interest. But too often, the larger the campaign purse, the greater the influence in the political process.

One of the finest persons ever to serve in the United States Senate, Paul Douglas, used to quote an unknown English poet:

> The law locks up both man and woman,
> Who steals the goose from off the Common.
> But lets the greater felon loose,
> Who steals the Common from the goose.

One of the influential men of the nineteenth century, British author John Stuart Mill, wrote:

> One of the greatest dangers of democracy . . . lies in the sinister interest of the holders of power: it is the danger of class legislation; of government intended for . . . the immediate benefit of the dominant class, to the lasting detriment of the whole. And one of the most important questions demanding consideration . . . is how to provide efficacious security against this evil.[6]

It is an evil we have not yet addressed effectively.

The old line of finding truth in humor is true in the observation of Ronald Reagan (though no friend of campaign financing reform): "I thought politics to be the second-oldest profession. I have come to realize that it bears a very close relationship to the first."[7]

Rush Limbaugh is not my favorite authority on most matters, but listen to his response to a question from a writer for the *National Review* on whether he would ever seek public office:

> I have no desire [to do it]. Primarily because . . . to be elected to anything, you have to walk around like this—with your hand out. And you have to beg people to put something in it. Somebody always does, and they want repayment. And not with dollars. It's going to be with your soul, it's going to be with a portion of your soul. I don't look at it as fun.[8]

But some who read these words may ask, "If the system is that bad, why do you use it?" Former Senator William Proxmire of Wisconsin is the only member in recent history who ran and got reelected without raising campaign funds. Had he not chosen to retire, he would have been reelected again. After my election to the Senate, I approached him about the idea of running without fund-raising in Illinois. In strong terms he advised me against it. In a state with a smaller population like Wisconsin, he told me, it is difficult but possible, but it would be impossible in a state with the population of Illinois. That means that unless a person considering a Senate race is independently wealthy—and I am not—a candidate depends on contributions to raise the money necessary for a campaign and has to use the present system, bad as it is.

There are those who argue that a change to public financing will help Democrats more than Republicans, because generally Republicans have an easier time raising money. Opponents of public financing for presidential campaigns used that same argument, because Republicans generally collected and spent more in presidential races than Demo-crats. Since the income tax check-off reform passed, we have seen three Republican presidential victories and two Demo-cratic wins, including yours. Because the House has been in Democratic hands since 1955, and because incumbents raise money more easily than challengers, it is probable that over time public financing would create a shift away from the Democratic lock on the House. But the electorate is not predictable under any system, and that is good. When Alaska and Hawaii were admitted to statehood, for example, Alaska had two Democratic Senators and Hawaii had two Republican Senators, and the political calculators predicted that the two states would remain in that position long into the future. They erred: Today Alaska has two Republican Senators, and Hawaii has two Democratic Senators.

A system of public financing will give incumbents less of an advantage. In 1974 the spending difference between House incumbents and challengers averaged $17,000. By 1990 it had reached $308,000. In 250 of the 435 House races that year, the winner outspent the loser by at least ten to one.[9] Opponents of public financing argue that incumbents have much greater name recognition and other advantages. But incumbents also have the disadvantage of a record that can be dissected, distorted, and criticized. Balancing spending in general elections will remove the financial advantage for incumbents.

One restriction that you are subject to, Mr. President, that House and Senate members are not, is term limitation. People who advocate a constitutional amendment for term limits in the Senate and House make a mistake, in my judgment, on the grounds of both merit and practicality. The merit argument is that to change officeholders simply for the sake of change is not wise in an increasingly complex world. (I confess some conflict of interest on this argument.) I could give many examples of members in both political parties who have mastered highly technical areas and whose loss to the Senate would be a loss to the nation. Senator Bennett Johnston of Louisiana is one. He can enter into an extremely sophisticated discussion with scientists on the merits of various technical projects that fall under his jurisdiction. His substantial knowledge in this area, unmatched by anyone in either the House or Senate, is a national asset.

The practical reality is that to enact term limitations requires a constitutional amendment and that takes a two-thirds vote of the House and Senate. You would probably get more votes in Congress to move the nation's capital to Las Vegas. It simply won't happen.

A system of public financing would make the reelection of incumbents less certain. That would bring meaningful and selective change. Incumbents would be forced to hold more town meetings in place of fund-raisers and pay more attention to weighty issues rather than hefty donors.

As candidate Bill Clinton pointed out during the 1992 campaign, we need to change the way we finance campaigns. You have shown your concern. Although it is a somewhat delicate matter involving congressional turf, you need to exert more leadership toward this end as President Bill Clinton.

Sincerely,

Paul Simon

Three

Strong Leadership Requires Conviction

Dear Mr. President:

Whether journalists favored or opposed the North American Free Trade Agreement (NAFTA), all were impressed with your leadership on this issue. It grew out of conviction. You didn't waffle. You set your goal, and you fought for it. You won. But whether you had won or lost, you provided a most impressive display of presidential leadership. I have served under five Presidents, and I have not seen a better effort.

Your leadership on this, and on the budget deficit, is impressive when it is remembered that we have had a twelve-year period without a Democratic presidency and you had no basic cadre of experienced White House staff to call upon. It is also impressive—and Trumanesque—that your election by a minority of American voters did not deter you from coming in and leading, shaping the battle on health care, as one example.

As President, you are in a position where criticisms abound no matter what you do. People who agree with you on issues are largely silent; they expect the finest from you. But when editorial writers, reporters, Senators, or House members disagree with you, they speak out. Senators face the same problem on a smaller scale, and you had similar difficulties as Governor of Arkansas. My own reading is that you communicate effectively with the public, that your appearances on the *Larry King Show* and similar programs during the campaign helped you immensely then and are helping you in your presidency. But it is not automatic that the public will like what strong leadership does. Secretary of State George Marshall and President Harry Truman proposed one of the finest acts in our nation's history, the Marshall Plan, which saved Western Europe from both economic chaos and communism. At the time they proposed it, opinion polls showed only 14 percent of the public favored it. Now we look back upon that action with great pride, justifiably so.

In my 1990 Senate race I remember being attacked for some unpopular positions—including my saying that the federal government had to have additional revenue and stating my opposition to capital punishment. One day a man stopped me on the street in Chicago and said, "I think I disagree with you on every issue, but I trust you, and I'm going to vote for you."

There is deep cynicism toward government, more than I can remember at any time in my years in public office. Much of it is caused by the fact that too many of us elected to public office are not telling people the truth, that we are pandering rather than leading. People should not want a physician who tells them just what they want to hear; ultimately, the same is true for those of us in politics. We all have weaknesses and strengths, and one of your long-time friends told me that you instinctively like to please people too much. That can be a weakness. It is a weakness all of us in politics have to a lesser or greater extent.

But it is not just a weakness in politics. It is a danger in any profession. Listen to TV reporter Leslie Stahl: "News judgments are being made on the basis of polls. For the last twenty years, we've been heading more and more in that direction, and not just the networks." *Time, Newsweek,* the newspapers: Everybody is asking, "What does the public want?"[1]

Don't Expect Popularity as President

What you did on the budget, forcing some cuts and revenue increases, and what you did on NAFTA, displayed genuine leadership. But that is not a uniform impression. Let me use a comparison with your predecessor, George Bush.

President Bush's major weakness was that outside of foreign affairs he had no clear direction, no strong convictions, and people sensed that. Craig Fuller, who worked with him, told the *New York Times*: "My job with Bush was telling him, in effect, 'This is who you are and this is what you believe.' "[2] Bush did better in foreign affairs because he had clearer goals. Historians will note favorably his response to the mass starvation in Somalia.

But he switched from a pro-choice stand on abortion to a pro-life stand when he became the vice presidential nominee in 1980, and it lacked conviction. He did not convey believability. His "Read my lips: no new taxes" made great campaign oratory, but when he then asked for a tax increase and later waffled on that, he came across to the public as something less than a strong leader. There are other examples.

Gradual changes in positions are part of the life of anyone who thinks and reads, but political leaders should not appear to be shifting position because a stand is unpopular. That leads to mistrust.

Stick to Your Guns, Mr. President

There has been a touch of this shifting by your administration, enough to temporarily placate your critics and sometimes make your friends uneasy. On one hand, there was an example of Bill Clinton the fighter that impressed many of us. It occurred when you stood before the joint session of Congress and waved that pen and told us that if we did not provide universal coverage on health care, you would veto the measure. I joined the hearty applause.

On the other hand, whether Lani Guinier should have been nominated for Assistant Attorney General for Civil Rights is a judgment call, but once you nominated her, you should have stuck with her.

There is no shame in defeat, and maybe she would have won. I did not know her before her nomination, but I read her controversial articles. I found them to be somewhat typical of academic journals and, like many academic articles, not particularly practical, but no cause to reject her nomination. She made a favorable impression on my staff and me and answered questions candidly and lucidly. Her hair style caused one junior member of my staff to comment, "She looks like a radical but she doesn't sound like one." She met for an hour with Senator Alan Simpson of Wyoming, a Republican with whom I sit on the Judiciary Committee. He told me he came away from his meeting with a good feeling about her and that he probably would vote for her. I know that one Democratic member of the Judiciary Committee recommended that you withdraw her name, and maybe that member would have voted against her, which put you in a bind. But even if that had happened, you hurt yourself more by withdrawing her name than you would have by standing solidly for her, even in defeat. My guess is that she would have made it and served the nation well. People are looking for a little more Harry Truman-type loyalty and feistiness from you in this type of situation.

I also have the feeling that an inexperienced staff may have advised you that it was not worth a fight with the Senate. "Give in on this and you'll build favors for another fight" is a political equation that is sometimes right and sometimes wrong. If you enter a battle, and you think a matter of principle, not personal pride, is at stake, then your credibility is enhanced, not diminished, if you stay in the fight. That is true whether you win or lose.

My colleague, Senator Howard Metzenbaum, is an example of someone who gets into many battles on the floor of the Senate, and he wins more than he loses because his colleagues know that he acts from conviction and that he is a bulldog. I cannot imagine any Senator coming up to Howard Metzenbaum and expecting to win with the argument, "Howard, you'll lose if you go ahead on this one." If he believes something strongly, he will go ahead if he is the only Senator who votes his way. That engenders respect. Your stand for direct lending on student loans, against the banks and the secondary-market people, took courage, particularly because it was not a widely understood issue. That was Bill Clinton at his best, and it did not go unnoticed in the House and Senate.

I applaud your meeting with Salman Rushdie, the novelist condemned to death by Iran's leaders for what many devout Moslems view as heretical writings. As the leader of a nation that believes in free expression for popular and unpopular views, you did the noble thing. But when it became clear that the meeting had offended many Moslem leaders around the world, your staff handled the matter inappropriately, noting a week later that you met with Rushdie for only "a couple of minutes," that you saw him in a corridor and that it really wasn't a meeting.

Rather than semi-apologize for a noble act on your part, your staff should have set up a meeting with some American Moslem leaders, indicating that you want to keep in touch with them, as well as with Moslems around the world, but reiterating to them your strong belief in freedom of expression and your equally strong abhorrence of views—including false views—being countered with violence by either government or individuals. This also would have given you an opportunity to address a largely ignored problem of prejudice against Moslems in the media and in our society. The United States has become more pluralistic, with more Moslems than Presbyterians, more Buddhists than Episcopalians.

Too often, the word Moslem—or Muslim—is tied to another word: Moslem fundamentalism, Moslem extremists, or Moslem radicals. (One of the few good things to come out of the Bosnian tragedy is that the Moslems we see on television appear to be sensible, tolerant people—unlike the image too often fostered.) Extremists or radicals pose problems no matter what their religious background. Moslem fundamentalism is, by itself, not a greater danger than Christian fundamentalism or Jewish fundamentalism or Hindu fundamentalism or any other form. The problem with any dedicated religious group arises if it goes beyond practicing its religious beliefs and tries to impose its beliefs on

others through government. That is true for Moslem fundamentalists in Arab nations, Christian fundamentalists here,
Jewish fundamentalists in Israel and Hindu fundamentalists
in India.

Someone on your staff, through lack of experience, mis-
judged the reaction to the Rushdie meeting. That's no great
problem; those things happen. But then the staff turned
lemonade into a lemon. Instead of a strong call for free
expression, your voice was muted. Instead of being an
opportunity seized to promote understanding and toler-
ance, the whole episode probably added to misunderstand-
ing. And what started out as a gesture of strength instead
conveyed weakness.

People want strength, sureness, and stability in leadership. You and I did not always agree with where Ronald
Reagan led us as President, but he had a strong sense of
direction and purpose. The public liked that; they followed.

Don't reverse or semi-reverse your decision unless you
really believe that you made a mistake. There is truth in the
biblical observation: "If the trumpet give an uncertain sound,
who shall prepare himself to the battle?"[3] Don't worry about
the headline the next day or the picture in *Time* magazine or
an unfavorable poll. David Gergen, who has always impressed me favorably, recently told the *New York Times*: "A
lot of what happens in Washington now is not about things
that have connections to people's lives. . . . It's all the ball
game now. It's not about whether an idea makes sense in
terms of changing the country. And through all these games
over the years, the country has been going down the tubes."[4]
On legislative matters you will have to work out practical
compromises. Everyone understands that. But when your
excellent mind and good political instincts bring you to a

solid decision, don't let staffers or pollsters or media critics or Senators or House members deter you.

Don't Worry About Labels

That also applies to those who tell you that you're becoming too liberal or too conservative, that you're creating this kind of an image or that kind of an image. Don't worry about whether you're pictured as an "Old" Democrat or a "New" Democrat. Politicians worry about labels; the public does not. They don't care whether the Democratic Leadership Council or the Americans for Democratic Action are for you or against you. They want honest, candid, gutsy leadership. They want you to do the right thing for the future of our country and, if it is explained to them, for the future of our world. If they come to trust your motivation, and if you give them a vision of what you want to do, they will follow, including making the sacrifices that are essential to building a better future for your daughter and my grandchildren.

Be President, Don't Run For President

Strong leadership sometimes means standing in what seems to be a lonely position, sometimes not pleasing the majority. By our nature, those of us in politics like to please people, and we have our morale reinforced by a big crowd or a good poll. At this midpoint in his presidency, George Bush drew great crowds—as any President can—and the polls looked marvelous. Mr. President, you reach the public most effectively when you take part in radio or television talk shows. I know of no American politician who does a better job. That is more important than the speech made to a cheering crowd, and it demands less of your time. When I asked one of my Senate Democratic colleagues what advice he would give you if asked, he observed: "Be President. Don't run for President." He did not mean that you should not run for reelection in 1996, but that the most effective way you can run is to play less to the crowd; make fewer speeches in Pittsburgh and New Orleans and San Francisco—and even in Illinois. These events are morale boosting for you and your staff, but much less significant than doing a superb job at 1600 Pennsylvania Avenue. Don't pay too much attention to running in 1996. What the American people want is a strong President, not a strong candidate. The cheers from a crowd make you feel good but mean nothing to Joe and Jane Smith who want their problems addressed. The best way to win in 1996 is to fight now for principles you believe in, no matter who is for you or who is against you.

Forget the Polls

I confess to being a little unsettled when I read that the Democratic National Committee has spent more than $900,000 on polling for the White House. Polling is like whiskey: A little may be okay, but it is easily abused. Polling to help determine how to frame a message to secure public approval has a legitimate place—but be careful even with that. Polling to determine in which direction to go is bad for a senator or a president. *The Los Angeles Times* reported that you meet with pollster Stanley Greenberg "several times a week." I like and respect him, but if the report is true, you are making a mistake. It reinforces what columnist Robert Novak calls "the power of public opinion in shaping Clinton's policies."[5] Leadership will not emerge from polls. In 1979, I served in the House, and in the weekly column I wrote for the newspapers in my district, I commented about another presidency:

> The Carter administration, to much too great a de-
> gree, has been determining policy by studying na-
> tional polls rather than national needs. That
> does not result in effective leadership. If the media
> reports are correct, the Carter decision to have a
> Camp David summit, and to fire some cabinet
> members after asking all to submit resignations,
> grew out of recommendations made by Carter's
> pollster. Two days after his resignation, Secretary of
> the Treasury Michael Blumenthal spoke in Chicago,
> generally supportive of the President's fiscal poli-
> cies, but he carefully worked in a criticism of "timid
> politicians and mindless pollsters." While this par-
> ticular criticism is directed at the President and Pat
> Caddell, the same criticism can be leveled at much
> of Congress. We are collectively holding our finger
> to the wind to learn the latest direction in public
> opinion. Then we act, or decline to act. The nation
> is ill served by that shaky type of performance. In a
> recent issue of *Foreign Affairs*, former Sen. J. William
> Fulbright speaks about this problem, and although
> he is writing of Congress, his words apply with
> equal validity to the presidency:
>
> > Our elected representatives. . . study and ana-
> > lyze public attitudes by sophisticated new tech-
> > niques, but their purpose has little to do with
> > leadership. . . . Their purpose, it seems, is to
> > discover what people want and fear and dislike,
> > and then to identify themselves with those sen-
> > timents. They seek to discover which issues can

be safely emphasized and which are more prudently avoided. This approach to politics is the
opposite of leadership; it is followership, for
purposes of self-advancement. . . .

I doubt that the President will move away from his
reliance on polling and Congress will have an
equally hard time extricating itself from the polling
quicksand, because members of the House and Senate have discovered that polling breeds success—if
you measure success by winning elections. But it
does not breed quality leadership. And, unfortunately, I could cite some "good" examples.
    We need people—in the executive branch and in
Congress—who are willing to sail against the winds
of public opinion, who are willing to make the tough
decisions this nation needs. We yearn for effective
leadership, and polls will not provide it.[6]

I should add that Jimmy Carter, freed from the pressures
of polls and other distractions, has performed more effectively in his public service since leaving the White House
than any former President in our history, with the possible
exception of John Quincy Adams. Jimmy Carter would have
been a stronger President if he had never taken a poll or read
one. I cannot imagine Harry Truman taking a poll to make
a decision or permitting a poll to play any significant role in
a decision.
    Almost two thousand years ago, the historian and biogra-
pher Plutarch wrote:

For this is indeed the true condition of men in public
life, who, to gain the vain title of being the people's

leaders and governors, are content to make themselves the slaves and followers of all the people's
humors and caprices . . . .These men, steered, as I
may say, by popular applause, though they bear the
name of governors, are in reality the mere under-
lings of the multitude. . . . As Phocion answered
King Antipater, who sought his approbation of
some unworthy action, "I cannot be your flatterer
and your friend," so these men should answer the
people, "I cannot govern and obey you."[7]

Winston Churchill observed:

Nothing is more dangerous than to live in the tem-
peramental atmosphere of a Gallup poll, always
taking one's pulse and taking one's political tem-
perature. . . . There is only one duty, only one safe
course, and that is to try to be right and not to fear
to do or to say what you believe to be right.[8]

And then there is the oft-repeated story of one of the
leaders of the French Revolution who said: "There go the
people. I must follow them, for I am their leader."[9] That
applies to too many "leaders" in American politics today.
This type of leadership makes your job more difficult because you have to convince members of the House and
Senate from time to time to take a certain position when the
polls show such action unpopular. An American historian
has noted:

As we look over the list of the early leaders of the
republic, [George] Washington, John Adams, [Alex-
ander] Hamilton and others, we discern that they

were all men who insisted upon being themselves.
. . . With each succeeding generation, the growing
demand of the people that its elective officials shall
not lead but merely register the popular will has
steadily undermined the independence of those
who derive their power from popular election.[10]

We need to listen more to the voices of our early leaders,
to Harry Truman, and to others such as Winston Churchill.
They provide examples of real leadership. We should also
listen to the people, and town meetings are an effective
mechanism to do that, for both a senator and a president.
The call-in shows help. We need to listen particularly to find
out the problems in our society, and then we should devise
solutions. Our system of campaign contributions often
mutes the voices of those to whom we should be listening.
But we cannot blindly follow the voices we hear, particularly
as we try to shape complex answers to society's difficulties.

What is good about your situation is that, despite the
polling, people do perceive that you really are in charge.
After an Eisenhower press conference in which he said
something out of line with his own administration policy,
James Reston remarked to Daniel Schorr as they were leaving, "President Eisenhower does not necessarily speak for
this Administration."[11] No one has that feeling about the
Clinton administration. We know that Bill Clinton is in
charge, and that is good.

I have found in my years in politics that I have always felt
comfortable with myself when I stood for what was right
but unpopular, and I felt even better when the right cause
had popularity; but I have felt worst when I have done what

all of us in politics sometimes do: cast a vote for something that was at best marginal but popular.

There is a Latin proverb of unknown origin: "An army of stags led by a lion would be better than an army of lions led by a stag." We want you to be our lion, standing without fear or wavering for what will build a better nation and world. Then the rest of us will follow.

To the extent that there is a problem in the White House, it is not because issues have been improperly packaged or that there has not been enough fine-tuning to the public will. I know you will have a hard time believing this, but the problem has been that you have not demanded enough of us.

If, for example, you had presented the health care package and said that it will require a one percent payroll tax and a one percent increase in the income tax, you could have sold it. Would there have been cries of anguish? Yes, but far fewer than you might expect. To present a health care package and say we will pay for it solely with a 75-cent increase in the price of cigarettes lacks credibility—and I favor such a tax. In wartime people make sacrifices and make them willingly, if not gladly. Why? Because they see a larger purpose and see themselves as playing a role in that larger purpose. Give us a noble cause, ask us to sacrifice, and we will. Do not fashion your programs and lower your vision and expectations to please the public relations packagers and the pollsters. Let them accommodate your program.

You have a great understanding of the aches and pains of this nation. There is no immediately popular way of dealing with these problems, of being an FDR or a Harry Truman, without talking about revenue. But if the American people see our money going for a specific need that will improve our lives and the future of our nation, we will follow.

You may or may not be elected to a second term. I hope you will be. Life is unpredictable and political life even more so. But if you do your best to be a good President, not a popular President, you will serve the nation well—and you may end up being not only a popular President but, more important, a great President.

I do not know you well, but I have been with you enough and observed you enough to know that your initial instincts and attitudes are sound. Follow them. Listen to people; read the memos; get solid information. But once you have made a decision, stick to it.

Sincerely,

Paul Simon

Four

Enjoy the Rush Limbaughs of the Nation, But Don't Let Them Get Under Your Skin

Dear Mr. President:

He is outrageous! He is entertaining! Sometimes he is right; sometimes he is mean-spirited. When he is far off base, occasionally the listener still has to chuckle. He is clear and decisive on every issue; his is a world not inhabited by any uncertainties. He writes that he was an offensive tackle in high school. He is still tackling, and he is still offensive. His books are well read: Rush Limbaugh sold more nonfiction books in 1993 than any other author in the nation—a commentary on his ability and on the cultural state of our country. He has a huge listening audience. His radio shows are on more than 600 stations, with estimates of as high as twenty million listeners. The show smothers rural USA and can be heard in almost all of our cities and suburbs. His television show airs on 220 stations but usually appears at less-than-favorable viewing times, but it adds to his audience. Fred Barnes of the *New Republic* calls him the loudest voice in the Republican Party today, and few would dispute that. My colleague, Senator Jeff Bingaman, recently complained to me, "When I travel in rural New Mexico, I can't get away from Rush Limbaugh." People who live in the big cities and their suburbs tend to underestimate his impact. Listen to former Vice President Dan Quayle: "It's only in the three months since I returned to Indiana that I've realized how big he is."[1] His combination of politics, show business, humor, and spontaneity has clicked with much of America. When, during his radio program, he gives the customary disclaimer that his "political view is not necessarily that of this station," he adds the uncustomary, "but it should be." And he means it.

Rush Limbaugh comes from Cape Girardeau, Missouri, a city of 34,438, not far from my home of Makanda in southern Illinois, population 402. Cape Girardeau, Missouri, Makanda, Illinois, and the surrounding territory are south of Richmond, Virginia, and south of Louisville, Kentucky. Culturally, they are also south of those two cities. Our area is not that far geographically or culturally from Arkansas. We had segregated schools in parts of southern Illinois and southeastern Missouri for several years after the 1954 Supreme Court decision on school desegregation. Rush Limbaugh grew up in a community where prejudice against African Americans dominated the culture—but virtually no one would admit to such prejudice or recognize it in himself or herself. Rush Limbaugh's Cape Girardeau roots are visible in his writings, even though I am sure he is sincere in believing that he has no prejudices. Limbaugh writes: "A program like mine could not have sustained such enormous growth and popularity for so long if I were a racist or a bigot."[2] (Limbaugh does not spew blatant racism, as did a radio priest in the 1930s, Father Charles Coughlin. But Father Coughlin's success suggests that appeals to the worst in us are no barrier to large audiences.) But in Cape Girardeau and much of America, those more fortunate economically—and that included Rush's family—often had prejudices against all poor people, not just African Americans. I received a note on a Christmas card from a woman in southern Illinois who protested "subsidizing Rush Limbaugh's broadcasts to the armed forces." She wrote: "I went to [high] school with his father. He was the rich, snobbish kid who wouldn't belong to our Social Science Club because we were all—perish the thought—New Deal liberals. While I was sweeping classroom floors and cleaning the blackboards, he was riding around in his new car." Of Rush she added: "I worry that so many can be so influenced by the meanness and shallowness of the man." He has learned what appeals to a segment of listeners in rural Illinois and rural Missouri, and he has spent enough time in the big cities to know what appeals there. He builds on the George Wallace base in a more sophisticated way and expands on that by touching the greed button that is in all of us. He puts it all together in such an outlandish fashion that even those of us who differ with him often are entertained. Journalist James Fallows describes him as "smart and funny—as opposed to shocking." Fallows also notes that he has listeners "who would never sit still for Pat Buchanan or Jerry Falwell."[3]

His first book, *The Way Things Ought To Be*, sold 2.5 million copies in hardcover, one of the largest hardcover book sales in history, and it is now in paperback. His next book had an initial printing of two million copies. (By comparison, the book you are now reading will have an initial printing of 10,000 copies. Rush Limbaugh would assure you that this reflects the relative merits of the two books and the two authors.)

He is alternately fun and galling to read, and there is enough of the latter that I confess to feeling guilty when I buy his books—I shouldn't be encouraging that nonsense!

You catch the spirit of his books with the dedication in his first: "Dedicated to my parents, whose love and devotion made me the terrific guy I am."[4] With tongue-in-cheek he has a quotation in one book followed by the comment: "Those are not my words. But they come from an equally great mind—Albert Einstein."[5] You catch the tone of things to come when in the brief introduction he says: "Chuckle when they blame you for hunger in Ethiopia."[6] And then he assures his readers: "You can no longer be an honest liberal after reading this entire masterpiece."[7]

Sometimes he builds his conclusions on inaccuracies. He mentions that Ronald Reagan created a record-breaking twenty million new jobs as President, and not "hamburger-flipping jobs" either.[8] However, these are the facts from the Bureau of Labor Statistics:

> 1980-1988...............14,804,000 new jobs
>
> 1972-1980...............16,731,000 new jobs
>
> 1964-1972...............15,392,000 new jobs

Not only were fewer new jobs created during the Reagan years than in previous eight-year periods, but because our population grew, the percentage of growth in jobs was the smallest by far.

Some of what he writes is outlandish fun. Occasionally he is even right. As the old saying goes, "Even a stopped clock is right twice a day." But in a nation that needs to be brought together, that already reads race into too many issues, that ought to be doing more to help the unfortunate, Rush Limbaugh sanctifies greed and our baser instincts. "The Fraud of Homelessness Advocacy" is the heading of one chapter.[9]

We Already Tax the Poor Heavily

After properly criticizing passage of the 1986 tax bill (which I voted against) for devaluing real estate and causing part of the savings and loan problem, and after thoroughly misrepresenting what brought on the basic savings and loan disaster, he takes out after the poor: "The poor in this country are the biggest piglets at the mother pig [government] and her nipples. The poor feed off of the largess of this government and they give nothing back. Nothing. They're the ones who get all the benefits in this country. They're the ones who are always pandered to."[10] This man, who makes well over $1 million a year (one report says $15 million), also writes: "It's time to get serious about raising taxes on the poor. . . . Let's balance this budget on the backs of the poor. Show them what life is like for the rest of us. . . . I'm sick and tired of playing the one phony game I've had to play and that is this so-called compassion for the poor."[11]

That suggestion of taxing the poor received so many adverse reactions—even from his audience—that he halfway retreated from the statement. Then in the midst of his attacks on the poor, this self-proclaimed seer writes:

> The Democrats reverted to their age-old theme of class envy. . . . Like so many other political tactics, it pits one group against another. . . . Bill Clinton may be the most effective practitioner of class warfare since Lenin.[12]

I confess to believing that there is too much class-bashing and race-bashing, but Rush's not-so-fuzzy line is that it is okay to bash the poor but not the wealthy. His ridicule of those less fortunate has with it what one writer describes as "a smiley sort of malice."[13]

We Already Subsidize the Rich

I would be interested in seeing Rush Limbaugh's tax return. I am sure it would show some special subsidies ("welfare," if you will) in the form of tax breaks that he receives that a waitress or carpenter in Cape Girardeau does not. *Forbes* magazine estimates that his 1993 pretax net income was $15 million. Another magazine reports that Limbaugh spends $90,000 a year on limousines.[14] He probably has some tax exempt bonds and some capital gains benefits and is able to write off a significant amount of taxes in one way or another so that the person in Cape Girardeau who makes $30,000 a year pays a higher percentage of income in taxes than does Rush Limbaugh. The subsidies that Rush receives—unless he is an exception to someone in his income category—are far greater than the benefits any poor person in this nation receives.

I don't want to make the mistake that Rush Limbaugh rightfully criticizes: pitting income class against income class. He criticizes it, but he does it. The reality is that all of us, regardless of income, will have to make some sacrifices in order to get our nation out of the fiscal hole into which we have dug ourselves. Listen to what Peter Peterson, former President Richard Nixon's Secretary of Commerce recently wrote: "The truth is that middle-income Americans, just like all other Americans, are on the dole—the entitlement dole. But few realize it. Facing up means facing the fact that we are *all* [emphasis in the original] on welfare of one kind or another."[15] And then Peterson adds:

> Everybody must be part of the solution to America's economic problems. . . . The "poor" have not caused the deficit. Those of us in the broad middle class have. The poor have suffered grievously from "fis-

cal austerity"; the rest of us continue to benefit from untrammeled public largess.[16]

Rush Limbaugh does not view what he receives as welfare. His programs are broadcast on government-sponsored airwaves; his books are mailed at a subsidized book rate. Each of us gets some benefits from the government, but we tend to view what another person receives, and we do not, as welfare. What *we* receive is never welfare. I remember meeting with a group of farmers who, among other things, complained about money the federal government puts out for welfare, meaning help to the poor. Within two minutes they then asked for an increase in farm subsidies and obviously saw no contradiction in their position. I remember going to a think-tank session at the lodge of Zion Beach State Park in Illinois. One of the participants said, "I suppose I'm like most people. I'm tired of seeing all my tax money going to help poor people." I asked him how he got to Illinois, and he responded that he flew into O'Hare Airport near Chicago. I asked him if he felt that they designed that airport primarily for poor people. Then I pursued the issue by questioning how he got from O'Hare to the state park, and he told me that he went on the interstate highway system, and I again asked if he felt they built that primarily for poor people. Then I asked him about the somewhat plush lodge at which we met, built at government expense.

The answers are obvious, but it is less obvious that most of what the federal government spends is not for poor people. The Assistance for Families with Dependent Children program, food stamps, and SSI (Supplementary Security Income)—the three major programs for the poor—total less than four percent of the federal budget. Indirectly, these programs also help the merchants who sell food and clothing, the people from whom the poor rent houses, and many others, including people who advertise on Rush Limbaugh's show and then deduct their advertising on their income tax, another indirect bit of welfare for Rush Limbaugh.

Government Can Create Wealth

Limbaugh modestly characterizes his second book as "loaded with insight, brimming with profundity."[17] In it he emphasizes one of his recurring themes: "Government can't create wealth; it can only destroy it or confiscate and redistribute it." That old saw has some initial appeal—until it is examined. The reality is that there are important roles for the federal, state and local governments, but where the private sector can do a better job, government should stay out.

If Rush Limbaugh believes that the interstate highway system has not added to the nation's wealth, he is almost alone in that belief. He is chauffeured around the streets of New York City and the highways of the nation, and while he does not like some of the potholes, my guess is that it does not bother his conscience too much to ride on government-created roadways. Federal assistance to students has made American higher education the envy of the world, and there is no question that the post-World War II G.I. Bill—a government grant to veterans to attend college—while designed as a gift to those who served our country in uniform, turned out to be a great investment in the nation's economy.

Like this author, Rush Limbaugh is a college drop-out, but my guess is that his time at Southeast Missouri State enriched him at least a little, and government dollars sustained that college, as they do the University of Missouri. I assume that he went to a public grade school and high school, government-run enterprises. We should do a better job in our schools, but I would guess that even Rush Limbaugh would not want to close them, simply because they are government run. Investment in research by the government-sponsored National Institutes of Health has returned benefits many times the original dollars to the people of this nation and of the world, in terms of better health and longer life. Thanks to government-sponsored programs, whooping cough has been almost eliminated in this nation—though it is still a problem in many countries—and the government-sponsored Centers for Disease Control have led the way in eliminating the scourge of smallpox from the earth.

When Social Security was enacted in 1935, the average American lived to be 58 years of age, and now the average U.S. lifespan is 76. Government research on disease, government assistance to farmers in the form of research and subsidies, and government warnings about cigarettes and other health hazards have all combined to enrich and lengthen our lives. It is true that research by pharmaceutical firms—the private sector—also played a major role. But sweeping generalizations about government automatically being a force for evil are inaccurate and deceptive. We should use government where it can do the best job and the private sector where it can, and frequently it will take a combination of the two to resolve our problems.

Name Calling

In one book Rush denounces "name-calling and ad hominem attacks."[18] But in the same book he refers to you, the President of the United States, as "Slick Willie"; he refers to the former Senator from California as "Alan (the Cadaver) Cranston." His descriptions of your wife, Hillary, can most charitably be described as rude. He refers to your brother Roger as "the President's half-witted half-brother." His name-calling probably appeals to some listeners and readers, but it adds nothing to constructive discussion of the issues. When Richard Nixon headed the nation, many

Democrats called him "Tricky Dick." But that type of rhetoric demeans not only the person named but the name-caller and the office of the presidency. Alan Cranston's strenuous exercising to keep a slim body should not detract from his views any more than Limbaugh's girth should detract from the Rush point of view.

James Fallows calls Limbaugh

> 100 percent predictable. He has not, as far as I know, said or written anything positive, ever, about Bill or Hillary Clinton. Not in the past year and a half has he said anything remotely critical or disrespectful about Dan Quayle, Jack Kemp, Clarence Thomas, William Bennett, or other inherently satirizable conservative characters.[19]

Limbaugh, of course, opposes your health care program. He says that we have "the best health-care system in the world," and he is correct—if you can afford it.[20] He opposes gun control legislation, the minimum wage and a host of other things good for the nation.

The Reagan Myth

Rush's hero is Ronald Reagan, and he is entitled to choose his heroes. What he is not entitled to do, without correction, is to warp the truth of what happened in those years.

Read through his books, and you would never guess that during Ronald Reagan's presidency the national debt grew three times as much as the total debt grew during all the presidencies from George Washington through Jimmy Carter combined. At the end of President Carter's last fiscal year, 1980, the debt stood at $908 billion. At the end of President Reagan's two terms, the debt stood at $2.9 trillion. Limbaugh is proud of the prosperity that Ronald Reagan brought us but neglects to say that either an individual or a nation can live "high on the hog" if you spend four dollars for every three dollars you take in. But the bills are starting to roll in on that great big national credit card that we've been using so irresponsibly. His book also does not mention that a study by the New York Federal Reserve Bank (not a Democratic institution) shows that the loss of savings during the decade of the eighties—primarily because of the federal budget deficit—cost the United States five percent growth in our national income. The Congressional Budget Office calculates that a loss of just one percent means losing 650,000 jobs.

Who does Rush Limbaugh say is responsible for all of this? "If Congress had made any strides toward curing skyrocketing spending during this period, there would have been no deficit by the end of the Reagan presidency."[21] You would never guess that every one of those spending bills was signed—not vetoed—by President Reagan and that in five of the eight Reagan years, Congress authorized less spending than the President requested. Does the Democratic Congress bear part of the responsibility? Yes. The Democratic House and the Republican Senate voted for the Reagan tax cut bill of 1981 (not with my vote), which caused a major part of the deficit.

And, of course, the women's rights movement bothers Limbaugh. He batters their leaders with names—"feminazis" he calls them—and with attempts at humor: "I love the women's movement . . . especially when I am walking behind it."[22] The women's political agenda is so bad, according to Rush, that "men can no longer enjoy themselves or tell jokes with a lot of women around, because anything they say within earshot of women can be construed as sexual harassment."[23] I could go on and on.

A small item in the *Washington Post* noted that the best-selling political button this past year reads "Limbaugh in

'96." In terms of winning an election, that would be great for you.

Mr. President, Rush Limbaugh will oppose you and support any Republican nominee in 1996. No matter what you do or say, you will not please him. So don't try. Just chuckle with him when he shows a sense of humor, but don't take him too seriously.

Sincerely,

Paul Simon

Five

Crime: The Choice Between Real Solutions and "Good" Politics

Dear Mr. President:

Our nation needs to focus more on what unites us. Unfortunately, one of those things is fear of crime. That fear immobilizes older citizens in inner cities, terrorizes mothers of small children in large public housing projects, and, in a hundred and one ways, has changed people's conduct in the cities, suburbs, and rural areas.

My real home is in Illinois—when I am not in Washington, D.C.—in the rural, southern part of my state. We have a burglar alarm system in our home now. For much of my life in small-town Illinois we did not even lock our doors unless we were going out of town for several days.

The nation's growing crime rate has not only prompted an increase in the numbers of police in most jurisdictions, it has also generated a huge increase in the numbers of private security personnel. There are now significantly more private security guards than the total of law enforcement personnel employed by federal, state, and local governments combined.

Crime has escalated, and so has it as an issue of public concern—and, therefore, as an issue for politicians. Rightfully so. But we can handle the issue responsibly or irresponsibly, and there has been far too much irresponsible conduct. It is an easy issue on which to demagogue, with quick fixes and slogans such as "Three strikes and you're out" being pushed as solutions. I'm writing to you because this is an issue on which you should take the lead from those who would scare us into expensive short-term action and even bigger long-term problems.

Crime stirs strong passions, and that is particularly true of the death penalty. When heinous—or even not so heinous—crimes are committed, the urge for vengeance often overwhelms reason. Throughout history executioners and legislators have been too ready to satisfy the immediate desire for retribution rather than the long-run need for justice and prevention.

In a quick glance through presidential speeches, the first address I found that dealt with crime was by President Benjamin Harrison more than a century ago. Our Constitution deals briefly with crime, and Alexander Hamilton wrote about it in two of the *Federalist Papers*. The subject of crime has caused comment over the centuries. The ancient Greeks and the Old Testament discuss crime.

Nations have punished criminal conduct with floggings, torture, loss of a limb or an eye or an ear, public humiliation in a stockade, and in a variety of other creative and sometimes cruel ways, including prisons. Four centuries before Christ, the historian Herodotus wrote about King Cambyses of Persia, who ordered the death of a judge who accepted a bribe and told the executioner to cut "his skin into strips, [and] stretch them across the seat . . . where he [sat when he] heard cases." He then appointed the judge's son to the same court "and bade him never forget in what way his seat was cushioned."[1]

The Death Penalty

In 1818, in England, hangings were the prescribed punishment for 220 offenses, the only exception being that a child under seven could not receive capital punishment. Thirteen people once suffered death by hanging on the same occasion "for associating with gypsies."[2] In 1833 nine-year-old Nicholas White received the death sentence "for poking a stick through a cracked shop window and stealing two pennyworth of paint." In 1748 a judge sentenced ten-year-old William York to death for murdering a five-year-old, but Chief Justice Sir John Willis postponed the execution to consult with his judicial colleagues on the matter. They ruled unanimously that the boy was

> certainly a proper subject for capital punishment and ought to suffer; for it would be a very dangerous consequence to have it thought that children may commit such atrocious crimes with impunity. . . . The taking away of the life of a boy of ten years old [might] savour of cruelty [but] the example of this boy's punishment [might] be a means of deterring other children from like offences.

Not only did public hangings offer—in the mind of policy makers—deterrence to crime, they also offered entertainment. Thirty thousand people attended one hanging, and at another the unruly crowd crushed twelve people to death. When a hanging victim convicted of pickpocketing stood before the crowd, others went through the crowd picking pockets. One prisoner, Jonathan Wild, in 1725 picked the pocket of a priest counseling him as he stood on the gallows and proudly waved his trophy to the assembled crowd in his last seconds.

We look back with incredulity that people in other nations could believe that their treatment of criminals in this manner would deter crime—unaware that other nations look to us in much the same way today, with just cause, and future generations of Americans are likely to be harsh in their judgments of our shortsightedness.

While few industrial nations, including those of Western Europe and our neighbors Canada and Mexico, have capital punishment any longer, there are still many countries that execute people. But among all nations, only seven continue to have legal execution of those under eighteen: Iraq, Iran, Pakistan, Nigeria, Saudi Arabia, Yemen and the United States.

That is a small but symbolic part of what is wrong with our criminal justice system. While you and I do not agree, Mr. President, on the death penalty (it is a penalty we reserve for those of limited means who cannot afford to hire the best attorneys), there are many other aspects of the crime problem upon which we should agree.

We agree on the staggering dimensions of the plague of crime that afflicts us. The Old Testament prophet Ezekiel sounds as if he is writing about us: "The land is full of bloody crimes, and the city is full of violence."[3] A few years ago, one author put it this way:

> The risk of being the victim of a violent crime is higher for an American than the risk of being divorced, being injured in a car accident, or dying of cancer. The risk of being robbed is 208 times greater in the United States than in Japan. . . . Japanese authorities recently expressed alarm about a rise in senseless street murders, which had brought the national total for the year to thirteen—about the total for a bad weekend in New York City.[4]

These statistics are disheartening, but almost as discouraging is our response to them.

We have reacted to the wave of crime by appearing to get tough and imprisoning offenders for longer and longer periods. We now have 510 people in prisons or jails per 100,000 total population, far more than any other nation. A 1991 study shows South Africa second with 311; Canada has 109, Australia 72, and the Netherlands only 40. In 1970 we had 134 imprisoned per 100,000 population, and because of a growing concern about crime, leaders in both political parties started making speeches about "law and order," wanting to sound tough on crime. Frequently, these orations were race-baiting, clear enough so that people understood the message but with a sufficient veneer that the speeches invited no editorial criticism. We started to "solve the crime problem" by putting more and more people into prison. And the cheers that greeted these political speeches and legislative actions resulted not in a reduction in crime but an increase.

Mandatory Injustice

For example, it sounds tough to be in favor of mandatory minimum sentences, taking this discretion away from judges. But the Justice Department study released February 4, 1994, tells a different story. (Incidentally, someone at the White House allegedly held up release of the report in the fall of 1993 because it might have harmed the chances for passage of the "get tough" crime bill in the Senate.) That report says that more than one-fifth of those in federal prisons are "low-level drug violators" with no previous prison record. Because of the mandatory minimums, they are sentenced to an average of 81.5 months—almost seven years—and serve almost six years with good behavior before release from prison. The majority have had no previous contact with the criminal justice system. According to the study, the "length of their incarceration does not positively or negatively influence their recidivism." What a waste of human talent and of taxpayers' money! In the fourth century St. Augustine wrote: "Thefts also I committed from my parents' cellar and table, enslaved by greediness."[5] Our prison cells may contain Augustines or even Einsteins, or at least people who could be contributing in a positive way, rather than draining public funds.

Pete duPont, the former governor of Delaware who served in the U.S. House and in 1988 sought the Republican nomination for President, was one of the more conservative but thoughtful presidential candidates. Listen to his comments:

> Given that the average Delawarean pays about $1,000 in state income taxes every year, it takes seventeen law-abiding citizens to support each criminal we incarcerate. . . . Despite its great cost, our present corrections system might be acceptable if it worked, but our crime and recidivism rates show it does not. The time clearly has come for . . . us in the United States to take a long, hard look at corrections philosophy. . . . There is no evidence that higher incarceration rates have any impact on the crime rate. . . . Building more prisons simply frees legislators, sentencing judges, corrections officials, and, yes, governors, from the difficult job of looking for less costly, and perhaps more effective, ways of dealing with offenders. If we cannot get free of the mind-set that building more prisons is the only answer to our overcrowding problem, then we can never hope to make the criminal justice system cost-effective.[6]

William French Smith, attorney general during Ronald Reagan's first term, has also called for examination of alternatives to incarceration for nonviolent offenders. Judges, conservative and liberal, are critical of mandatory minimum penalties. While making clear that this is a policy decision for Congress, Chief Justice William Rehnquist said such laws are often "the result of floor amendments to demonstrate emphatically that legislators want to 'get tough on crime.' "[7] When a federal district judge sentenced a quadriplegic user of a wheelchair to five years in prison followed by five years of home confinement, the appellate court sent the decision back to the lower court because the law required ten years in prison. One of the appellate judges, Nathaniel Jones, wrote:

> By concurring in this court's majority opinion, which the law requires me to do, I am joining in a result that is neither rational nor honest. . . . It may yet dawn on makers of public policy that an unacceptable social price is being paid for this folly.[8]

Upon sentencing a twenty-year-old to ten years in prison, Judge Alan H. Nevas of Connecticut observed:

> The sentence which I am being forced to impose on you is one of the unfairest sentences that I have ever had to impose. . . . I resent the fact that the Congress has . . . put me in a position where I have to send a young man like you to jail for ten years for a crime that doesn't deserve more than three or four. I know what ten years in jail is going to do to you. . . . [Congress does] it for political reasons. It looks good when some candidate stands up and says, 'I voted for a ten-year mandatory minimum.' I wish that candidate could come into the courtroom and sit here and have to sentence this young man to ten years in jail.[9]

Senior Judge Vincent Broderick, a former deputy police commissioner and prosecutor, testified before a House committee: "Mandatory minimums are the major obstacle to the development of a fair, rational, honest and proportional federal criminal justice sentencing system."[10] At least one federal judge, J. Lawrence Irving of California, has resigned to protest the mandatory minimum sentencing laws. In a sentencing opinion of Judge Robert Sweet of New York for a man found guilty of importing heroin, the judge said:

> The defendant Kwok Ching Yu does not face me for sentence but rather unseen Members of Congress. . . . This first offender, 42 years old, must be sentenced—as a matter of law—to life imprisonment. This is a decree imposed arbitrarily without any knowledge about Kwok Ching Yu or any consideration of his circumstances. . . . Congress has concluded that arbitrary sentences, which they require to be imposed without consideration of the individual, best serve justice and society. . . . Despite my concerns regarding the efficacy, justice and constitutionality of mandatory minimum sentences, I am bound to impose the sentence that Congress has imposed.[11]

A *Time* magazine article on our prison system concludes: "More prisons and longer sentences likely point in only two directions: larger inmate rosters and a higher crime rate."[12] That article begins with this story:

> For years, Tonya Drake struggled from one welfare check to the next, juggling the cost of diapers, food and housing for her four small children, all under eight. So when Drake, 30, was handed a $100 bill by a man she barely knew in June 1990 and was told she could keep the change if she posted a package

for him, she readily agreed. For her effort, Drake received $47.70 and assumed that would be the end of it. But unknown to Drake, the package contained 232 grams of crack cocaine.

Although she had neither a prior criminal record nor any history of drug use, the judge was forced under federal mandatory sentencing guidelines to impose a ten-year prison term.

At the sentencing, District Judge Richard Gadbois Jr. lamented, "That's just crazy, but there's nothing I can do about it."

Now, while Drake serves her time in a federal prison in Dublin, California, at a cost to taxpayers of about $25,000 a year, her children must live with her family 320 miles south in Inglewood. "How are you going to teach her a lesson by sending her to prison for 10 years?" demands her attorney, Robert Campbell III. "What danger is she to society?" Penologists have a ready answer: The danger is that while Drake monopolizes a scarce federal prison bed, she enables a more dangerous criminal to roam free.

There is also the real danger that Tonya Drake will learn the drug habit in prison, as well as emerge embittered and prepared for a life of crime taught her by the professionals with whom she serves time.

In a 1993 national conference held at Dana College in Nebraska—composed of corrections officials, prosecutors, judges and others—the overwhelming sentiment was that mandatory minimums are serving the national passion but not the national interest.

The theory is that by establishing mandatory minimums there is an added deterrent, but it does not recognize that criminals do not expect to be caught. A study in New York City in the 1970s found that of 1,000 felonies committed, only

540 are reported to the police, and some believe that today that figure is as low as 333. Of the 540 reported in the 1970s, 36 resulted in arrest and conviction, and of that number only three of those convicted served a sentence of a year or more. That's three-tenths of one percent. And many who committed these crimes acted impulsively or under the influence of drugs or alcohol. Yes, judges should be tough on those who commit crimes of violence. But if we were to triple the rate of arrest and sentencing, the deterrent effect would be small compared to the effectiveness of crime prevention. We must shift our attention from policies that don't work—like mindlessly building more prisons—to less dramatic answers that we know are effective, even though they have less public appeal.

Build More Prisons?

As spending for prisons escalates, governors and presidents and legislators defend their actions by grabbing a few isolated statistics to make it appear that we really have made progress on the crime and drug problems. In 1973 President Richard Nixon announced, "We have turned the corner on drug abuse."[13] In his 1976 State of the Union message President Gerald Ford assured us: "We have cut the growth of crime by nearly 90 percent."[14] A few years later, President Ronald Reagan told us: "We see . . . three straight years of falling crime rates."[15]

But the overall statistics are not encouraging, under Democratic or Republican presidents, under Democratic or Republican governors. The speeches escalate but so do the crime rates. Two years ago a San Francisco lawyer wrote:

> California has just admitted its 100,000th prisoner, the prison budget is $2.6 billion and expected to

triple, all the prisons are terribly overcrowded, and there has been no impact on the crime rate.[16]

Even the few statistics on crime that are encouraging are questioned by some, who say people have just given up hope of getting action from the police or the justice system. "Call the police, and call Domino's Pizza, and you know who responds first," they assert.

Yes, there are people who commit violent crimes who should be imprisoned to protect society. One of the ironies of our present situation is that many who are guilty of crimes of violence are walking the streets because our prisons are overcrowded with nonviolent offenders. Those who commit nonviolent crimes probably should feel the clank of the prison doors and serve a sentence. But instead of taxpayers footing the bill for their room and board for five years, for example, at a cost of $20,000 a year—and $100,000 per cell to build—we could have that prisoner work at a shelter for the homeless or provide some other type of required public service that would be much less costly to the taxpayers and might actually do something toward rehabilitating the prisoner. Charles Colson, who has made the remarkable journey from White House staff to prisoner to founder of a program called Prison Fellowship, says: "In work programs, inmates feel like they're paying back society. Work restores their sense of dignity—and it's useful to society."[17] Too often, our prisons do nothing to rehabilitate but are schools for crime. One warden commented, accurately, "Our system nurtures criminals with the same care the Air Force Academy uses to turn out second lieutenants."[18]

For many, the alternative of a prison to a terror-filled neighborhood or home is not that bad. Kathleen Hustad of Indiana interviewed some inmates of a female reformatory as a high school project. She commented: "These girls were not bad people. They lived in bad environments, and, to get away from that, they would commit a crime. Then they were guaranteed to go to Girls School, have a bed, have a warm place to live, have hot meals. They were guaranteed that and they didn't get that at home. What has society become when there are children who prefer to be living locked up because it's safer there than out on the streets?"[19]

Another irony of our present situation is that because prisons are so overcrowded, sometimes those who have committed crimes of violence are released early to make room for non violent criminals. Listen to this description of the Louisiana situation:

> By the end of the first [Governor Edwin] Edwards administration, the state was generating 50 more inmates a month than it was letting out. Then came the [Governor David] Treen administration [which] felt that they could squeeze more people into existing facilities and solve the problem that way. . . . During the same time that they stopped building, they systematically . . . supported every bill that came along that either did away with good time, did away with parole eligibility, did away with pardon eligibility, or lengthened sentences. . . .

The problem is that the state is using up the jail beds at the rate of fourteen hundred a year. So, as Department of Corrections prisoners back up into the jails, the judges, district attorneys, and sheriffs must have a meeting every Friday to decide who[m] they are going to let out of jail [because of a court order on overcrowding] so that they can arrest somebody on the weekend. Then on Monday, they meet again and decide who[m] they are going to let out of jail so they don't violate the court order.[20]

Not surprisingly, the Assistant U.S. Attorney General for Civil Rights wrote to the Governor: "We have concluded that conditions at Louisiana State Penitentiary deprive inmates of their basic constitutional rights."[21] Louisiana has the third highest imprisonment rate in the nation.

Wilbert Rideau, a prisoner in that state, wrote in an essay in *Time*:

> I was among 31 murderers sent to the Louisiana State Penitentiary in 1962 to be executed or imprisoned for life. We weren't much different from those we found here, or those who preceded us. We were unskilled, impulsive and uneducated misfits, mostly black, who had done dumb impulsive things. . . . The vast majority of us are consigned to suffer and die here so politicians can sell the illusion that permanently exiling people to prison will make society safe. . . . If getting tough resulted in public safety, Louisiana citizens would be the safest in the nation. They're not. Louisiana has the highest murder rate among states. . . . The idea of punishing the few to deter the many is counterfeit because potential criminals either think they're not going to get caught or they're so emotionally desperate or psychologically distressed that they don't care about the consequences of their actions. The threatened punishment, regardless of its severity, is never a factor. . . . Prisoners kept too long tend to embrace the criminal culture, its distorted values and beliefs. . . . This prison houses 4,600 men and offers academic training to 240, vocational training to a like number. . . . It is essential to educate and equip [young people] with the skills to pursue their life ambitions in a meaningful way. . . . We must address the adverse life circumstances that spawn criminality. These things are not quick, and they're not easy,

but they're effective. Politicians think that's too hard a sell. They want to be on record for doing something now, something they can point to at reelection time. So the drumbeat goes on for more police, more prisons, more of the same failed policies. Ever see a dog chase its tail?[22]

Equal Justice?

An unpleasant reality is that if you are an African American or a Latino American, you are more likely to be found guilty by a judge or jury and more likely to receive a harsh sentence. The racial imbalance in arrests and convictions for similar crimes is unquestioned. Part of that is prejudice, and part of it is economics. The young man or woman from the suburbs who is arrested on a drug charge probably can select and pay for a good lawyer who knows how to get the best possible deal for his or her client. Overworked prosecutors don't want to face a formidable trial and are more likely to work out a fine or a guilty plea on a lesser charge or to drop the charges.

The suburban youth with a problem is less likely to even enter the criminal justice system because his or her difficulties are frequently defined as "a problem" requiring drug treatment. A far smaller percentage of young people in the inner-city receive that consideration. The inner-city youth also may be unable to hire a lawyer and is likely to be assigned a court-appointed attorney with a huge caseload who may or may not take an interest in his (and, increasingly, her) case. African Americans and Latinos make up 60 percent of the prison population.

These are among other realities about prisons:

☐ **Eighty-two percent of those in prison today are high school dropouts.** That has been a fairly constant figure: In 1970 the former director of the Federal Bureau of Prisons reported the identical number.[23] Only a small percentage will add to their education during their incarceration. A Minnesota study found a greater relationship between high school dropouts and crime than between cigarette smoking and lung cancer.

☐ **A majority of those in our prisons cannot read** a newspaper or fill out an employment form. Many are totally illiterate. If they go into prison without these basic skills, they probably will come out without them. Most prison officials feel they are fortunate just to maintain "law and order"; wardens let others in society provide any significant social services.

☐ **Sixty percent of those who enter federal prisons and about 25 percent in state and local prisons and jails are there for drug-related charges.**

☐ Alcohol is a problem for many who are incarcerated, but alcohol treatment programs are successful only if the person is a volunteer genuinely committed to change, and even then recovery from alcoholism is far from certain. But drug treatment, whether voluntary or involuntary, has a reasonable chance of success. Only a small percentage of federal prisoners participate in drug treatment programs, yet the Institute of Medicine reports: "Prison-initiated treatment can reduce the treated group's rate of rearrest by one-fourth to one-half."[24] The answer should be obvious: We need more drug treatment investment. But as one of my Senate colleagues told me, "How can I defend voting for drug treatment programs for prisoners when we don't provide them for non-criminals who need help?" We should provide this assistance to anyone who needs treatment, in or out of prison. To fail to do so is an extremely expensive "savings."

Former labor leader Jimmy Hoffa may not have been reliable on many things, but he did bring practical experience on one issue:

> Prisons are archaic, brutal, unregenerative, over-crowded hell holes where the inmates are treated like animals with absolutely not one humane thought given to what they are going to do once they are released. You're an animal in a cage and you're treated like one.[25]

That is an exaggeration but not a great one. Too often prisons create opportunities for connections between prisoners whose plans afterwards—nurtured with plenty of time on their hands—are not how to abide by the law and make a decent living but how to evade the law. These people hope to avoid making the same mistake again, and for too many the mistake is not committing the crime but getting caught. Drug sales in prison are common. Prison sexual attacks are often brutal. One observer noted: "America has the longest prison sentences in the West, yet the only condition long sentences demonstrably cure is heterosexuality."[26] That inaccurate statement illustrates a truth.

Crime Prevention

We also have to look beyond prison to solve crime and do what we can to prevent criminal tendencies and actions before they occur. We are still looking for a dramatic way to reduce the crime rates—in what author Lisbeth Schorr calls "the search for shortcuts"—but there is no such thing. And those of us in public office must be candid about lowering expectations.[27] Then we must address the real problems that can gradually—and it will be gradually—turn trends in a more positive direction.

Turning things around requires facing our inconsistencies. To illustrate the contradictions in our society, the magazine *Mother Jones* featured a teddy bear and the assault weapon frequently used in crime, a handgun called the tec-9.[28] For the teddy bear, the magazine found:

1. At least four broad types of federal safety standards cover teddy bears: sharp edges and points, small parts, hazardous materials, and flammability.

2. The Toy Manufacturers Association has maintained a safety standards committee since the early 1930s. In 1976 the toy industry issued a comprehensive voluntary toy safety standard.

3. Six separate stuffed toy models were recalled in fiscal year 1992 alone.

4. Keeping a teddy bear in your home does not increase the chance that someone will be killed there.

5. Teddy bears killed nobody last year. Only eight child deaths from all accidents involving toys were reported in the first eight months of 1993.

For the tec-9, *Mother Jones* found that:

1. There are no federal safety standards for the domestic manufacture of guns.

2. There are no voluntary, industry-wide safety standards for the manufacture of guns.

3. Approximately one gun model is recalled every three years.

4. Keeping a gun in your home makes it three times more likely that someone will be killed there.

5. In 1990 guns killed 37,184 people in the United States.

A Roman Catholic chaplain, Rev. Gregory J. Boyle, asked a class of forty convicts serving time in a California state prison what could be done to reduce crime. All forty are in a way real experts on crime, not academic experts. Their answers differed fairly dramatically from the provisions of the crime bill that passed the Senate in 1993. Father Boyle writes:

> My students, virtually all life-termers, many without the possibility of parole, were amazingly well informed about the bill.... Not a single one thought that longer sentences stop crime. Not one juvenile, they insisted, will be deterred by the fear of being tried as an adult. We could triple the number of prisons in this state ... and not one of my 40 students believes that it would make a criminal think twice. . . . My students know that there exists in this country no real will to stop crime. Legislators herniate themselves to be seen as "tough" on crime while sidestepping every conceivable approach that would be "smart" on crime.

Of the suggestions of this class of 40, only one—getting guns off the street—is addressed in any meaningful way in the 1993 Senate crime bill. These are among their suggestions:

☐ **Address the pervasive hopelessness among the inner-city poor.** Money spent on jobs for the unemployed will make the streets safer than all the prisons in California.

☐ **Promote mentoring programs** to tackle the issue of so many fatherless sons. Seventy percent of all juveniles detained in the United States know no father.

☐ **Convert prisons from punishment warehouses to rehabilitation centers,** for one day these inmates will walk free.

☐ Conceive ways to offer meaning to inner-city poor youth who have lost the ability to imagine a future.[29]

Of these suggestions, the only one that is in the crime bill is one on which you have shown leadership, Mr. President—guns.

The simplistic but popular response to the crime problem of building more prisons brought this response from a House witness: "Nowhere in President Clinton's plan or any competing plan has anyone suggested that the solution to the health care crisis is to build more hospitals. It is universally acknowledged that prevention is the most effective tool in providing good health care, and that hospitals should be used only as a last resort."[30]

One of the difficulties of opposing the build-more-prisons approach is that political opponents then try to paint you as "soft on crime." William Bradford Reynolds, counselor to Attorney General Edwin Meese, served as a key person in the Reagan Justice Department. He circulated a memorandum urging "polarization" of the issue "to further our agenda." He added, "We must take the side of more prisons, and to polarize the issue we must attack those by name, such as Sen. Paul Simon, who take the other approach."[31]

The nation needs more than a public relations effort to appease the electorate on the crime problem. If we are to solve this problem, we should stop doing short-term patchwork and undertake a complete, long-term renovation. We should:

☐ **Follow Attorney General Janet Reno's advice to provide prekindergarten help to children in disadvantaged areas.** Criminal careers do not start at the age of

16. In speaking of inner-city youth, the *New York Times* accurately observed in an editorial: "No one pays much attention to them until they get into trouble."[32] Harvard's Deborah Prothrow-Stith has written much the same: "The criminal justice system is fundamentally reactive. Little happens until a crime has occurred. By then it is too late for prevention strategies."[33]

☐ **Strive for quality education in all our schools.** Too many schools have library shelves with few or no books and are run by disheartened and dispirited teachers and principals. When second and third graders show signs of problems, special help must be provided immediately. By the time they get to be high school sophomores, it is often too late to intervene. Schools in areas of special need should have additional resources, not fewer. One Chicago elementary school I visited in a high crime area, where drugs are a major problem, had one half-time counselor for 831 students. I am reminded of the words of a 17-year-old prisoner: "I know if somebody cared for me, I wouldn't be in here."[34] I wonder if he ever talked to a school counselor in even a rushed five-minute session.

☐ **Help adults who cannot read or write or who have extremely limited skills.** Approximately 23 million adult Americans fall into this category. Not only are they more likely to be unemployed and desperate, they are also unable to help their children, and illiteracy is then passed from one generation to another like a disease. And their children may be destined for trouble with the law.

☐ **Stress education in prisons.** I once visited a state prison in Illinois with more than 800 inmates. I asked the warden to see their classroom facilities, and he took me to a room with eighteen desks, empty desks.

I asked how often the facilities were used, and he told me that two of the prisoners had bachelor's degrees and taught a little, and that Tuesday evenings the assistant county superintendent of schools came to teach a class. What are the chances that those in that prison will eventually return after committing further crimes? Overwhelming. A former director of federal prisons believes a good prison education program could cut the federal recidivism rate in half.[35]

☐ **Inaugurate a job guarantee program for anyone out of work five weeks or more.** This is discussed in more detail in my letter to you on welfare reform. Roughly half of those in prison were unemployed when arrested. People need pride in themselves and they must have hope, and too many have neither. Show me an area with high unemployment, and I will show you an area with high crime. There is no better social program—and no better anticrime weapon—than a job. In a lengthy editorial reflection on the problem of crime, the magazine *Tikkun* gave as its first recommendation: "Create full employment, guaranteeing every American a job."[36] Virtually no one questions that there is a significant connection between poverty and much of our crime. More than a century ago, an American economist wrote: "How vainly shall we endeavor to repress crime by our barbarous punishment of the poorer class of criminals so long as children are reared in the brutalizing influences of poverty."[37]

☐ **Change welfare so that we encourage parents to stay together rather than discouraging them from doing so.** The large majority of those in single-parent families do not involve themselves in crime, but the chances are greater than in two-parent homes. Children need love and stability. We all need it.

☐ **Outlaw many popular military-style street weapons**
that are now legal, following the good example of the
enactment of the Brady Bill, with its waiting period for
handguns. My home is on twelve acres next to the
Shawnee National Forest in deep southern Illinois. On
those all-too-rare days when I am home, I ordinarily
see more deer than people. I am around hunters a great
deal. I have yet to see a hunter with an Uzi or an AK-47
or a tec-9 or any of the other weapons that gangs and
drug kingpins and professional criminals favor. We
should outlaw the sale, production, and importation
of these types of weapons. The action by both the
House and Senate during the first half of 1994 has not,
as this is being written, yet reached the status of law
but it does suggest that the forces of the National Rifle
Association can be defeated and that reason may
gradually flourish in this emotion-charged policy area.

As Marc Mauer of The Sentencing Project has noted:
"Seattle and Vancouver [British Columbia] . . . are quite
comparable on most demographic factors and have similar
crime rates for assaults without firearms, [but] the murder
rate in Seattle is almost twice that of Vancouver, with the
entire difference explained by gun-related homicides."[38] He
attributes the difference to "strict Canadian gun control
laws." The Los Angeles area and Sydney, Australia, are in
many ways similar, though they differ in ethnic population.
The burglary rate in Sydney is approximately ten percent
higher than in Los Angeles. But the murder rate from firearms in Sydney is only seven percent of that in Los Angeles.
The reason: gun control laws. Or look at handgun deaths in
1990: Australia, 10; England, 22; Canada, 68; the United
States, 10,567. In 1992 the U.S. total reached 13,220. Listen to
the testimony of Marian Wright Edelman: "The 560 American 10- to-14-year-old children who died from guns in 1990
were twice the number of handgun deaths of citizens of all

ages in all of Sweden, Switzerland, Japan, Canada, Great Britain and Australia combined that year." She called upon the religious community to be "the moral locomotive, not the moral caboose, on the gun issue."[39]

☐ **Clamp down on fly-by-night gun dealers,** Mr. President, as you and Treasury Secretary Lloyd Bentsen have suggested. I have been able to get some changes in the law that have improved the situation, but we must go further. We have just raised the license fee for becoming a gun dealer from $10 a year to $66 a year and that helps slightly. My amendment to require gun dealers to live up to local ordinances and state laws helps a little, as does my amendment to require the federal government to notify local police of who is a gun dealer. Three-fourths of all gun dealers do not sell from stores, but from their kitchens, their basements, or the trunks of their cars, and rarely does anyone undergo any type of inspection of records—the average now is one every 22 years. This is an invitation to trouble-making.

☐ **Place higher taxes on handguns and bullets,** as your Working Group on Violence recommended in January 1994. Set the fees on a per-gun and per-bullet basis, because inexpensive handguns can do as much harm as their more costly counterparts. That will not pay for even one percent of the economic damage of handguns, but it may prevent both human and economic tragedy. The *Star-Tribune* of Minnesota carried a story about Silas Coleman, a 21-year-old whose spinal column was severed by a bullet. He now speaks by blinking his eyes. The estimated cost of his medical care for the next five years: $3.6 million.

☐ **Intensify drug education.** It's not dramatic help, but it gradually pays off, just as education on smoking cigarettes has slowly reduced that health risk.

☐ **Make drug and alcohol treatment available** to anyone who needs it, in or out of prison. In a few states you have to wait nine months after you sign up for drug treatment to start the program; that is nine months of dynamite. For those in prison on drug-related charges, drug treatment should be mandatory, as it should be for anyone who serves a prison term of six months or longer—half of those in prison for a crime of violence committed it under the influence of alcohol or drugs. In addition, those under the influence of alcohol or drugs are much more likely to abuse or neglect children, and childhood abuse or neglect dramatically increases the probability of eventual criminal behavior by those children.

☐ **Continue to push the television industry to reduce glamorized violence,** and applaud those who have now turned the corner and are getting messages in stories and public service announcements that discourage violence as an attempted answer to problems. Old movies and television shows have our heroes and heroines constantly smoking cigarettes and drinking heavily. To the credit of the film industry, that portrayal has changed and has helped to change our habits. Thirty seconds worth of glamorizing a bar of soap often persuades us to buy a bar of soap; 30 seconds glamorizing a pair of shoes often persuades us to buy those shoes; and 25 minutes glamorizing violence, conveying the message that violence can solve problems and is fun, often persuades people to use violence. The evidence that the wrong type of TV violence portrayal adds to crime is at least as strong as the evidence that cigarettes do harm to our health, though some leaders in both industries deny it.

In addition, the Nielsen surveys show that the lower our income, the more television we watch. That partially explains the increase of average television watching time for

African Americans compared to all others. This is particularly striking for children and teenagers—varying from 28 percent more to 245 percent more, depending on the time of day. Part of the reason is not simply income. Children in rural or suburban communities who have limited income still have the ability to go outside and play with others in safety. In many high-rises in urban America, the only safe place is an apartment, and often the only entertainment there is the television set that too frequently teaches the lessons of violence.

☐ **Create a greater police presence in high-crime areas.** Critics argue that this doesn't make a difference. They say that some of the cities with the highest ratios of police to population have some of the highest crime rates. They do, but it is not because of the numbers of police. The Cabrini-Green public housing units in Chicago had a high crime rate, extremely high. When authorities put more police into the complex, crime rates dropped significantly. Even in the highest crime-rate areas of our cities, the large majority of the population is law abiding. They need protection. Your efforts, Mr. President, to provide more police are meaningful to those who now live in fear. Most crimes are black on black, white on white, Hispanic on Hispanic. But the minority crime rate is higher, and those neighborhoods are particularly in need of assistance.

☐ **Eliminate mandatory sentences for nonviolent crimes** and offenses committed without a weapon. Mandatory sentences sound tough, but judges need to be given more discretion. In the last years of his life, more than three centuries before the birth of Christ, Plato wrote: "We should exhibit to the judges . . . the outline and form of the punishment to be inflicted. . . . But when a state has good courts, and the judges are well trained and scrupulously tested, the determination of the penalties or punishments which shall be inflicted on the guilty may fairly and with advantage be left to them."[40]

☐ **Give alternative forms of sentencing** to those who are not repeat offenders and have committed nonviolent crimes. For example, someone who has embezzled money from a bank should serve 90 days to six months of a five-year sentence in prison, to understand the severity of the crime, and the balance of the term working in a school for children who are mentally retarded or in any one of a number of private or public institutions, subject to good behavior. If the offender does not work hard, or in any way violates sensible rules of behavior, the balance of the term should be spent in prison. That change will save money and lives.

☐ **Go slow on programs with popular slogans like "Three strikes and you're out."** Most crime is committed by males between the ages of 15 and 24; the peak age is 17. By the age of 30, the crime rate is diminishing rapidly and is negligible by the age of 40. Housing people between the ages of 50 and 70 in prison will cost at least $500,000 per prisoner and will have no impact on the crime rate. The young males who commit most of the crimes usually act under the assumption that they will not be caught, and usually they are not. Jerome Skolnick of the University of California writes about the new California "three strikes" law:

> During the past sixteen years, [California's] prison population has grown 600 percent, while violent crime in the state has increased 40 percent. . . . To pay for three strikes, California expects to spend $10.5 billion by the year 2001. . . . Will California be better off in 2027—indeed, will it have less crime—if it has twenty more

prisons for aging offenders instead of twenty more college campuses for the young? Of course, [Governor Pete] Wilson and other politicians are worrying about the next elections, not the next century."[41]

☐ **Reduce the case load for parole supervisors** so that they really can supervise, as well as help on job placement, social problems, and counseling.

If we were to enact such a series of programs, we would gradually but substantially reduce crime in our nation. Would it cost money? Yes. Would it be cheaper in the long run than investing billions more in prisons each year? Yes. Would it reduce heartache and fear for our people? Unquestionably. Would it make ours a more productive nation? Of course. Will we have the wisdom to do it? I don't know.

There is the beast and the noble in each of us. It is politically easier to appeal to the beast, and the results of that we can see. What we need is an appeal in concrete terms to what Abraham Lincoln called "the better angels of our nature."[42]

We need your leadership, Mr. President.

Sincerely,

Paul Simon

Six

Welfare: Confronting the Disgrace of the Nation's Poverty

Dear Mr. President:

People who are not or have never been poor do not understand the harshness of poverty. We may smile when we read Gene Fowler quoting an old reporter:

> There are many in the old world of ours who hold that things break about even for all of us. I have observed, for example, that we all get the same amount of ice. The rich get it in the summertime and the poor get it in the winter.[1]

But that does not convey the grimness and hopelessness of so many people. Their feelings are conveyed with a little more meaning by a Catholic priest who works with youths who are having trouble. "These young people," he comments, "have no good memories of the past."[2] That is true for many adults also. When the poverty of dollars is compounded with a poverty of spirit, breaking the welfare cycle becomes many times more difficult.

Here are a few of the grim statistics:

☐ In 1980 29.5 million Americans (13 percent) lived in poverty. By 1992 that figure had climbed to 37 million (14.5 percent).

□ In 1970 there were 7,429,000 welfare recipients; in 1993, 14,128,000.

□ According to UNICEF, the U.S. child poverty rate is more than double that of any other industrialized country. Forty percent of our poor are children.

□ One in four children under the age of six lives in poverty. One of seven U.S. children is on welfare, meaning that almost half the children living in poverty in this country are not supported by welfare.

□ A State of Washington survey found that 52 percent of the women on welfare were originally teenage mothers.

□ What most people consider welfare, Assistance for Families with Dependent Children (AFDC), is paid two-thirds by the federal government, one-third by state and local governments. The federal share is $13 billion, less than one percent of the federal budget. If you add food stamps and SSI (Supplemental Security Income), welfare amounts to less than four percent of the budget.

□ A 1986 study found that seven percent of welfare recipients stay on welfare for less than two years; 11 percent, three to four years; 17 percent, five to seven years; 65 percent, eight or more years. Because of the turnover of the first seven percent, the majority of recipients are not on welfare long. You can with accuracy shift the statistics around to make them look much better. For example, roughly 35 percent of all recipients are on welfare 24 consecutive months or less. The majority of those receiving welfare stay on it less than four years. Mary Jo Bane and David Ellwood have an excellent chapter in a book spelling out the statistical realities and apparent inconsistencies.[3] But the overall picture is anything but heartening.

There is too much truth to Senator Paul Wellstone's comment: "When you are poor and dependent in America, you are despised."[4] Who can question John Kenneth Galbraith's conclusion about our society: "The comfortable are now in control."[5] He implies words not added: And much too insensitive.

Who Are the Poor?

Disproportionately the poor are women, children and minorities. The reasons for poverty are often identified with perceived racial characteristics. In much of the nation the not-so-quietly whispered, negative descriptions are of African Americans, but in some regions the prejudice shifts to Latinos or Native Americans or Asian Americans.

I am old enough, Mr. President, to remember vividly the elation I felt when the 1954 Supreme Court decision on school desegregation came down. I recall being heartened by Branch Rickey's courageous decision to bring Jackie Robinson to the Brooklyn Dodgers and going to St. Louis from my southern Illinois home to cheer Jackie Robinson when he made his first appearance there for the Dodgers, even though he played against the Cardinals, "my" team. I remember the "white" and "colored" signs in the South and the practice of segregation, even in Illinois, the Land of Lincoln, as we boast on our license plates. I recall flying from St. Louis to Atlanta with Dr. Martin Luther King, having a great visit with him—my first—and then getting to the Atlanta airport where we both decided to head for the men's room. Suddenly I stopped at the "white" sign and hesitated, and Dr. King smiled and said to me quietly, "This is not the battle we want to fight."

The Civil Rights Act finally passed, and much of that obvious and superficial discrimination disappeared. I did not expect the United States to instantly become a semi-paradise, but I felt that we were about to make tremendous strides toward having a country that lived up to its ideals more effectively. In some ways, that has happened, far more than younger people can imagine. But in some ways, that has not happened, and that concerns me.

The civil rights struggle galvanized our conscience and our attention because of the harshness and crudeness of the manacles of segregation. But the more sophisticated restraints of discrimination that remain offend a much smaller body of social activists. The glamour is gone, and when the Supreme Court hands down a decision in the *Crosson* case, on minority set-asides, or the *Ward's Cove* case, on employment discrimination, each of which partially undermines civil rights gains, the number of those concerned is relatively small.

Under one of your predecessors, President Lyndon Johnson, we had what we called a "war on poverty." In a war, we galvanize all the resources of a nation to defeat an enemy; the action taken against poverty cannot be stretched into a "war," but it was a battle. Despite all the criticisms— and mistakes were made in this burst of activity—the battle made a dent in poverty. We had reached the point in 1964 where 23 percent of all children lived in poverty. But thanks to the Johnson-led initiatives, that figure gradually went down to 14 percent in 1969. Unfortunately, in recent years it has been creeping back up and is now at almost the same 23 percent as in 1964. From 1965 to 1974 the percentage of our total population below the poverty level fell from 17.3 percent to 11.2 percent. What a difference that represented for millions of people.

Perhaps equally important, our leadership sensitized us to the problems of those less fortunate. By only a few votes, the nation missed the opportunity of having the leadership of Hubert Humphrey for President. But even under Richard

Nixon, the nation moved ahead, though less dramatically, with the Head Start program, for example. Gerald Ford and Jimmy Carter made additional programmatic progress. While all of this was happening, however, the population shifted more and more into economic ghettos negating many of the gains we had made.

Our housing is slightly less racially segregated than it was few decades ago, but our neighborhoods are more segregated economically than at any time in the history of our nation. Small communities are much less likely to be segregated by economics. I have spent most of my life in small-town, rural southern Illinois. People in small towns usually know when someone down the street faces problems. In small communities that are racially diverse there is usually less of a segregated racial pattern than in large cities.

I have never visited Hope, Arkansas, but I have looked at the census data, and about 40 percent of the 9,636 population is African American. I talked to Wanda Hays, executive vice president of the Hope Chamber of Commerce. She tells me that there is a "somewhat mixed" residential pattern. In the schools, there is a good economic mix. More than a quarter of the population of Hope has income below the poverty level, a higher percentage than the national average of 14.5 percent. Thirty-nine homes have no indoor plumbing, and 719 homes have no telephone. Of those residents over 25 years of age, more did not graduate from high school than did. In Hope there is some segregation by race and some segregation by economics. But in this community of 9,636, there is generally more integration of both kinds than in most of the nation.

Urban America

But economically integrated small-town and rural America is a decreasing percentage of our population. The big shift: We have increasingly stockpiled the poor into urban America, then ignored the cities and their problems. An Associated Press story of May 23, 1994 (no author indicated), tells part of what has happened:

> CHICAGO (AP) A new study has found that poor people are becoming increasingly isolated from prosperous people in Chicago and its suburbs, mirroring a worrisome national trend. From 1970 to 1990, the segregation of poor in the area increased 20 percent, according to the study by Alan J. Abramson and Mitchell S. Tobin of the Washington-based Urban Institute. Nationally a rise of 13 percent was recorded. . . . "We seem to be becoming a really stratified society. It's an ominous trend," said Douglas S. Massey, a University of Chicago sociologist. Separation of the poor and the prosperous makes it harder for the poor to rise economically. It also has an effect on local economies, where concentrated poverty tends to be accompanied by lack of political clout, substandard schools and minimal city services. In such areas, social problems such as crime, drugs and welfare dependency reinforce each other. And the costs spread to the rest of society in the form of an unproductive labor force, crime that spills outside the ghettos, and taxes for public aid, police and prisons.

The study found that half of all Chicago-area residents would have to move to new neighborhoods to become economically integrated. But Chicago is not alone. In Milwaukee 55 percent are economically segregated; Hartford, 53 percent; Cleveland, 51 percent; Detroit, 51 percent; and the list goes on.

New York City in 1955 had 150,000 people on welfare; today it has 2.1 million receiving food stamps, 1.6 million of whom receive direct welfare payments. We still have sub-stantial numbers of rural poor, but many have moved to the cities, sometimes in desperation, sometimes because they hear of a friend or relative who is doing better, sometimes because they hear of a job opportunity. The demand for unskilled labor has diminished dramatically in agricultural America, and the lights of the big city have an allure—and, unfortunately, sometimes they ensnare in tragedy those ill-prepared for city life.

Us Versus Them

A less measurable but equally significant attitudinal change added complications to the population shift. As the poor were less and less our neighbors, it became easier and easier to ignore them. People in Illinois outside of Chicago were never in love with that big city; people in New York City, Los Angeles, and other major population centers faced similar attitudes. As the poor became a greater part of the city population, problems of education, crime, and housing escalated. Middle- and upper-income citizens fled to the suburbs, cities became more and more African American and Latino and more isolated.

As you know well, Mr. President, the stereotypes of African Americans and Hispanic Americans are like all stereotypes, negative and inaccurate. But as long as "they" are an increasing percentage of the city population, it be-comes easier and easier to ignore the urban plight. The fact that city problems in schools, housing, and crime are grow-ing reinforces prejudices and political indifference. People may work in the city, or attend a symphony concert in the city, but urban difficulties seem so gargantuan that people dismiss them with the hope that somehow, in some way, they will get solved—but "Don't use any of my tax money to do it." That is particularly the case if the tax money should go to help minorities. While relations between middle-income people of various racial and ethnic backgrounds have improved—where they have the opportunity of working together—much too much of this nation is a mini-Bosnia in terms of race relations. Even a superficial scratching of the surface evokes ugly racial and ethnic prejudices that need to be stamped out. Prejudice compounds the difficulties of the cities and threatens the future of our nation.

A 1994 Louis Harris poll of 2,755 people, a large sampling, shows in statistical language that we have difficulties. Here are the results by ethnic background of people who believe certain statements:

"Muslims belong to a religion that condones or supports terrorism."

Hispanic Americans	48%
Whites	41%
Non-Muslim African Americans	39%
Asian Americans	30%

Blacks "want to live on welfare."

Non-black Hispanic Americans	26%
Asian Americans	31%
Whites	21%

Roman Catholics "are narrow-minded because they are too controlled by their church."

Non-Catholic Asian Americans	57%
Non-Catholic African Americans	49%
Non-Catholic whites	34%

Hispanics "tend to have bigger families than they are able to support."

Asian-Americans	68%
Non-Hispanic whites	50%
Non-Hispanic African Americans	49%

Jews, "when it comes to choosing between people and money, will choose money."

African Americans	54%
Hispanic Americans	43%
Asian Americans	34%
Non-Jewish whites	27%

Asian Americans "are unscrupulously crafty and devious in business."

Hispanic Americans	46%
African Americans	41%
Whites	27%

In addition, the largely inaccurate stories of abuse of food stamps or welfare make the rounds from barber shop to beauty shop and, ultimately, into public policy. Politicians and office-holders respond more to a public perception of reality than to reality itself. That causes our problems to multiply.

Not only that, as sociologist William Julius Wilson has pointed out, the good news of gradually desegregated housing brought with it bad news for the toughest neighborhoods, where the African-American physician and lawyer and business person formerly had to live. The new residential freedom brought the opportunity for a better neighborhood for those families, but it sharply reduced the numbers of people who could provide responsible neighborhood leadership to the poor. Instead of people who don't know how to solve problems living next to people who do, the neighborhood changed—public housing too often being a striking example—and people who don't know how to solve problems now live next to people who also don't know how, and the problems are compounded. The insightful academician and activist Roger Wilkins, looking back over 25 years, observed: "There's been progress for the black middle class but the isolation of the black poor is worse."[7]

In the midst of shrinking civil rights gains and growing perceptions of "us versus them," the nation elected Ronald Reagan as our leader. His stories about welfare queens and abuse of public assistance meshed with the nation's prejudices. He gave us an excuse to spend less on our cities and to feel good about it. As the cities' problems multiplied, the federal government cut off revenue sharing for the cities. "They should learn to help themselves" became the prevailing mood. Instead of resources to help cities and states solve their problems, the federal government offered them mandates that pre-empted local laws—these were much less expensive to the federal government and gave the appearance of not ignoring problems of poverty. The *New York Times* reported: "In the nation's history, one-fourth of all the federal actions pre-empting state and local laws occurred during the Reagan years."[8]

Insensitive Policy–Makers

Policy-makers and the public are not heartless but they are insensitive. Few outside the cities understand the nature of the problems, and even within the cities the barriers imposed by race, language, and economics become impos-

sible for most of the nonpoor to surmount. Politicians of
both political parties find it easier to appeal to prejudices,
however subtly, than to tell people the realities. While
politicians often have a slightly better understanding than
the electorate, many public officials view the high-crime,
impoverished areas of the cities as places to avoid, and as
they evade being there, they also evade understanding. The
Reagan-era worship of rugged individualism shoved the
nation's powerful middle class away from a sense of community, and that became "cancerous," according to one
prominent sociologist.[9] Poll-taking public officials followed
the middle-class lead.

Family Status

Complicating all of this is another factor: family status.
My colleague, Senator Daniel Patrick Moynihan, has written
eloquently about the problem of family status and he bears
some scars for his candor. He stirred the nation with his first
report in 1965. A more recent book of his, published in 1986,
Family and Nation, is as insightful today as when it first
appeared. The statistics in it have changed for the worse, but
the drumbeat of messages resounds with even greater rele-
vance today. I ask you to look at these disturbing realities
from his book and other sources:

☐ **Children from one-parent homes are less likely to do
well in school** and more likely to have medical problems; a higher percentage will have trouble with the
law. (As you know from personal experience, Mr.
President, the majority of those from single-parent
homes fortunately struggle through satisfactorily.)

☐ **There are dramatic increases in the numbers of children in one-parent families,** and children from one-
parent homes are much more likely to fall below the
poverty line. Quoting from an Annie E. Casey Foun-

dation report, columnist William Raspberry notes: "Of those who finish high school, get married and reach age twenty before having their first child, eight percent of their children are living in poverty. Of those parents who don't meet these criteria, seventy-nine percent of their children are living in poverty."[10]

☐ **We have significantly reduced the problem of poverty among the elderly,** thanks largely to Social Security and Medicare, but poverty among children has markedly increased.

☐ **The majority of children born today will live in a one-parent household** before reaching the age of 18, unless present trends are reversed.

☐ **The out-of-wedlock birth rate is higher in the United States than in any other Western industrial nation—** and perhaps higher than in any nation.

☐ **Children born into poverty are more likely to have drug or alcohol problems.** The United States has "twice the poverty rate of Canada, three times the rate of Western Europe."[11]

☐ In early 1994 the *Peoria Journal Star* published a remarkable series about Illinois' third-largest city. The appalling figures include: seven out of ten children in that city live below the poverty line; 87 percent of teen births are out of wedlock, and 41 percent of all births are out of wedlock.

☐ In Illinois families started by teenage mothers cost the state well over $1 billion a year.

☐ **A teen mother will earn approximately half as much** during her lifetime as a woman who does not become a mother until the age of 20.

☐ **Children of single parents are twice as likely to drop out of high school** and 2.5 times as likely to become teenage parents.

☐ **High school drop-outs—boys or girls—are more likely to become parents as teenagers.** Some of it is predictable: they have poor grades or poor attendance or are a year behind their age peers in school. Any one of these factors puts them at high risk for becoming drop-outs and teen-age parents.

☐ Of the one million teen-age pregnancies each year, approximately 400,000 end in abortions.

☐ **Teenage pregnancy follows the unemployment statistics, regardless of ethnic background.** In Alexander and Pulaski counties in Illinois, which have large African American populations, there is a high rate of teenage pregnancy. In Pope and Hardin Counties in the same state, with virtually no African American population, there is a high rate of teenage pregnancy. What all four counties have in common is a high rate of unemployment.

☐ **The rate of teenage pregnancy drops dramatically when either or both parents have finished high school.**

☐ In 1940, 3.8 percent of all births occurred out of wedlock; in 1965, 7.7 percent; and in 1990, 28 percent. Skewing those figures slightly, however, is the decline in numbers of children for those who are married, making the out-of-wedlock births appear more dramatic.

☐ Of births to teens in 1940, 13.5 percent were out of wedlock; in 1965, 20.8 percent; and in 1990, 67.1 percent.

- For white teens, 59 percent of births occur out of wedlock; for Hispanic teens 61 percent; for African American teens, 92 percent.

- The average annual number of births to teen mothers per 1,000 children born in the industrialized nations is thirty-eight; for the developing countries, 58; for the United States, 62.

- Single women who have been married are much less likely to remain on welfare for a lengthy period of time than single women who have never married.

A 16-year-old Los Angeles girl gave this nonstatistical insight: "Out of the funerals [I have attended], I never seen a father right there, crying. Only the moms, crying and crying and crying at the funerals and afterwards."[12]

Regrettably, Mr. President, these are reflections of our culture that are not easily or quickly changed. Like the problems of crime—and these trends are related to crime—there are no quick fixes. Answers like school prayer and cutting people off welfare may bring applause at a suburban civic club or votes at the ballot box, but by diverting attention from possible real answers, they only add to the misery of the already miserable.

That the family situation has direct bearing on the ability of people to cope is underscored by a 1990 U.S. Census study of African American families in the northern and western states of our nation. Where the African-American couple was married and under the age of 35, they had a mean income of $48,220, while a white family in the same region with the same conditions had a mean income of $48,260—almost identical.[13] Combine opportunity (the West and North are better on that) and family stability, and people of all ethnic groups do well.

Resolving our welfare difficulties is like resolving most complex problems: Sensible answers are entwined with other issues. Like almost all difficulties, real solutions on welfare will not be quick and dramatic. If we can provide slow, steady, solid answers, the public will be well served. The danger is that the public appetite is for quick answers; the less people know about an issue, the easier it is for them to believe there are easy solutions. We do know that the simplistic approach offered by a few—get tougher on welfare recipients, cut back their benefits—will not solve our problem. In inflation-adjusted figures, in 1970 the average family on welfare received $644 in benefits and in 1993, $366. If reducing benefits were to give us the answer, our welfare rolls would be going down; instead, they increased from 7,429,000 to 14,128,000, almost doubling.

Welfare assistance is much higher for recipients in Western Europe than in the United States, but they have nowhere near our teenage pregnancy rate or welfare rate or poverty rate. We have to look for answers other than the simplistic, meat-axe approach to cutting benefits. Few go on welfare because it is attractive; almost all go on welfare because they see no alternative. However, there are things you, together with Congress and the American people, can do to improve the situation. And the medicine we must take has to be stronger than your administration has recommended, good as that is. For example, to spend $1.2 billion over a five-year period ($240 million a year) for jobs for those who have been on welfare for two years or longer, won't begin to cut into the problem.

To spend $60 million a year (or $300 million for five years) for pregnancy prevention education will help, but just a little. Your people have put together a plan that can be described in three words: good, but timid. You can make speeches that you have a program, but it will come nowhere near "ending welfare as we know it" as you pledged. And the portion of the plan that permits states to take punitive action against welfare recipients is more likely to increase the crime rate than decrease welfare costs.

What should we do? As William Sloane Coffin has written, "It is one thing to say with the prophet Amos, 'Let justice roll down like the mighty water,' and quite another thing to work out the irrigation system."[14] Lofty rhetoric must be replaced with hard-headed solutions that can work.

An Eight-Step Program

1. Provide jobs for people in need. There can be no significant welfare reform without a meaningful jobs program. Anything less tinkers at the edges of reform and cannot accurately be labeled reform. There is some truth in Rush Limbaugh's comment: "We need to teach self-reliance. We need to re-establish the American work ethic. It's a fact of life that when something is given to someone, he values it far less than when he earns it through his own sweat."[15] I do not suggest that he endorses what I recommend in the following paragraphs—though it has appeal to some conservatives—but he has touched on a raw nerve, a weakness in our present approach.

New York financier Felix Rohaytn, a thoughtful observer, believes that "it is government's responsibility to step into the jobs breach because private institutions alone can't handle the problem."[16] He would downplay the role of retraining. "Retraining for what?" he asks.

I could give you heartbreaking letters from people out of work, but rather than that, here is a more typical case from a woman in Alton, Illinois:

> I wish we could get some jobs for older people in this area. I will be 60 years old in January and have

no income and can't get any help or assistance. I had 25 years of experiences and can't find a job since Mom died. When I go back to places where I applied, they [have] hired younger people.

Right now, Mr. President, our answer to her is that she must first become a pauper, then we will pay her for doing nothing. She deserves better. Our society deserves better.

Large numbers of unemployed people can be turned into an asset to the nation with constructive programs, or they can become a liability to the nation. We can adopt policies that pay people for doing something or pay them for doing nothing; pay them for being productive or pay them for being nonproductive. We have chosen the wrong path—wrong for people who are on welfare, wrong for taxpayers, and wrong for the future of our nation. It is ironic that we have made the bad choice, because we have in our history a rich example of leadership that took the great liability of unemployment and turned it into a huge national asset.

During the Great Depression of the 1930s, the nation had millions of disheartened, hopeless people who had given up on themselves and their country. While the percentage of our unemployed population then exceeded current numbers, today we also have millions of Americans who lack hope and have given up on themselves, and their sense of pride in our country is minimal; they see the nation's policies and policy-makers turning away from the desperation of the unemployed.

In May 1935 President Franklin Roosevelt issued an executive order creating the Works Progress Administration, better known by its abbreviation, the WPA, and by December of that year, 2,667,000 formerly unemployed people were at work, an amazing feat. But even more amazing is what they did. They built 125,110 buildings—schools, libraries, and lodges in parks; they installed 24,300 miles of sewer line and 16,100 miles of water line; they helped start hot lunch programs in thousands of schools; and they taught more than 1.5 million adult Americans how to read and write. The WPA encouraged the creative arts by sponsoring musicians, playwrights, and authors. Two of the authors to emerge from the WPA were Arthur Miller and Richard Wright. The list of accomplishments and those who benefited directly is lengthy. People who participated received a small amount of money, but much more important, they received hope and found pride in themselves, two things lacking for many of today's welfare recipients.

Our culture is different today. Thanks in part to the leadership of FDR, many construction jobs, for example, are now held by union workers. The WPA was an overwhelmingly male-oriented effort, while today's work force is much more diverse. But the idea of providing work for everyone did not die with the WPA. The Employment Act of 1946, introduced under President Harry Truman's leadership, called for a national policy of full employment. By the time Congress passed the measure, it had been weakened appreciably. As on so many things, Harry Truman had the right idea.

There have been other small-scale experimental jobs programs. A four-year New York City program working with long-term drug addicts from disadvantaged areas gave jobs to the addicts and compared the results with a similar cross-section who were not given jobs. The work varied from doing clerical service in a library, to painting in public schools, to translating for a district attorney. Called Wildcat, the program's results are described by one author:

> The stereotype is that the kind of people who abuse drugs do not want to work, but of one group of over

three hundred addicts offered jobs in Wildcat, all
but thirty showed up for work . . . . More than half
of those who started work stayed on the job for at
least a year. . . . Disadvantaged addicts flocked to
the program, and, from its first day of operation,
Wildcat attracted more applicants than it could accommodate. . . . Almost half (46 percent) of them
received no welfare at all while in the project, versus
only 6 percent [of the control group]. . . . A smaller
percentage were arrested during the three-year [pe-
riod of studying the results]. . . . Those who worked
[in either the control group or the project] during
more than half of the three-year study period were
arrested less than half as often as those who worked
less. . . . Those who worked more than half of the
time were much more likely to cut back their drug
use. . . . participants more often married or entered
common-law relationships; they were more likely
to be supporting dependents and living with their
children. . . . Wildcat appears to have provided a
head start for some and been the critical vehicle of
rehabilitation for others.[17]

I have introduced legislation that would take some of the
basic concepts of the WPA and adjust them to today's
realities. Senator David Boren of Oklahoma has taken the
same idea and suggested a more limited demonstration of
the proposal to see what works well and what does not, a
good suggestion. Senators Harry Reid of Nevada and Harris
Wofford of Pennsylvania are also supporters. Here is the
rough outline of the idea:

☐ Anyone out of work five weeks or longer is eligible,
including people not on welfare. We make a mistake
when we pauperize people before we give them help.

☐ Those who are eligible can work four days a week at the minimum wage, or for ten percent above what they draw on welfare, or for ten percent above what they draw on unemployment compensation. Four days a week at the minimum wage amounts to $535 a month—not much money, but the average family of three on welfare in Illinois receives $367 a month, and the average family on welfare in Mississippi receives $120 a month. Nationally, the average is $388.

Here is a breakdown for monthly dollar payment for all of the states for a family of three on AFDC as of January 1993:

State	Amount	State	Amount
Alabama	164	Montana	390
Alaska	923	Nebraska	364
Arizona	347	Nevada	348
Arkansas	204	New Hampshire	516
California	624	New Jersey	424
Colorado	356	New Mexico	324
Connecticut	680	New York	577
Delaware	338	North Carolina	272
D. C.	409	North Dakota	401
Florida	303	Ohio	341
Georgia	280	Oklahoma	324
Hawaii	693	Oregon	460
Idaho	315	Pennsylvania	421
Illinois	367	Puerto Rico	180
Indiana	288	Rhode Island	554
Iowa	426	South Carolina	200
Kansas	429	South Dakota	404
Kentucky	228	Tennessee	185
Louisiana	190	Texas	184
Maine	453	Utah	402
Maryland	359	Vermont	659
Massachusetts	539	Washington	546
Michigan	489*	Virginia	354
Minnesota	532	West Virginia	249
Mississippi	120	Wisconsin	517
Missouri	292	Wyoming	360

Because of relatively higher welfare payments in a few states, the federal government would pay more to those states under this jobs plan, but because of the welfare formula on federal matching funds, the national government is already paying some states more than others. The disparity between states for both the federal government and recipients would be reduced under this jobs program.

☐ At $535 a month, families will still be eligible for food stamps, just as many who work in the private sector at low wages are now eligible.

☐ Those with a Medicaid card keep it. People should not lose money or health coverage because they work.

☐ More than one person in a family can work. If two work, for example, the family income would be $1,070 a month. Unlike the present welfare program, this approach would encourage families to live together. And as a friend, Herman Bodewes, has observed: "If your income is there, it's easier to maintain family values." The relationship of income to family values is clear when we look at the numbers of out-of-wedlock births of white women. For white women who lived below the poverty line the year before a child was born, 44 percent gave birth to children out of wedlock. Of white women who lived above the poverty line the year before the child's birth, six percent gave birth to children out of wedlock. Ignoring the tie between poverty and many of our problems is extremely shortsighted.

☐ Participants are eligible for the Earned Income Tax Credit.

☐ The fifth day of each week, the participant has to try to get a job in the private sector. If someone finds a job, even at the minimum wage for 40 hours a week (rather than 32 hours under this program), that represents an increase in income of 25 percent. The plan encourages people to get private sector jobs.

☐ This program is project oriented, with a local committee of 13 people choosing the projects. One of the 13 is a labor union representative, and another a representative of the business community. Either can veto a project to avoid problems with either unions or businesses. The jobs could be teaching adults how to read and write, tutoring young people in school who need help, escorting children to school in crime-ridden neighborhoods, cleaning up a park, cleaning up vacant lots that are eyesores, planting trees, assisting in day care centers for children or seniors, developing an arts program and a host of other useful projects local people will suggest.

☐ People are screened as they enter the program. If they cannot read and write, or can barely do so, they are enrolled locally to acquire those skills. If they have no high school diploma or have not passed a GED test, they are encouraged to work on this. If they have no marketable skill, they are required to try to acquire one in a local community college or technical school.

There is Work to be Done

We have millions of Americans who want to work, but cannot find a job. We also have a host of things that need to be done in our communities. Meshing the two makes sense and gives people pride and hope, which we now deny too many Americans. Adopting such a program would be real welfare reform. Hoping that the private sector will suddenly boom and provide the needed jobs is unrealistic. A large number of major corporations, such as IBM and General Motors, have announced scaled-back employment. Do the financial markets view this as grim news? Frequently, the day after such announcements, the stock of the corporation rises. Today, more and more can be produced by fewer and fewer. That trend is not going to change.

Those who preach only the doctrine of retraining (and I strongly support retraining) fail to recognize the basic loss of jobs.

Like any investment, initially this jobs plan will cost more than simply continuing the status quo. But the present program is so massively flawed, as both recipients and taxpayers know, that if the American people are told why we are investing a little more initially, they will be receptive. In 1987 the Congressional Budget Office estimated that if the jobs plan outlined here were to be adopted nationally, its net cost above the present programs would be $8 billion. Inflation has increased that number. But all studies suggest that this plan will save money in the long run, and, more important, we would be preparing people to become useful, contributing citizens—good for them and good for all of the rest of us.

It is a program that you can sell easily, Mr. President. When I talk to the most conservative Chamber of Commerce and tell them we have a choice of paying people for being productive or nonproductive; for doing something or doing nothing, I ask the soft question: What is your choice? Their answer is the expected one, and they are enthusiastic about the alternative. They are also willing to sink additional tax dollars into the right choice.

Social Security has been a great government program— "social engineering," if you will—that has cut the number of elderly living below the poverty line by more than 50 percent and channeled funds into the communities where they live. Now we must build on that good experience—not attack it or take from it—and devise programs that can lift many of the non-elderly above the poverty line, particularly our children—our future. One of ancient Rome's most famous women, Cornelia, wife and mother of Roman leaders, was visited by a neighbor who proudly displayed her jewelry and asked Cornelia, "Do you have any jewelry?" Cornelia replied, turning to her children, "These are my jewels."[18] The same is true for the United States, and we are not protecting our jewels well.

This jobs proposal will also put more money into communities, particularly those in states with low welfare payments. In Mississippi, with its average payment for a family of three of $120 per month, shifting to $535 would not only improve the quality of life for that family but also add to the income of grocers, clothing store merchants, and others. Ultimately, that will improve the income of the federal government.

Another not-so-small advantage of the program is that it will permit many who live in small communities, who have their roots there, to remain where their families are. This type of job opportunity does not pay much, but it is enough to permit people to hang on while something else develops. Part of the nation's urban problem is caused by the flight from small-town and rural America, where there is nothing to hold people economically, and when they move to the big city, they are often ill-prepared for its problems.

In the book *A Nation of Strangers*, Vance Packard advanced the theory, which I accept, that one of the reasons for our high crime rate is that we are too rootless, that what we regard as a great national asset, our mobility, is also a great national liability. People move so much that they lose a sense of responsibility to their family and neighbors. Neighbors in the new environment may be strangers. There is a complete loss of restraint from "I don't want to do this because I will embarrass my family or myself within my community." A good jobs program can, at least slightly, reduce mobility that is not healthy. And because there is such a close nexus between unemployment and crime, this jobs program would at least slightly reduce the crime rate.

The present system of unemployment compensation still works in more cyclical industries, such as construction, but the assumption that virtually everyone who is unemployed will soon find other employment is no longer valid. We have moved from covering the large majority of the involuntarily unemployed with unemployment insurance to protecting less than half. A guaranteed job opportunity plan like the one described here is not a substitute for permanent employment at better wages, but it is much better than no employment and the loss of self-esteem that goes with it.

This jobs proposal would also be counter-cyclical, softening the blow of recessions to the nation's economy.

The great division in our society is not between black and white, between Hispanic and Anglo or the other divisions about which we read. The great division is between those who have hope and those who have given up. This is our chance to give people hope, to help them and the nation. The bottom line is: The most important single action that can be taken to reduce welfare costs long-term, and break the welfare cycle, is a jobs program.

2. Create stand-by authority for the President to create more conventional jobs programs. One way to reduce welfare is to prevent people from getting there. Education programs (see page 150) are part of that. But we also need to create a more rapid federal response when there is a dip in the economy. The deficits we have created and learned to tolerate not only have cost us millions of industrial and construction jobs, as well as other positions, they have also limited the ability of the federal government to respond to a recession. When we tried to pass an $11 billion jobs bill for you, Mr. President—which is not large in a $6.5 trillion economy—too many members of Congress showed a reluctance to support it because of our already huge deficits, and it failed.

To achieve flexibility for jobs programs, the deficit has to be substantially reduced, or better yet, eliminated. Fred Bergsten, Assistant Secretary of the Treasury under President Carter and one of the nation's finest economists, made a suggestion that ties in with my deficit plan (see Chapter Eight). He suggested that a pool of up to one percent of the economy, $60 billion, be created to use to stabilize the economy when and where needed. For example, the plan might authorize you to issue grants to state and local governments when the unemployment in any area exceeds ten percent. State and local governments would have to show that the money could be put to work to create jobs within sixty days. These would be jobs paying the prevailing union wage within an area. They might be highway projects, mass transit efforts, sewer and water plans, school construction, park improvements, or similar efforts; but state and local governments would have to ensure that a healthy percentage of the participants would be women and minorities, who tend to represent the poorest in our society. Highway jobs, for example, have traditionally been overwhelmingly male and white, though that is changing.

By having this authority for spending on job creation on a stand-by basis, you and your successors could move quickly on soft spots in the economy. One of the criticisms of Congress—a legitimate criticism—is that we move far too slowly to respond to recessionary pressures. If the $60 billion figure frightens people, we could try at least a $15 billion stand-by effort, supported by a small, dedicated tax such as a gasoline tax increase.

By moving in with projects that communities need at the time unemployment is high, the federal government will help to stabilize the economy and reduce the numbers of people who are compelled to turn to welfare.

3. Actively discourage teenage pregnancies. The immediate and most obvious need in some schools is for sex education, including counseling and candid information about avoiding pregnancy and, for someone from a low-income family, how to get birth control pills or other effective means of contraception. Sex education should include lessons in how to say no, as well as encouraging abstinence, but communities must recognize that protective measures are necessary for those who will not abstain. Whether to have sex education is a decision local school districts should make, and the federal government should not impair their ability to make it. The *Peoria Journal Star* did a study of teenage mothers in its circulation area and found that approximately ten times as much is spent on the results of teenage pregnancies as is spent on preventing them. One successful program they do have is called Young Teen Sisters, a program run by Planned Parenthood that works with the younger sisters of teenage mothers. The statistical odds are high that these younger sisters will become teenage mothers also. They see the pride and attention that motherhood brings, but the program provides them with a more balanced view of the hope and opportunity that later motherhood can give. In Atlanta's schools a course/program titled "Postponing Sexual Involvement" is offered. It has caused eighth graders to "wait at least until the end of ninth grade to start having sex. A study showed that kids not in the program were five time more likely to become sexually active than those taking the five-week course."[19]

While sex education and other activities are desirable in many areas, there are other actions that should be taken everywhere.

Girls who drop out of high school are much more likely to become pregnant, and boys who drop out are much more likely to father unwanted children. Reducing drop-out rates must start with intensified preschool education programs in disadvantaged areas and tutoring and mentoring programs for first, second, and third grade students who show signs that they need help in school. That help must be there through succeeding years. That is easy for me to write, but it is not easily done. Whenever possible, those who drop out of school must be lured back.

By executive order you could appoint a commission of ten or fifteen people, chaired by someone like Marian Wright Edelman of the Children's Defense Fund or Roger Wilkins of George Mason University to report back in six months what should be done to discourage teenage pregnancies. My observation is that commissions that do the best job are of short duration, are not heavily funded, and have good people on them. If unwanted teen pregnancies could be substantially reduced in number—and they can be—that would be good news for the people involved, for welfare financing, and for our crime rate. A special commission could focus on this singular problem much more effectively than those who are viewing this as part of overall welfare reform.

One footnote that underscores the importance of dealing with this issue is that births are occurring to girls at an earlier and earlier age. We now have children of nine-year-olds on welfare. A gradual improvement in nutrition is making the citizens of many nations taller, and that same factor may be lowering the age for childbirth. Senator Moynihan observes that infants are being born to girls at an age "the [human] species has not seen before."[20]

4. End the isolation of the poor. Not only do we have the economic residential segregation that I have already mentioned, but too often that segregation isolates people of limited income from jobs. Where are the poor? Overwhelmingly, in the central cities. Where are the jobs being created? Overwhelmingly, in the suburbs. Employers are leaving the cities because of high taxes, weak schools, crime, and what they consider a better quality of life. Early in the morning in Chicago, I have seen the stream—slightly more than a trickle—of African Americans going to work in the suburbs, some as maids and some to work in other situations. They overcame the barrier. But for many inner-city residents, that barrier between the city and suburbs is too high a hurdle. There are the costs of transportation to pursue an opportunity, travel time with children to manage, and the fear of the unknown about which they have heard stories—usually exaggerated—about treatment of minorities; they may have limited reading skills, which makes public transportation forbidding, or simply lack self-confidence, not an unknown quality among people who have experienced more failures in life than successes.

A significant experiment called the Gautraux Program is at work in the Chicago area. It takes families who live in high-rise housing projects, occupied in Chicago almost entirely by African Americans, and moves them in a carefully planned way to private housing—not public housing—in the suburbs. Frequently, it also provides suburban mentors. Robert Greenstein summarized the results:

> Before the program started, the families who moved
> to the suburbs closely matched the families who

lived within the city. But after moving, their experiences diverge sharply: the suburban-movers achieved much higher levels of employment; their children had substantially lower school drop-out rates and higher rates of college attendance, sharply higher employment levels, and much higher average wage levels.[21]

Started in 1976, by March 1994 the program had moved 5,400 families to 114 suburban communities and to other neighborhoods in Chicago. The suburban experience clearly is better for the families involved. They are required to move to neighborhoods that are not more than 30 percent minority. The program's appeal can be easily judged: Each January the office establishes a bank of twenty phones to take new applicants. Two thousand families are successful in getting through for this first part of the process—but the telephone company monitors unsuccessful attempts to get through and reports that more than 10,000 people tried to call.

This is not an answer for huge numbers of city dwellers, but it is an insight into the answer for many. It is one piece of a mosaic that we should put together to significantly reduce poverty and its accompanying ills in the nation. From 1955 to 1992 unemployment for white young people grew from 36 percent to 46 percent, but during this same period unemployment for young African Americans grew from 34 percent to 70 percent. While there are many causes for these figures, a significant factor is proximity to entry-level jobs. White youth grow up where there is a supply of jobs; black youth grow up in areas of high unemployment.

The evidence from many perspectives is that building more public housing that stockpiles the poor in central cities compounds the problems of poverty. An *Atlanta Constitution* study of the 33,400 residents of public housing in that city found only one out of twenty employed and 98 percent of the families headed by single mothers.[22] Programs like Section 8 grants that encourage subsidies for the use of private housing rather than public housing are helpful, particularly if people are encouraged to move where jobs are being created. Wherever politically possible, housing authorities should encompass a larger jurisdiction than the central city so that this type of movement is eased.

Enlightened private housing developers also should be encouraged to plan so that there is some economic mixture of housing. Properly done, it can add to a development, not detract. Housing subdivisions don't have to have a dull, monotonous sameness. Former HUD Secretary Jack Kemp, a conservative with sensitivity to the poor, suggested tax credits for housing developers who followed a mixed pattern.

There are other ways to avoid isolating the poor, including creative transportation between the jobless and the jobs. Isolation of the poor adds to their inability to extricate themselves from the quicksand of welfare.

5. Consider a modest increase in the minimum wage. I use the word "consider" rather than "enact," Mr. President, because of the uncertainty of health care reform and the nature of that legislation as I write to you. If health care reform adds a significant burden to small businesses, which does not appear probable, then the increase in the minimum wage should be temporarily postponed. But assuming that is not the case, a sensible increase in the minimum wage will encourage more people to work rather than struggle on welfare. Three decades ago the minimum wage supported a breadwinner for a family of three above the poverty level. Today that worker falls far short. The evidence that an increase in the minimum wage discourages employment is not strong except for teenage employment, where the results of studies are mixed. But a modest increase, depending on the health care reform situation, should create no barrier to employment.

6. Provide enriching child care. Most industrial nations are ahead of us on this. It is fine to say to a woman on welfare, "Go to work." Even if she has the opportunity, what does she do with her three children? Too many children are unsupervised because of terrible choices faced by desperate parents. To do what we should for the nation, however, child care should be more than custodial. It should help prepare children for kindergarten, help them recognize numbers and letters and become eager to read. We need trained child care providers.

7. Toughen child-support legislation and rules. Those who father children, whether in their teens or in their sixties, should understand that this has economic consequences. Two of the abler members of the House, former Representative Tom Downey and Representative Henry Hyde, introduced legislation that in modified form has become law. It has helped. An additional $2.5 billion has been collected from fathers for child support, and 86 percent more absent fathers have been located since 1988. Further steps can be taken by the states. In theory, if all fathers could be located and forced to pay, an additional $34 billion could be collected.

Toughening child support requirements should mean more than going after financially negligent fathers. Children should be removed from homes—whether of natural parents or foster parents—where children are abused. Some experts say that will lead inevitably to some form of institutionalized care, similar to the orphanages of another era.

Some of this is occurring now. Unfortunately, it is expensive. But not as expensive as tolerating child abuse.

8. Strengthen the use of existing programs. The Job Opportunities and Basic Skills (JOBS) Program pioneered by Senator Moynihan is not an elixir for all our ills, but the evidence is in that it helps. However, only about 15 percent of those eligible under the AFDC programs are involved. If we combine greater coverage with a plan for the individual, a genuine plan that the recipient helps to shape but that also uses counseling to form, we can lift more of our people off welfare and out of poverty.

"Open your hand to the poor and the needy in your land," is an Old Testament admonition we are inadequately heeding.[23]

We Must Have Courage

The levels of poverty this nation tolerates should trouble our conscience. Your leadership, Mr. President, to expand the Earned Income Tax Credit, moved tangibly in the right direction. But we must take steps to do for the nonelderly what Social Security did for the elderly: dramatically reduce the percentages of people living in poverty. Representative Ray Thornton of your state has suggested that the United States needs a domestic Marshall Plan. I agree. It took courage for Harry Truman to suggest the then-unpopular Marshall Plan. At its height, we spent 2.9 percent of our national income annually for the Marshall Plan, the equivalent of $180 billion today. I do not suggest that grand a vision today, but we do need significantly more than just tinkering. The least expensive answer short-term is to maintain the status quo, but that is the most expensive answer long-term. An open, direct discussion of what is happening to the impoverished in our nation, an appeal to the noble in us, led by you as President, would stir the American people. If you combine that appeal to the best in us with necessary political refrains about "cleaning up welfare," it would carry the day, even if it includes a spending/revenue program somewhat larger than your more cautious advisers like. They and you must decide whether welfare reform will be a public relations slogan or a reality. If it is the latter, it will take resources—and courage. I would love to join with you in such a fight.

Sincerely,

Paul Simon

Seven

Education: Building for the Future

Dear Mr. President:

The key to economic opportunity and a more enlightened life for young people and adult Americans is education. For many, it's like turning on a light in a dark room. Someone asked Aristotle how much people with an education are superior to those without it, and he replied: "As much as the living are to the dead."[1] That exaggeration illustrates a truth. There are few issues that have been stressed so consistently throughout history as the importance of education. And for a democracy like the United States, it is essential that men and women be able to understand our world and to think independently—difficult to do without a good education. Four centuries before Christ, Plato referred to ignorance as a "disease of the mind."[2] On another occasion he wrote: "You ask what is the good of education in general, the answer is easy—that education makes good men, and that good men act nobly."[3] Several centuries later, St. Augustine confessed—as many of us could—that "by playing at ball, I made less progress in studies," but added: "In boyhood . . . I loved not study, and hated to be forced to it. Yet I was forced; and this was well done towards me . . . for unless forced, I had not learned."[4] In the year of our country's independence, Edward Gibbon published his *Decline and Fall of the Roman Empire*. In it he observes:

The use of letters is the principal circumstance that distinguishes a civilized people from a herd of savages. . . . Fully to apprehend this important truth, let us attempt, in an improved society, to calculate the immense distance between the man of learning and the illiterate peasant. The former, by reading and reflection, multiplies his own experience, and lives in distant ages and remote countries; whilst the latter, rooted to a single spot, and confined to a few years of existence, surpasses but very little his fellow-labourer the ox in the exercise of his mental faculties.[5]

In 1917, Alfred North Whitehead wrote: "The rule is absolute, the [nation] which does not value trained intelligence is doomed."[6]

Virtually all of our presidents have stressed education. Eighteen months before he became President, Abraham Lincoln wrote: "[Since] the Author of man makes every individual with one head and one pair of hands, it was probably intended that heads and hands should cooperate as friends . . . and that being so, every head should be cultivated, and improved, by whatever will add to its capacity for performing its charge."[7] John D. Rockefeller III, the father of my Senate colleague from West Virginia, summed it up well: "We can maintain a democratic system and move toward a progressively more humanistic society only to the extent that we increasingly have citizens who are alert, intelligent, informed, and involved in the real issues of our time."[8]

This morning—as I am typing this—I told political columnist David Broder that I thought one of your most significant and lasting contributions as President will be in education. It does not receive the media attention of health care or foreign relations, but it does play a huge role in shaping what kind of nation we will become.

Not only are your contributions significant, being with you on a college campus or at a school is an encouraging experience because you obviously feel at home, and when you speak about education, you are not simply reading a speech some staffer wrote for you. You speak from the heart. You know your audience, and you know your subject.

During the 1992 campaign, the *Chronicle of Higher Education* had this summary of your record as Governor of Arkansas:

> Mr. Clinton has made education the central focus of his administration and has built a substantial record. At his direction, the state raised teacher salaries and required teachers to pass a competency exam to keep their jobs. Arkansas instituted standards that required all public schools to offer college preparatory courses in mathematics and sciences and pushed laws to make colleges accountable for what their students learn. Mr. Clinton has encouraged students to go to college by establishing new scholarship programs [and] revamping technical colleges. . . . Two of the three times he tried, Governor Clinton even managed to get money for his reforms by pushing tax increases past a stubborn General Assembly. . . .The result was a sweeping package of school reforms, financed with a one-cent increase in the state sales tax. . . . In 1982, 35 percent of all high schools didn't offer advanced mathematics, 32 percent didn't offer chemistry, 54 percent didn't offer physics, and 47 percent didn't offer foreign languages. Today all high schools offer these subjects . . . . The college-going rate. . .has increased from 38 percent to 51 percent since 1983.[9]

That is an impressive record, and we need the same kind of leadership and doggedness to achieve equally dramatic results in the nation.

Extra-Curricular Activities

One education difficulty that we have in this country is that we tend to become obsessed with less-than-central issues, both at the national and local levels. Who the basketball coach is will stir a community far more than who teaches English; whether the band has adequate uniforms is likely to cause much more discussion than the adequacy of chemistry lab equipment. Many other illustrations abound at the local and state levels. That is where most education change must take place, but it will happen only minimally unless there is national leadership.

Across the country the great dispute these past 12 years has been over whether school vouchers should be available for nonpublic schools, and because of our preoccupation with that, little of substance has happened in areas that really matter, that could lift public education. This has happened before. Former Speaker Carl Albert recalled that "for years, general aid to education had stalled because of the church-state issue" until Lyndon Johnson pushed through a measure in 1965.[10] All too predictably, in recent years this public vs. private issue ignited passions again and got media attention—and too little happened. The fourth-grade student at a miserable school on the West Side of Chicago experienced no change and no improvement in opportunity and saw little to give him or her hope for an education or a future. The less emotional issues in education receive little public attention, but they are the fundamental changes that can improve our product.

In 1983 under President Reagan and the leadership of Education Secretary T. H. Bell, a report on education titled

A Nation at Risk shocked much of the United States. In response, editorials all said the right things, and all of us in politics made lofty speeches praising the report, assuring the American public that we would pay attention to its words. At that time, elementary and secondary school funding coming from the federal government had slipped from almost ten percent to 7.1 percent. Eleven years after that report, after thousands of speeches and editorials, 5.6 percent of that funding comes from the federal government, and the nation is more at risk than we were in 1983. We have three million more children living in poverty than we did then, and almost none of the problems mentioned in the report have been seriously addressed.

In fact, the shifting of responsibilities to state and local governments and the withdrawal of resources have aggravated school problems. Libraries are open fewer hours and have decreased their acquisition of books. Many schools have more students and fewer teachers. As resources per pupil in some schools diminished, so did the quality of service, complicated by the increased presence of drugs and crime; thousands of students shifted to nonpublic schools. More than half of California's school libraries have closed in the last ten years. A person serving time in one of that state's correctional facilities has a greater chance of access to a library in a prison than the average California student does to a library in a school.

College Tuition

At the college level, tuition has increased faster than inflation, but the reduced federal role of support for state and local government, as well as education, caused resources at the college level in many states to shrink. In California alone approximately 1,000 full-time college instructors lost their jobs, as did 2,000 part-time instructors.

The lack of federal support, plus the recession, plus increased tuition caused a drop in the percentage of men going to college. Kevin Phillips noted: "In 1990, 31 percent of men between the ages of thirty-four and forty-five had completed four years of college; in the younger twenty-five to thirty-four-year-old group, only 25 percent had done so."[11]

British author H. G. Wells wrote: "Human history becomes more and more a race between education and catastrophe."[12] In our country, it is not clear which is winning the race. And who can deny the assertion of former Atlanta Mayor Andrew Young: "Poverty cannot be wiped out as long as a significant portion of a population cannot obtain a quality education."[13]

Human Resources

When we discuss schooling in the United States, we ordinarily think of kindergarten through college, and that is a big part of education, but if we are to really change the nation, it must be more encompassing. Preschool efforts are now generally accepted as important, particularly in economically disadvantaged areas, though the gap between acceptance of the idea and acting on it is still huge. The other great, barely-met need is in adult education, particularly for those who lack fundamental skills. Teaching a preschooler but not reaching that preschooler's parent or parents greatly hampers the child's future as well as the adult's.

As a fourth-grader, I remember reading in a geography book that the United States is a rich country because of all our natural resources. I believed that until about 15 years ago when I suddenly realized that the nations moving ahead economically more rapidly than the United States—including Japan, South Korea, Sweden and Taiwan—had relatively few natural resources. They developed their human resources. They invested more in their people than we did. In higher education we remain ahead of other nations, though the gap is narrowing, but outside of higher education, we trail many nations. Secretary of Labor Robert Reich is fond of saying, "If you are well prepared, technology is your friend. If you are poorly prepared, technology is your enemy. We have too many people who are poorly prepared." How right he is, and how little we are doing to change that!

The demand for high-skill labor will continue to rise; the demand for low-skill labor will continue to drop. No administration will change those trends; no economic resurgence will alter that picture. Economist Lester Thurow puts it this way: "A worker has two things to offer—skills or the willingness to work for low wages. . . . The unskilled who live in rich societies must work for the wages of the equally unskilled who live in poor societies. If they won't . . . unskilled jobs simply move to poor countries."[14] If the United States is to be as productive as it should be, we cannot have millions of Americans unable to contribute in a significant way to our productivity. The key to improvement is education.

In viewing productivity growth in the United States since World War II, economist Charles Schultze observes: "The intellectual nonmaterial elements of our productive system—the combined effects of increased education of the work force and advances in knowledge—are overwhelmingly the main sources of American growth in productivity and living standards."[15] Those elements need to be improved—most of that improvement will come at the state and local levels. There is no substitute for leadership there. But we also need leadership at the national level. Here are practical, achievable steps that you as President can take at the federal level to improve the nation's education.

Literacy is the Key

Launch a national crusade to see that all Americans have basic literacy skills. Approximately three million adult Americans cannot recognize their name in block print, and twenty-three million adult Americans—the most conservative estimate—cannot read a newspaper or fill out an employment application. Worse, they cannot help their children with their school work. Most hide it; they are embarrassed about it. Their neighbors do not know. They often try to conceal it from their own families. No other major industrial nation has a similar problem.

The national unemployment rate for people with no high school diploma is 12.6 percent; for those with four years of high school, 7.2 percent; for those with four years of college, 3.5 percent. Those statistics hint at the literacy problem and the related loss to the nation. And, obviously, it is a huge loss to individuals.

Illinois is fairly typical of the nation. Of the twelve million people in the state, 26 percent of the adult population has not graduated from high school, and 786,000 adults have eighth grade schooling or less. That represents huge potential for the nation. Think what could happen in Illinois and the United States if we got even one-fourth of them interested in improving their education!

No one can disagree with the conclusion of one study: "Remedial education is essential if disadvantaged youths and adults are to attain any employment beyond low-skilled, entry-level positions."[16] It is essential not only for those youths and adults. Since only two to three percent of the work force is new each year, to lift the abilities and productive capacity only of those who graduate from high school and college means decades before the national picture is changed appreciably. To regain and maintain a competitive stance with other major industrial nations will require attention to a huge, almost untapped resource the nation has in its education-limited adult population.

We take pride in calling ours a classless society and in many ways it is. There is no caste system, no titles of nobility that can be passed from one generation to another within a family. But it is also true that our pride in economic mobility sometimes masks the reality that people are usually destined to remain in the general economic status of their parents. The big tool for breaking that mold is education. Universal education is the product of democracy, but it is now imitated by almost all dictators. We need to make literacy in the United States universal.

We now have a National Institute for Literacy. It needs to be used in a major way. Your leadership, Mr. President, is critical to really doing something about this massive problem. Here are some of the things you can do:

☐ Make a national speech calling on those who cannot read and write, or who barely can, to get help. Urge those who have not completed high school to get their high school equivalency, a GED.

☐ Ask the nation's libraries and community colleges to serve as centers for this training. Many are doing it already. Almost all could. Adults who cannot read and write rarely will walk into a grade school or a high school. It is too embarrassing. They do not feel embarrassment, however, walking into a library or community college.

☐ Ask the churches, synagogues, mosques, and PTAs of the nation to serve as a resource for getting people to confront their deficiency. This is a natural for these groups. They can also recruit volunteers to help tutor.

- Ask the schools to become involved. Teachers of elementary school students can often accurately guess what the home situation is. A few schools are doing a great job of getting parents into programs, handling it delicately so that there is no shame for them. But most schools are doing little or nothing.

- Ask agencies that deal with welfare and unemployment compensation to become more aggressive in finding out who needs help, and get help for them. It's tough to get off welfare if you can't fill out an employment form.

- Have the National Institute for Literacy work with states to make sure that testing is available for those who may have learning disabilities.

I have worked with a number of people on adult literacy, including a former NFL football player, now playing in Canada, who attended Oklahoma State University for four years—and later tested at the second-grade level. He discovered that he had a learning disability; eventually he not only took the usual classes to overcome his reading disability, but he ended up studying Japanese! I talked to a 59-year-old man who had just written the first letter of his life, to his daughter. How proud he is, and he should be! A Chicago woman told me about accidentally giving her daughter poison because she couldn't read the label and thought she had given her daughter needed medicine. A marvelous 45-year-old woman in rural southern Illinois, Gloria Wattles, stood up at a town meeting in a small community and read the first letter she had ever written. The letter thanked me for establishing the VISTA Literacy Corps, through an amendment, and told her life story. By the time she finished reading her letter, she was crying, and half the crowd was in tears—tears of happiness.

In teaching basic skills to adults, the opportunity is also presented to stress the importance of education for their children. Reaching out to the nation's adults with literacy is an area where you can accomplish a great deal for the nation, Mr. President, at virtually no cost.

In communities where there are large numbers of legal immigrants who want to learn English, make sure that classes are available. It is superficially appealing to talk about making English the official national language, and for all practical purposes, it already is. To function effectively in our country, you must be able to use English. But there are Americans whose mother tongue is Navajo, Spanish, Vietnamese, or some other language, whose English language skills are almost nil. Many of them enroll to take a class in English as a second language, then discover that rosters are already full. In some areas there are waits as long as eight months to get into a class.

That is eight months of less help for their children, less likelihood of getting a job, and greater likelihood of being on welfare. Adult education generally needs more emphasis, but no part of it pays off more quickly for our society than teaching people English.

Parents Have A Role

Encourage parents to get involved with their schools. That happens in rural Makanda, Illinois, and I am sure it also takes place in Hope, Arkansas. But in the larger cities parents too often feel helpless, uninvolved, and ill-equipped to contribute anything meaningful to the cause of education. Frequently, there is a single parent whose own memories of school are anything but pleasant, and who may well be illiterate. Reaching that parent—difficult as it is—could change life for her, as well as her child.

Not only do we need to get parents interested in helping themselves, we need to get them to push their children, and there is no substitute for that. In Taiwan, "fifty-one percent of the parents purchase an extra workbook to help their children in science; only one percent do in Minneapolis. Japanese students do five times as many hours of homework per week as their American peers. American students read only one-third as much as those in Switzerland."[17] Greater parental involvement in education is essential.

The General Assembly in Illinois passed a law establishing Local School Councils in Chicago. They have limited authority, but they do have the ability, among other things, to fire a principal. Councils are elected by the people in that local school district. Initially, I did not get excited by the idea. I thought it more a gesture than anything meaningful. But during the 1992-93 school year, I visited 18 schools on the West Side and South Side of Chicago, the poorer areas, and I came away with a different impression. A poll shows that 82 percent of the principals, 87 percent of the parents, and 68 percent of the teachers believe it has helped. They are right. Chicago's schools still have a long way to go, but I know now that any small steps we take at the federal level to encourage more parental involvement in the schools is helpful. Tie this in with the idea being promoted in New York City to have smaller schools and that can significantly improve what the schools can do.

Public Preschool

Preschool education for all—but particularly in disadvantaged areas—is vital. The evidence is overwhelming that this pays off in the long run, but not quickly. It is not as simple as some suggest. No one in the nation has worked harder to promote this idea than a remarkable philanthropist and creative thinker, Irving Harris. Among other projects, he helped create a school in the Robert Taylor homes, a dismal high-rise public housing project on the South Side of Chicago where the statistics on crime, poverty, and single parenting are grim. I asked him how the project was doing, and he responded, "It's going well, but it's harder than we thought."

That sums up all of these programs. They do well and give opportunity to young people whose future is as bleak as their neighborhoods. The cultural gap is great for many whose parents, often struggling alone, have given up. Teaching a child from a home where a parent is drug-addicted or an alcoholic or deeply depressed is not easy. But giving up on that child cannot be an option.

Minorities in the central cities face overwhelming problems. Listen to this report from Milwaukee: "Of the city's 5,716 African American males in high school, only 135 earned a B average or higher last year."[18]

A second-grade teacher in an urban school district told me, "Most of my children are behind first-graders in the suburban district." That is not the fault of the school; it reflects a lack of cultural investment that has been made in those children, often the offspring of parents unable to contribute much. We should get some volunteer tutors and other help for those second-graders now, but reach future second-graders before they reach that stage. The federally funded Head Start program, which gives an assist to children in poorer neighborhoods before kindergarten—as early as the age of three—gives necessary help and will benefit the children and the nation. We know that. But it is not available to all who need it. Almost all Head Start programs have a waiting list. One Head Start program I visited in Rock Island, Illinois, had a waiting list, and, even worse, those who came attended one day a week. One group of students came on Monday, a second on Tuesday, and so on through the week.

I asked the woman in charge what it would mean for these children if they could come five days a week. She smiled and replied, "You couldn't believe the difference it would make in their lives." We are "saving money" by not providing this help each day but at a huge cost to those children and the nation. In 1992 the United States spent $17 billion for the defense of the northern part of Norway, a sensitive military spot. Extending Head Start to all who are eligible would cost an additional $10 billion. I favor an adequate defense, but the long-run interest and security of this nation rests with those children.

More than Head Start is needed. Unbelievable as it may sound, reaching many children at the age of three may be too late. We now know that having programs to see that youngsters have adequate nurturing for both their bodies and their minds very early is important. Observing that drop-out prevention must start much earlier, former New York City Superintendent of Schools Anthony Alvarado commented: "It's strange. We know what to do; we just don't do it."[19]

An impressive and disturbing report issued by the Carnegie Corporation, *Starting Points*, underscores the need for our nation to do much better. No plan is a substitute for good parenting, but early childhood intervention can be of real help to a home with inadequate parenting. The finest programs try to reach the parents also. Somewhere, somehow, the message has to be given to all young people: You have potential. The child of a parent with low self-esteem is likely to carry the same burden, unless a teacher or counselor or volunteer tutor or someone gives that child greater expectations, and lifting the vision of a parent is one way of doing that. Dr. Paul Dudley White, a famous heart specialist, used to say, "Tell me how your legs are and I'll tell you how your heart is." We can modify that by saying, "Tell me how your economically disadvantaged children are doing, and I'll tell you the future economic health of your nation." Or as Solomon wrote in the ancient Proverbs: "Train up a child in the way he should go: and when he is old, he will not depart from it."[20]

More School

The school year must be extended. In Japan elementary and secondary school students attend 243 days a year; in Germany, 240. In the United States we average 180 days, and our school days are shorter. We can delude ourselves into believing that we can learn as much in 180 days as they do in the longer period, but we are only fooling ourselves. Particularly at the elementary level, teachers have to spend valuable time when school starts each fall refreshing students, repeating lessons learned the previous year. With a shorter time between the end of one school year and the beginning of the next, that is less of a problem in other nations.

An alternative that a few schools have accepted is to have year-round school but with three-week breaks scattered through the year. I have talked with the teachers, and they like it, as do most of the parents and students. But it is not a substitute for more days of school.

Mr. President, we know it will cost more. A Japanese student who has finished the twelfth grade, for example, between the extra days and extra hours, has at least two more years of schooling than our average high school graduate, and the Japanese student tests four grades higher. That's worth a few dollars! If the federal government were to provide states with a per capita grant to schools that extend their school year to at least 210 days, with a provision that the states would have to match that in a grant to local school districts, for a relatively small amount of money the nation could be launched in a better direction. The first schools that would take advantage of this probably would be the wealthier ones, though the formula could give a somewhat greater incentive to the less wealthy districts. But the reality is that if we can get some schools started on this, whether wealthy or not, it would not be long before it would be demanded for all schools. Federal leadership—your leadership—is required to initiate this in a significant way.

Unfortunately the situation is even worse than the number of days suggests. In the spring of 1994 the National Commission on Time and Learning reported that the time spent on academic subjects during four years of high school showed these averages: Germany, 3,528 hours; France, 3,280 hours; Japan, 3,170 hours; the United States, 1,460 hours. You don't need to be an Einstein to understand why we have slipped.

More and Better Teachers

Recognize the need to stimulate teachers. The most important ingredient in a good education, outside of parents, is a quality teacher. Harvard did a study on the new audio-visual and other aids for foreign language students to test the impact of these technical marvels. After a lengthy study they concluded that if a student has a good teacher, he or she will do well, and if the teacher is not of high quality, the student is not likely to do well, despite all the mechanical assistance.

Teaching is an isolated profession. Teachers need more opportunity to consult with one another, to have a colleague come into the classroom and make evaluations and offer suggestions, to have the chance to observe a master teacher in a classroom. One area where the federal government could learn from its own experience is in summer seminars for teachers. I don't know how many teachers I have heard say that the summer seminars provided by the federal government under the National Defense Education Act passed in 1958 really inspired them. French teachers polished their French and learned more teaching techniques. Chemistry instructors learned the latest scientific developments, as well as clues on dealing with uninterested students. Teaching became exciting once again for those getting bored, experiencing a gradual burn-out. The federal government now assists in a small number of these, but we should expand the program to reach many more, as we once did. This is a practical way for the federal government to help the most essential ingredient in a good education, teaching.

We pay too little attention to our teachers. Some years ago I accepted an invitation six months in advance to speak at the commencement of the Scholl College of Podiatric Medicine, at the request of a long-time friend. The six months quickly slipped by, and suddenly, with no experience in foot problems, I had to speak to a group of graduating podiatrists. In doing research for my speech, I discovered Illinois (and probably all states) has much stricter standards for those who take care of our feet than those who take care of our children. Something is wrong with our priorities. We need high standards for both professions.

One economist has noted:

> Quality education is simply not possible without a cadre of well-prepared and competent teachers at all levels. . . . In the United States, teaching has not been seen as an attractive occupation especially up through the secondary level. Qualifications are relatively low [and] pay lags well behind industry.[21]

School Financing

Encourage greater equity in school financing. Sweden does not have the huge differences between wealth and poverty that we have, but the Swedes devote two to three times as much in education dollars to the poorer areas as they do to the more affluent areas, believing that the needs are greater among the poor. That is logical. We do the opposite. The wealthier areas have more resources and spend more on education, and the poorer districts suffer. Part of that is because in so many states we are excessively dependent on the real estate tax for the financing of education.

Illinois is an example. The difference in assessed valuation per student in school districts varies from $5,300 to $880,000. And that is reflected in the educational offering and the educational product. Impoverished East St. Louis, Illinois, is an example of the imbalance. It has every problem—high crime rates, high unemployment, drugs, alcohol . . . the list goes on. And partially because of these grim realities, almost all the industry has left the city, as have most of the middle-income African Americans and whites. For a city that once boasted a population of almost 90,000, the latest census shows 40,944. In order to continue the struggle to maintain its schools, it has one of the highest tax rates in the state and still lacks fundamental resources. And partially because of the high tax rates, it is difficult to get a business or new home-owners to come into the city.

Unfortunately, the inequity in opportunity is often compounded by racial realities. A study by Gary Orfield and Carole Ashkinaze notes: "People who would be outraged by a proposal to provide unequal education by race within a school district accept without question unequal schooling among separate white and black districts built on residential segregation."[22]

Mr. President, you have shown courage by advocating a change in the formula for the Chapter One program for impoverished areas, which calls for more assistance to the areas of greater need—logical, but education is no different than other jurisdictions: The "haves" don't like to give up anything for the "have nots." We need your similar attention to the total picture of inequity in school financing.

Encourage Racial and Economic Integration

It remains vital to the future of the nation that youngsters learn respect for "different" people. Diversity as an educational tool is important. That is often difficult to accomplish in urban districts, and some exchange with suburban schools is desirable for both the suburbs and the city. It is not easy to achieve politically, either, but in isolated areas there has been progress, and the idea needs further encouragement. Where this has happened, there has almost always been an unusually enlightened and courageous school superintendent or some state funding incentives or both. Federal funding incentives would be helpful. "Separate but equal" is as inoperable today as when the Supreme Court struck it down in 1954.

Diversity should be more than across racial and ethnic lines, however. Economic integration is also important. Secretary of Education Richard Riley observed in an interview: "Poor children [attending] a more wealthy school, surrounded by kids who are well-educated . . . do better."[23] A University of Georgia study of Atlanta area schools found that "racially integrated suburban schools scored much better than their black suburban counterparts despite the fact that they had almost as many low-income students."[24] A more integrated housing pattern in both race and economics is desirable but will take decades to achieve. In the meantime, there are practical ways to provide greater opportunity to all students.

Patricia Graham, who has headed research efforts with the federal government and at Harvard, points to another area that is a need and an opportunity: "By the end of the century it is estimated that between 30 and 40 percent of school children will be from minority groups, yet the current percentage of minority teachers is less than 10 percent and dropping."[25]

Challenging Students

Teachers should be encouraged to challenge students more. This costs no money. Senator Claiborne Pell of Rhode Island has a question he asks student groups, "How many of you feel you should be challenged to do more?" A huge majority raise their hands. I have stolen this question from him, and I find the response is the same, particularly at the junior high and high school levels, and it is true regardless of the ethnic makeup or economic status of the area around the school.

The best example of this is the visit by a remarkable, successful industrialist, Eugene Lang, to the old grade school he had attended in New York City. The school, which once had a predominantly Jewish and Italian ethnic mix, had shifted to African American and Latino, and the community moved from struggling middle-class to struggling poor. Seventy-five percent of those who attended his school now dropped out before graduating from high school. Lang visited the school and told the sixth graders that he would guarantee a college education to all who completed high school. But he did more than that. He became enmeshed in their lives, helping them with problems they had at home or with juvenile authorities or at school. Suddenly that group of young people who had little hope saw their lives turn around, and instead of 75 percent dropping out before high school graduation, two-thirds went on to college.

There were discouragements; not every young person met the challenge, but many did. Eugene Lang recognized, however, that the main aim of what became known as the "I Have a Dream" program should not be college, but for each student to acquire the basic skills needed to function effectively in our society. More than 90 percent of his students—he calls them dreamers—earned high school diplomas or GED certification in a school that formerly had a 75 percent drop-out rate.

Others heard about Eugene Lang and what he did and have followed in his footsteps. They formed an "I Have a Dream" Foundation to encourage others to do the same. By early 1994 the program had spread across the nation, with 156 "I Have a Dream" projects established involving more than 12,000 students ("dreamers") in 55 cities. In addition, thousands of individuals and institutional supporters—colleges, corporations, religious, and civic groups—have in smaller ways either become involved in these projects or assumed some responsibilities for students. Modest steps also have been taken in the federal law to encourage such private sector involvement. And the state of Texas has started a Partnership and Scholarship Program that takes Eugene Lang's idea and applies it to at-risk students in that state.

It would help, Mr. President, if you devoted one of your Saturday radio messages to the Eugene Lang story. But more than that, we have to see to it that all young people get that spark of hope that Eugene Lang instilled in those students.

Address Curriculum Weaknesses

Too many students cannot write a decent sentence and have never been seriously challenged to do so. True/false tests and multiple choice questions are easier than essays to grade. But students do not sharpen their writing and language skills that way.

There are more school districts in the nation than physics teachers.

Only 15 percent of high school students take an advanced math course, and only three percent take calculus.

Foreign language instruction is almost nonexistent in our grade schools, while in almost every elementary school in other nations students learn foreign languages. I have visited primitive schools—in terms of physical facilities—in situations as remote as nomadic groups traveling in the Sahara desert, in what was once Spanish Morocco, and found young people gathered in a small tent studying a foreign language. It is impressive to visit a fourth grade class in another developing African country, Botswana, and see students in their fourth year of foreign language study. We consider that nation "a developing country," and by most economic measurements, it is, but those fourth-graders have had more foreign language study than the average college graduate in the United States. We have the only foreign service in the world that you can enter without the knowledge of a foreign language. I have pushed several secretaries of state on this and, through amendments, encouraged more language competence for State Department personnel. The situation is gradually improving. The secretaries of state acknowledge our weakness, but all have said, "Don't expect us to do what our schools have not done." Our businesses also are hurt. There is a simple rule in business: You can buy in any language, but if you want to sell, you have to speak the language of your customer. We can't speak the languages of our customers. There was a time when the United States could wait for the world to come to us, and then we would sell to them. That world has changed dramatically, but our school curriculum does not reflect the new realities.

Bloomington, Illinois, offers a small vignette on the importance of quality education and of foreign language study. Japanese and American officials of Chrysler-Mitsubishi selected Bloomington and its adjacent city, Normal, as the site for a major automobile plant. After some ceremonies in the Capitol in Washington, I invited the Chrysler and Mitsubishi officials to my office and asked the Mitsubishi executive why they had chosen Bloomington-Normal. "It is a beautiful community, and your state made us a fine offer," he replied in that formal, polite manner that Japanese leaders have.

"Yes," I responded, "but there are many beautiful communities in the United States, and many states made fine offers. What made you pick this community?"

"There were two small factors that impressed us," he replied. "One was that the Bloomington Chamber of Commerce, for twenty-five years, had a sister city relationship with a community in Japan, and the other was that two years ago, one of the schools in Bloomington started teaching Japanese. We thought we would be welcome there." People in Bloomington who wanted to enrich their school curriculum landed 3,600 jobs for the area, plus many more indirect jobs.

In the United States we leave virtually all curriculum decisions to state and local governments, contrary to the practice in almost all other nations. The French Minister of Education could boast that he "could look at his watch and tell you exactly what was being taught in every classroom in the country."[26] We have avoided anything even approaching that. There is much that is good about our more unstructured approach, but there are also national needs, and the national government must indicate through financial incentives and in other ways what those needs are.

Learning by Doing

The school-to-work bill that you signed into law, which I had the privilege of sponsoring in the Senate, will help the curriculum in many schools. We devote much attention in high school to that one-fourth of the student population who will go on to get a bachelor's degree in college and not enough attention to those who will not. The school-to-work bill encourages schools and businesses and labor unions to work together more, and that is to everyone's advantage. This is "hire" education that helps young people learn by doing. They chart their own paths to real, high-skill, high-wage jobs. Students who work at a business or industry suddenly find their math or English or other course has new meaning. As a general rule, students who find one course of interest stay in school. One-fourth of our students now drop out before graduating from high school. Most students who work part-time at a business do better at school and are less likely to drop out. Some will go on to college, but all will learn from the process. Businesses are pleased because they find some valuable future employees through this process, in addition to the satisfaction they receive from helping the local schools.

Education Needs Tools

We should ensure that all schools get the technology and books they need. The computer world is one that young people of all backgrounds grab onto quickly and eagerly. Visit a school in the poorest areas of our big cities, and it is heart-warming to see how those computers excite young people. But some schools have none, and some only a few.

4

I have made phone calls to St. Louis corporations for contributions so that the East St. Louis schools could have computers, but those students shouldn't be dependent on my phone calls.

What is true of computers is also true of books. To see a "school library" with empty shelves, not because the books are on loan but because there are no books, is disheartening. It is discouraging to see elementary school pupils with workbooks where answers from two previous holders have been partially erased.

Let me add, however, that it is impressive to see remarkable and dedicated teachers sometimes doing a great job despite these handicaps. Sometimes teachers pay out of their own pockets for books and equipment.

Education Costs Money

Education needs more money. After World War II the nation's most prominent journalist, Walter Lippmann, wrote: "We are quite rich enough to defend ourselves, whatever the cost. We must now learn that we are quite rich enough to educate ourselves as we need to be educated."[27] But we are not doing it. Our expenditures at the higher education level compare favorably to other nations, though we are slipping, but among the 18 major industrial and advanced nations at the precollege level, we rank somewhere between tenth and fourteenth, depending on how the calculation is made.

Federal support of education is not new. The Continental Congress passed the Northwest Ordinance of 1787, which provided a direct subsidy for education. The two great federal strides forward since then were the College Assistance to Veterans program under President Harry Truman and 60 education bills signed into law under President

Lyndon Johnson and the more than quadrupling of federal aid to education during his five years as President.

The federal government should do more. In the 1870s and the 1880s, the Republicans in Congress attempted to pass the Hoar and Blair bills that would have provided federal aid to education, but the Democrats successfully resisted their efforts. In recent decades the general pattern has been reversed, with Democrats leading the charge for federal aid to education and Republicans dragging their feet. In fiscal year 1949, nine percent of the budget went for education. Today it is two percent.

We have passed legislation titled "Goals 2000," and you have signed it into law. I cosponsored it, and I believe in its aims. Establishing voluntary national goals, creating learning standards—touching on the equity of school financing—and expanding testing programs are all steps forward. I applauded when President George Bush said that by the end of the century our students would be number one in the world in science, mathematics, and other disciplines, and I have applauded your earnest exhortations on education.

Those of us in political life, whether officeholders or candidates, love to be shown in a television shot or a newspaper picture taken at a school. These "grip and grin" shots are pure gold politically. However, Senators, House members, and state legislative bodies are much less eager to be visible voting the funds and taxes that are essential for improved schools. Unless education receives significantly greater resources, not only will we not achieve the lofty goals spelled out, we will be fortunate not to fall back further in relation to other nations.

We should also monitor federal education funds more closely; monitoring will save dollars and improve the education product. Economist Lawrence Summers commented: "Increases in the level and *efficiency* [emphasis mine] of our investment in education are essential."[28] Literally hundreds of millions of dollars were wasted over the decades because the Department of Education did not carefully watch the accrediting process of some of the less reputable proprietary, for-profit schools. That hurt the taxpayers, the students, and the reputable proprietary schools. More than 15,000 grants have been given under the Chapter One program designed to help the economically disadvantaged. But not one school has been cut off the grants, no matter how weak the performance. The message to school leaders clearly is that they will receive money whether they do well or poorly.

If American students fare meagerly compared to many nations—and they do—then at all levels of government we must ask what changes, including structural changes, we should make. The standards that states are expected to adopt for themselves in the Goals 2000 legislation are fine, but if the states simply accept the status of our culture and our education and work a little at the edges, we will have failed our test as government leaders. Yes, we have to fund education better. But we also have to ask ourselves whether we are using the money wisely. In advocating more dollars for education, I also advocate more care and more creativity in the use of funds.

Senator James Jeffords of Vermont introduced a resolution in the Senate in 1993 calling for an increase of one percent of the total federal budget to be added each year for education until education reaches ten percent. That is approximately $15 billion additional annually, and since our education expenditure at the federal level is close to $30 billion, that would be a hefty increase. Exciting things could happen if we started down that path, and in a $1.5 trillion budget, it can be done. Just as one example, that amount could ensure that no classroom in the nation had more than fifteen students. Or we could launch a 210-day school year. Or other enriching options.

"Money won't solve our school problems," I can hear people say as they read this. Some even cite studies to prove no relationship between spending and results, but an article in *Education Week* says that researchers have found that the studies prove the opposite, that "strong ties are shown between student achievement and both per-pupil funding levels and teacher experience."[29] It is true that money alone will not solve our problems, but we need to devote greater resources to education as a significant part of a national effort at revitalization. The plant in which this nation does its business has been good to us, but unless we modernize it, we will slip behind the competition. We are like the grand old steel industry whose glory days have been succeeded by good days, but they are no longer glory days. The giant steel plants of America did not modernize quickly enough, and many closed because of more modern foreign competition. We have to invest in modernization, and part of that has to be in education.

I applaud your move for a $1.7 billion increase in education for fiscal year 1995, Mr. President, but we really ought to do better than that. That sum is roughly one-ninth of one percent of the federal budget—an improvement, but a long way from a dramatic one. If we believe our future is dependent on what we do in education, we should reflect that in our budget and not just touch the outer edges in our expenditure priorities. This is something in which Bill Clinton by instinct believes, Mr. President. We get there by shifting other spending to education, or by a tax specifically dedicated to education that the public would support, but the third option—not providing more funding for education—really should not be an option for this nation. Don't let the cautious types in the White House and the Office of Management and Budget restrain you on this!

Let's Use School Buildings After Hours

Encourage schools in poorer urban areas to use their school buildings more effectively. In many areas, when the school day ends, young people go out into the street. There is no alternative. The schools are open for the school day. Period. Parents cannot use the school for an evening meeting. The gym cannot be used for basketball or sports. The area community college is not permitted to offer any classes there. Students who want to stay later and catch up, working with teachers who are willing to remain an extra hour or two, cannot do it. It is a massive waste of a potentially helpful resource in communities that desperately need help. A small federal carrot to encourage school boards and principals to work with area social agencies and colleges to make the school a more positive force in the community would be helpful.

Support Higher Education

Keep the higher education priority high. The one education area where the United States is ahead of other nations is higher education. In England, Oxford and Cambridge were the only universities there until early in the nineteenth century, and the schools, founded by the Church of England, for many years theoretically excluded Catholics and Jews.[30] In contrast the economically weaker American colonies started nine colleges before the Revolution. Yes, there are areas of weakness in U.S. higher education: Those entering college too often reflect the inadequate quality of the elementary and high schools they attended; graduate education in some areas is slipping; and there are other problems.

When there is boasting about U.S. higher education, the claims usually ignore our heavy dependence on those who graduated in other nations and immigrated here. More than half of our Nobel Prize winners in the sciences are not native-born Americans; many of our top engineers and architects are fluent in their skills but not in the English language, because their first language was learned in another country; approximately 16 percent of the physicians in our nation are not citizens of the United States by birth and they graduated from foreign medical schools. We have an excellent system of higher education, that has contributed to other nations, but we also have benefited enormously from the higher education offerings of other countries.

We have come a long way. When our present structure of government was formed, attending Columbia University's commencement that year (1789) were the President, Vice President, and Senate (Columbia's president also served in the Senate)—for ten graduates.

The access our people have today to schooling after the high school years has been a great economic boon to the nation and to those individuals. Other nations are copying parts of our higher education format.

When you stuck to your support of direct student lending, Mr. President, in the face of strong opposition from the banks and the Student Loan Marketing Association, which had heavy government subsidies for fully guaranteed loans, you not only emerged victorious, but, more important, future students of the nation emerged victorious. And the taxpayers could claim a victory too.

Student loans under direct lending are now shifting from being available only to those of severely limited income to being offered to anyone who wants the loans, and that should permit hundreds of thousands more to prepare themselves through higher education. The program also shifts from a system that allows only the flat monthly payment that former students make on their loans, regardless of their employment status or income, to one that includes an income-contingent repayment option with a basic poverty level income exemption. Instead of banks and collectors going after individuals, the Internal Revenue Service will probably collect—and they're pretty good at it. This decision is not finalized, though IRS Commissioner "Peggy" Richardson is willing to do it. The combination not only will help students but saves the nation more than $1 billion a year in the subsidies to banks and guarantee agencies that we now provide. Students will save an additional $500 million or more in reduced fees and interest rates, and income-contingent repayments will reduce default rates.

This is not a widely understood victory for the nation, but most people in higher education know that it is a victory. I'm proud that you stood up to the pressure on this!

Weaknesses remain in higher education and one is that college technical and library and physical facilities are often outdated. I serve on the board of regents of a small, liberal arts college in Nebraska that I attended, Dana College, and to bring its campus-wide computer system up to date—now the most modern in that state—took a hefty investment of limited resources that many schools cannot afford. Colleges and universities, caught in a financial squeeze, too often are letting their library collections and periodicals suffer, and once-grand buildings are becoming less grand.

While the new direct loan program will be a significant improvement for students and colleges, grants to students have suffered over the years. After World War II the nation decided it should provide a generous gesture to its veterans and we launched the G.I. Bill of Rights, which pays basic college costs, including room and board, for all veterans. What was conceived as a gift to veterans turned out to be a huge investment in our national prosperity. But if the inflation factor were added to the benefits then available, that would mean a grant today averaging just over $8,500 a school year. Veterans received that regardless of family income. Today, we have the Pell grant, named for my colleague from Rhode Island, but it is only for low-income families, and the maximum grant is $2,300. In the 1980-81 school year, the average of federal grants and loans to students amounted to 81 percent of their costs at a public college or university, and a decade later it averaged 60 percent; at private colleges and universities 1980-81 federal aid averaged 33 percent of costs, and ten years later, 20 percent. Slippage in aid is clear, and in the long run that harms our nation's productive capacity.

Many other issues are generally state and local matters. A particularly important one is more adequate pay for teachers while at the same time we gradually raise standards. Others include forming smaller schools where greater intensive attention and genuine reform are more possible; studying the possibility of making high school grades available to potential employers, making them meaningful for first-time employment rather than meaningless; involving parents much more in the schools; and encouraging minorities to go into teaching where they are now badly underrepresented.

And—though this is slightly controversial—education should teach values, something that must be handled with great care but cannot be ignored. Education that only instills facts and skills is empty, or worse. Sensitivity to people of other backgrounds, for example, must be part of a rounded educational product. One of the great prodders of the conscience of nations, Elie Wiesel, noted: "If in Europe, in the most educated nation in the world [Germany], they could have reached such a stage of violence and hatred, something was wrong with education."[31] As we see racial, religious and ethnic strife in our country, we should be pondering Elie Wiesel's words.

These matters generally should be handled by state and local governments, not the federal government.

The bottom line in all of this, Mr. President, is less in the particulars of the programs, than in the reality that we must make education a much greater priority. It is something in which you believe. It is your strong suit, and your leadership on this can become a huge asset to the nation.

Sincerely,

Paul Simon

Eight

The Deficit:
Our Not–So–Hidden Cancer

Dear Mr. President:

We're like a person who has lung cancer—and keeps on smoking. It defies all logic, but it's hard to "kick the habit."

What is the harm in our deficit habit? It has already hurt us a great deal and will do much more damage if it is not arrested. But this is clear:

☐ **It hurts our ability to compete with the rest of the world.** Each dollar we add to the deficit may temporarily help some cause we applaud, but in the long run, it makes our society less competitive, less prosperous, less progressive, and, ultimately, less responsive to those who are in need.

☐ **We are on the path to printing worthless paper dollars.** Even if the present, most optimistic forecasts by your administration are correct, we will end up monetizing the debt, attempting to escape our problems by printing more money, risking the economic future and political stability of the nation with devastating inflatin. We are headed on that course, unless something major changes our economic policies.

☐ **The deficit kidnaps our natural savings,** making it more difficult to refurbish our industrial base, slowing economic progress, and lowering our standard of living significantly.

☐ **The budget deficit is the single biggest cause of the trade deficit** and transfers jobs from the United States to other nations.

☐ **Our independence is limited,** each year the debt grows, and, as the dollar total we owe to those outside our nation grows, we are put in greater jeopardy.

I will explain all of this in more detail, but I believe these points are irrefutable.

Your record as President in this field merits one huge plus and one huge minus.

The plus is your willingness to take on a fight to reduce the deficit in your first year as President. Even among some of my Republican Senate colleagues who voted against you on this there is a willingness to admit privately that what you did was needed, that it turned out to be a great asset to the nation. Senator Robert Kerrey of Nebraska described it as "a modest step," and that is an apt description; but that modest step showed courage and a leadership quality for which the nation's financial markets and business community have yearned. The pleasing lines in a speech that win applause won't turn our economy around, and sensible leaders know that. The applause that counted came with the drop in interest rates, which did far more to improve our economy than any stimulus package could have done. Political applause for your action is minimal: You're going against public opinion. As George Bernard Shaw wrote: "A government which robs Peter to pay Paul can always depend on the support of Paul."[1]

George Bush deserves part of the credit, for the budget agreement he worked out with Congress helped, but most of the credit rests at your feet. And for the first time since Harry Truman's presidency, we will have three years in a row of reduced deficits. That's the good news. The bad news is that the Congressional Budget Office projections for the years after the turn of the century show record-breaking deficits and an upturn in the deficit soon. We have started to tackle the problem, but only started.

I agree totally with former President Gerald Ford: "Unless we as a nation face up to the facts of fiscal reality and responsibility, and the sacrifices required to restore it, the economic time bomb we are sitting on will do us in as surely as any sudden enemy assault. We cannot go on living beyond our means by borrowing from future generations or being bailed out by foreign investors."[2]

A century ago, Illinois had one of its few great governors, John Peter Altgeld. After leaving office he wrote a small volume of reflections on life and included this story:

> The writer recently heard a young man laughingly tell of his outwitting a [street]car conductor, and succeeding in riding into the city without paying the usual fare. He told the story in great glee, thinking it, no doubt, an evidence of his astuteness and cleverness. This seems a trivial thing, and yet that little dishonest trick may be the beginning of that young man's ruin. He is cultivating a desire to get something for nothing.[3]

As a nation, we have learned a "little dishonest trick" of living on a national credit card, telling our creditors to send the bill to future generations, trying to get something for nothing. It is already hurting us as well as those who will follow us.

Let me return to the points I made at the beginning of this letter and explain the background for each one.

The Long Run

Each dollar we add to the deficit may temporarily help some cause we applaud, but in the long run, our society becomes less competitive, less prosperous, less progressive, and, ultimately, less responsive to those who are in need.

We make annual choices on spending, some of which I favor and some I don't. But each $1 billion in deficits creates spending of approximately $50 million in interest next year and every year thereafter in perpetuity. The next result is to make all interest rates higher than necessary or desirable, largely to the benefit of those who are more fortunate in our nation and other nations. Not only is it a generous and unwise gift to those who do not need our assistance, but, more importantly, it crowds out our ability to respond to the needs of those who do need our help. More and more, high taxes are necessary simply to pay for interest, to pay for last year's—or the last decade's—spending. My former House colleague, Mayor Andrew Young of Atlanta, recognized this reality: "Housing low- and moderate-income citizens has traditionally been a federal responsibility, but budget deficits at the national level make that a rapidly diminishing option."[4]

You and I are believers in the cause of education, Mr. President, and between fiscal years 1981 and 1993, spending for education rose. But when adjusted for inflation, spending for education actually dropped eight percent over that period. What increased? In inflation-adjusted numbers, defense went up 16 percent (less than many people think), and entitlements 32 percent (because of growth in the numbers of eligible people and inflation of health costs), but the big increase was in gross interest—91 percent. Interest is now roughly $300 billion, more than we spend on defense, nine times as much as we spend on education, and twice as much as all of our poverty programs combined. The biggest "welfare" program the nation has is welfare for the wealthy, in the form of interest, and to pay that interest we take taxes primarily from people of modest means and hand it in the form of interest payments to the wealthy, including the wealthy beyond our borders. Interest payments continue to grow and will continue to grow until we signal to the financial markets, in terms that are stronger than we have so far, that we are serious about the deficit.

Harry Truman's budget in 1950 totaled $42 billion. In 1962 we had a total federal budget of $100 billion for the first time. In fiscal year 1993 the federal government spent $293 billion on interest, more than the total amount of the federal budget when I was elected to the House in 1974.

Social Programs are in Jeopardy

A 1992 General Accounting Office report suggests that if the budget is not balanced by the end of the century, social programs will eventually have to be cut by one-third because of the growing interest expenditure.

The Milton Eisenhower Foundation issued a report, *Investing in Children and Youth,* on the twenty-fifth anniversary of the Kerner report that had called our nation deeply divided between black and white, poor and nonpoor. The more recent report makes recommendations for high-risk children, high-risk youth, and the inner city. Significantly, however, it says that we cannot carry out these recommendations when "the biggest competitor" for those funds is growing interest on a growing national debt. "The costs of servicing the debt are consuming larger and larger portions of the government's resources."[5]

New ideas to deal with our social ills are frozen by rising interest costs.

Almost a decade ago, Nobel Prize-winning economist Paul Samuelson wrote: "The end of the world is not at hand. Yes, the public debt will continue to grow and will do so for as far ahead as we can now see. But those who study the lessons of history realize that economic law will exact its retribution, not in the short run of 1986 and 1987, but in the shape of the less progressive society we carry into the next century."[6] A Tokyo-based economist wrote a magazine article, the title of which summarizes where we are: "America's Budget Deficits . . . They Redistribute Income to the Rich."[7]

Even if the present, most optimistic forecasts by your administration are correct, there is a significant risk—many would say a virtual certainty—that we will eventually monetize the debt (that is, try to escape our problems by printing inflationary money), risking the economic future and political stability of the nation through devastating inflation. We are headed on that course—unless there is a major change.

The good news is that thanks to your courage on the budget, the deficit in relation to our national income is down. The bad news is that it will soon go back up—and up and up. The General Accounting Office (GAO) estimated in June 1992 that by the year 2020 deficits relative to gross domestic product (national income, GDP) would reach 20 percent. That has to be revised downward after the budget action Congress took under your leadership in August 1993. The GAO has no revised estimates, though I have met with them to discuss the matter. One informal estimate is that the deficit relative to GDP should be dropped by 3.7 percent to 16.3 percent. I have seen other estimates as low as 10 percent. But forget all those estimates. "Maybe they're from opponents of my administration," you may be saying to yourself. Instead, look at the following chart from the budget submitted by your Office of Management and Budget.

LIFETIME NET TAX RATES UNDER ALTERNATIVE POLICIES			
BirthYear	Before Clinton	After Clinton	With Healthcare Reform	With Healthcare/ Inflation
1900	23.6	23.6	23.6	23.6
1910	27.2	27.2	27.2	27.2
1920	29.0	29.0	29.1	29.1
1930	30.5	30.6	30.9	30.9
1940	31.6	31.9	32.4	32.2
1950	32.8	33.2	34.0	33.5
1960	34.4	35.0	35.9	35.2
1970	35.7	36.5	37.6	36.6
1980	36.0	36.9	38.2	36.7
1990	35.5	36.5	38.3	36.0
Future	93.7	82.0	66.5	75.2

You will note that since you were born in 1946, your lifetime net tax rate will be approximately 33 percent. I was born in 1928, and if you follow on the line for 1930, you will see that my tax will be approximately 30 percent. But go down to the line for future generations at the bottom. You will note that, without the passage of your budget reconciliation proposal, the lifetime tax rate would have been 93 percent. With the passage of your budget proposal, it dropped to 82 percent.

Under the optimistic projections of your budget, with ten years of prosperity without a dip—rather than the usual six-and-one-half-year cycle—and assuming all the savings you predict from your health plan that I am cosponsoring—even with these factors, future generations, including my new granddaughter and Chelsea's children, will pay 66 to 75 percent of their lifetime earnings in taxation, largely because of the debt service we are piling on them.

Whether we use your figures or others, however, that just won't happen. Before we reach that point, we will start the presses rolling to print money. That is the history of nations. We may think we'll be the first country in history not to follow that path, but to assume that is to take a huge gamble with the future of our country. The nation's most watched business investor, Warren Buffett, wrote in 1993: "Monetizing the debt is where we will end up unless Congressional behavior is modified by amending the Constitution."[9] Economic analyst Kevin Phillips writes that the deficit hangs "like a sword over U.S. prospects for renewed economic growth."[10] He talks about the "Brazilianization" of our economy.

A study of industrial nations shows that monetizing the debt occurs when the deficit gets to be around nine percent of national income. The exception is a wartime situation when both business and consumer credit are dramatically restricted. Nations during wartime have amassed temporary deficits as large as ours relative to national income, but no major country has ever amassed such debt during peacetime. We are the first major nation to move so significantly from creditor status to debtor status in peacetime. For a nonwar situation, the nine percent figure for monetizing generally holds. The ten to 16.7 percent predictions for the United States clearly surpass that ratio. And the assumptions of OMB anticipate surpassing it.

The stories from Germany after World War I of people taking wheelbarrows full of money to go to a grocery store to buy milk and bread—and the political chaos that followed—are lessons we should absorb. Our closest neighbor to experience something similar was Mexico, which in 1988 reached the 12.5 percent ratio of deficit to GDP. That year Mexico had an inflation rate of 114 percent. For us that would mean cutting the value of the Social Security Retirement Fund in half, cutting family savings in half, shifting the basis of international commerce from the dollar to the yen or deutschmark, and causing a scurrying of foreign investors to other nations as they dump our bonds. The General

Accounting Office's description of what will happen if we reach that deficit point is "economic catastrophe."

The short-term advantage of inflation to a government with high debt is that 20 percent inflation, for example, reduces the government's debt by 20 percent. But it also creates many long-term problems. Adam Smith, in his classic *The Wealth of Nations*, published in 1776, makes clear that the economic history of nations is that they pile up more and more debt, then in one way or another renounce the debt, salvaging political careers but ruining the economy of the nation. For those interested in history, Oxford University Press has published a book by Michael Veseth, titled *Mountains of Debt*, a study of the fiscal policies of several governments, starting with the Italian city-state of Florence. What is so clear is that we fail to study history and learn from it, and the parallels with what we are experiencing in the United States are powerful and ominous.

The Deficit Holds Our Savings Captive

The deficit kidnaps our natural savings, making it more difficult to refurbish our industrial base, slowing economic progress, and lowering our standard of living significantly.

Harvard's articulate Benjamin Friedman summed up the problem in one sentence: "The main reason budget deficits are unhealthy is that they eat the economy's savings and therefore starve the economy's investment."[11] Our abysmal savings rate and the problems that it causes are dealt with in more detail in my next letter, but the New York Federal Reserve Bank study mentioned earlier, suggests that our lack of savings in the 1980s cost us the loss of five percent in national income (GDP). The principle villain: the debt of the federal government. The study suggests that the damaging trend can be reversed "by pushing the government balance into surplus and buying down some of the debt accumulated in the 1980s."[12] Of the seven leading industrial nations of the world, the only one to accumulate sizable deficits from 1983 to 1993 was the United States, and the only one to experience loss in inflation-adjusted income during that period was the United States.

The General Accounting Office said that if by the end of this century the budget is balanced, by the year 2020 the average American will experience an increase in income, adjusted for inflation, of 36 percent. A pattern of drift will mean a gradual and continuing decline in our quality of life and standard of living.

The Concord Coalition, headed by former Senators Warren Rudman and Paul Tsongas, says that the median family income today of $35,000 would be approximately $50,500 but for the deficit of the last two decades. That is a substantial loss suffered already.

When money goes for interest rather than more productive use and when savings go to pay for a government deficit rather than building a manufacturing base, we suffer. Even among those who are uncertain that calamity awaits us if we continue down our current economic path, there are few who would dispute that the continuation on our present course will result in making the United States a significantly diminished player on the world scene, with many more nations surpassing us in per capita income.

But it is not only people in our country who suffer. The managing director of the International Monetary Fund, Michel Camdessus, generously invited me to have breakfast with him. At that point a $12 billion guarantee for the IMF was slated to come before the Foreign Relations Committee. Since I am only midway in the committee in seniority, I thought he was reaching fairly far down the ranks, but I happily accepted. It turned out that he had a greater interest in our deficit situation than with the loan guarantee. Perhaps in exaggeration to make a point, he said that if we faced a choice of balancing our budget or eliminating foreign aid, we should balance our budget, that our dominance in the world economic market and our forcing international interest rates up with our heavy borrowing placed a great burden on the poor nations. A 1993 report by the International Monetary Fund calls the need for the United States to reduce our fiscal deficits "urgent."[13] It describes the United States as having "a relatively steady erosion of its fiscal position."

Not only are we harming the people within our country with our heavy borrowing, we are harming the poor around the world.

The Twin Deficits

The budget deficit is the single biggest cause of the trade deficit and transfers jobs from the United States to other nations.

Studies report that 37 to 55 percent of the trade deficit is caused by the budget deficit. That is not the public perception. A Congressional Research Service study concludes:

> Many observers contend that two factors—restrictive foreign trade practices and the falling efficiency (productivity) of American workers and factories— are causes of the trade deficit. The facts do not support these contentions.

The author suggests that these factors are marginal, that our lack of savings has escalated the value of the dollar, hurting exports and stimulating imports. "We are left with one [major] course: to continue to reduce the trade deficit requires raising domestic savings. The most viable policy path to increased savings is through reduction of the federal budget deficit."[14]

Combine three things: 1) A New York Federal Reserve Bank study that the savings loss from 1978 to 1988 cost us a loss of five percent of GDP, primarily because of the federal deficit; 2) the studies on the trade deficit and its direct attribution to the federal budget deficit; and 3) the Congressional Budget Office study that a one percent loss of GDP costs us 600,000 jobs. That combination suggests clearly that the federal budget deficit has cost us, by the most conservative estimate, hundreds of thousands of jobs, probably millions. The deficit has cost us significantly in industrial investment, making our work force less productive and shifting higher paying manufacturing jobs to other nations.

Our Independence is at Stake

Each year the debt grows, and the dollar total we owe to those outside our nation grows, our independence is limited and we are put in greater jeopardy.

This problem is creeping up on us—it's more like a cancer than a heart attack. It is not putting us in danger today or tomorrow, but unless our habits change it will eventually put us in great jeopardy.

"We owe it to ourselves" is an old line once used to defend deficits, a defense that did not stand up to solid scrutiny but one that had a modicum of legitimacy. It no longer has any legitimacy. Now, 17 percent of our publicly-held bonds *that we know of* are owned by foreign governments, corporations or citizens. Some nations have laws prohibiting citizens or corporations from investing outside of their countries, and that causes a hidden amount of bond holdings. It is probably not large but it is an additional factor. Using only the known foreign-held bonds as a base for calculation, we send approximately $30 billion in interest to other nations each year—twice as much as our foreign economic aid budget.

"Trickle-down economics," the theory that if you help the wealthy, economic gain will trickle down to the rest of the population, never impressed me, but even its advocates can hardly claim that if we help someone in Japan, Great Britain, or Saudi Arabia, it will help the average citizen in our country.

The 17 percent of U.S. bonds held by foreign entities underscores our dependence, not only because of the hidden bond holdings: We also have significant foreign private sector loans to U.S. corporations, as well as savings accounts and ownership of certificates of deposit in U.S. banks.

A study published by the New York Federal Reserve Bank, mentioned earlier, warned: "At current rates of net capital inflow, in ten years the United States will pay more than one percent of its annual income to service this foreign debt, an exact reversal of its position ten years ago."[15] In three years during the early 1980s, we moved from being the number one creditor nation to being the number one debtor nation, the first time we have been a debtor nation since World War I. Economist Lester Thurow observes: "In late 1983 . . . Americans owned $152 billion more assets in the rest of the world than the rest of the world owned in the United States. At the beginning of 1991, the rest of the world owns about $757 billion more assets in the United States than Americans own in the rest of the world."[16]

Imagine, Mr. President, that you headed the First National Bank in Hope, Arkansas—and I am sure there are days in the White House when that would look attractive. Suppose I come to you and say that I want to spend more next year than I take in, and I would like to borrow some money. You would look at my asset sheet and, if it is healthy, you would lend me the money. And then imagine that next year I come back with the same request; and a third year; and a fourth year. At some point, you as a prudent banker will say to yourself that you would be wise to make your loans elsewhere.

We have come to the world's bankers twenty-five years in a row, asking to borrow money so that we can spend more than we take in, and sooner or later prudence will dictate that our lenders go elsewhere. We need to slow our borrowing and reinforce our capacity to carry the debt, or we are headed for trouble.

As our economic picture becomes grimmer—and it will unless we take the action I recommend in a few pages—foreign purchases of our bonds will either gradually or precipitously decline. Lester Thurow says the question is not *whether* those who hold our bonds in other nations will abandon us but *when* they will abandon us. He writes: "Eventually the rest of the world will be unwilling to lend the necessary sums. Nations will refuse to lend because the risk of not being repaid by the Americans in currencies of equal value to those that were lent is too high."[17] Then we will either start the printing presses, or we will borrow money from our people at higher and higher interest rates, money that cannot go to increasing the productivity of our industrial base or into improving the quality of our life, such as housing.

If the Simon family gets too deeply into debt, we start to lose our independence. The same is true of a nation. And it is difficult to get tough with your banker, for an individual or a nation. One of the reasons we have been able to be a little firmer with Japan in our trade negotiations recently is that the percentage of our bonds held by Japan has gradually declined. Some years ago, I indicated opposition to an arms sale to Saudi Arabia. Then I had a visit from a representative of the Treasury Department who pointed out to me, among his other arguments, that the Saudis held many of our bonds, and it would hurt us if they stopped buying them or dumped them (an unlikely circumstance, unless they saw other nations doing it, because it would have depreciated the value of their own holdings). That puts us in the position of basing an American defense policy on Saudi, or some other, financial considerations—clearly absurd.

The dollar amount held by others has risen since then, and our independence is slowly declining. We cannot be strong internationally if we are weak economically at home. In writing about America's failure to invest in itself and about the sale of our assets to other nations, Martin and Sue Tolchin added: "Presidents Bush and Reagan feared that restricting the sale of America's technological base would send a negative message to foreign investors, on whom the United States has become increasingly dependent for money to underwrite the deficit."[18]

Almost forgotten is what happened in 1956. Shortly before the U.S. election—a time when our nation frequently becomes immobilized, particularly on foreign policy—the British, French and Israelis invaded Egypt. They had done this because Egypt's President Nasser had seized the Suez Canal. The United States objected to the invasion and threatened to dump the pound sterling on the heavily indebted British, with the implied threat of blocking any international rescue efforts of the British currency. Our friends—and they were and are our friends—had no alternative but to withdraw from what had been a clear, decisive military victory. The three nations counted on the combination of our friendship and the approaching U.S. election to prevent any U.S. response. But the United States did respond and won a military victory without firing a shot—because of British indebtedness. The lesson from this for the United States ought to be clear, but nations are slow in learning lessons from history.

We are pious and resolute in telling developing nations to balance their budgets and not become too dependent on foreign support. Now the world's biggest debtor nation—by far—is the United States, and our message to others rings hollow. As economist Alice Rivlin, the number two person in the Office of Management and Budget, notes: "It is hard to preach responsible fiscal policy to developing countries when the United States is running huge deficits in its federal budget."[19] She called ours "a paralyzing deficit." International economist David Calleo observes: "To many it seemed . . . obscene that the world's richest country should also be its biggest borrower."[20]

How Do We Turn the Budget Deficit Into a Surplus?

It is easy to do on paper but extremely difficult to do politically, as you discovered, Mr. President. Logically, the step you took in 1993 on the deficit should be followed by further steps. But the 1993 action came with a new President still basking in much goodwill and his political party controlling both houses of Congress—and even then it took a huge effort by you and your cabinet and congressional leaders—the Vice President had to break the tie in the Senate. That combination of happy circumstances will not be with us often.

What makes it difficult is that all of us in politics like to do what is popular, and there is no popular way of reducing the deficit. We must cut spending and raise revenue, though the sacrifice in either area would be small compared to what other nations have done and exceedingly small compared to the dangers the nation faces.

The only answer that will work is a constitutional amendment that requires us to balance the budget except for unusual circumstances. Can the budget be balanced with this? Yes. Will it be done without this? No. That is part of the reality that some economists, academicians and media people are not willing to face.

Let me give you a practical example of how the system works now. I introduced a measure for long-term care, a problem that will balloon on us in the next decade. I included in my bill a provision for a 0.5 percent increase in the Social Security tax to help pay for it. Two of my Senate colleagues came to me and said they really liked my proposal and that if I would just drop the tax to pay for it, they would become cosponsors. That is easy to do now! If we want a long-term care measure, however, we should be willing to pay for it, and if we are unwilling to vote for the taxes ("Send the bill to our grandchildren"), we should not have the long-term care plan. That's the essence of this constitutional amendment proposal. Liberals and conservatives should be able to disagree on whether or not we should have such a long-term care plan; we should not disagree that if we have one, it should be on a pay-as-you-go basis.

The idea for a constitutional amendment on this subject is not new. Thomas Jefferson was in Paris in 1787, negotiating for our nation, when James Madison and others wrote the Constitution. When Jefferson returned, he said that if he could add one amendment to the Constitution, it would be to prohibit the federal government from borrowing money. He wrote: "We should consider ourselves unauthorized to saddle posterity with our debts, and morally bound to pay them ourselves."[21] On another occasion, Jefferson wrote: "We must not let our rulers load us with perpetual debt."[22] During his first term as President, he cut the national debt in half. Those who fed the fires of revolution against the British said: "Taxation without representation is tyranny."

For future generations, that is exactly what deficit spending is.

Jefferson and Alexander Hamilton frequently disagreed, but as secretary of the treasury in 1795, Hamilton called for "incorporating as a fundamental maxim . . . that the creation of Debt should always be accompanied with the means of extinguishment." In explaining the need, he observed this about political leaders: "It is no uncommon spectacle to see the same men Clamouring . . . against a Public Debt, and for the reduction of it as an abstract thesis; yet vehement against any plan of taxation . . . [or] defraying expenses."[23] As secretary of the treasury, Hamilton wrote that growing debts are "the NATURAL DISEASE [his emphasis] of all Governments."[24]

Even the lead witness against the amendment in a 1992 hearing, Professor Laurence Tribe of Harvard, said:

> Despite the misgivings I expressed on this score a decade ago, I no longer think that a balanced budget amendment is, at a conceptual level, an ill-suited kind of provision to include in the Constitution. . . . The Jeffersonian notion that today's populace should not be able to burden future generations with excessive debt does seem to be the kind of fundamental value that is worthy of enshrinement in the Constitution. In a sense, it represents a structural protection for the rights of our children and grandchildren.[25]

A Constitutional Amendment

What some of us have proposed is an amendment that requires a balanced budget unless there is a 60 percent vote of both houses of Congress to the contrary. A 60 percent vote is not easy to obtain, but in times of emergency we can secure it. There are times when a deficit is wise, but it is not wise year after year after year—every year since 1969.

For most of our history we needed no such amendment because both Congress and the President exercised self-restraint. We had an unwritten barrier to having deficits except for wars or major economic downturns. Both political parties followed this understanding. Typical of this thinking was the Democratic platform of 1896, which stated: "We are opposed to the issuing of interest-bearing bonds in time of peace."[26]

Andrew Jackson wrote: "I am one of those who do not believe that a national debt is a national blessing, but rather a curse."[27] And Jefferson stated that a generation should be no more willing to accept a debt from a previous generation than from another nation. Even Cicero, in the century before Christ, said: "The budget should be balanced, the Treasury should be refilled, public debt should be reduced . . . lest Rome become bankrupt."[28] George Washington helped to set the tone for the nation with his farewell address, warning the nation against piling up debt. From George Washington through Jimmy Carter, the nation accumulated less than $1 trillion in debt. In 1994 it is $4.6 trillion and climbing. Another gauge of how rapidly our problem is growing is that from fiscal years 1981 through 1993, our gross expenditure for interest was $1.7 trillion. During the next five years it will be $1.7 trillion. The problems and interest mount.

Some argue that families, businesses, and local and state governments borrow. Shouldn't the federal government be able to do the same?

First, families and businesses don't borrow unless there is some advantage in doing so. They don't borrow to get by until the next election! When they borrow, it is generally for capital projects, not operating budgets. They don't ordinarily borrow for groceries and school supplies. The federal government is borrowing for our operating budget, for our groceries. School districts and cities borrow—sometimes needlessly, but usually because they have to—and states borrow, though again it becomes an easy way for an incumbent governor or legislature to "do something" and pass the bill on to future officials. In a state like Illinois, for example, there is virtually no excuse for borrowing, but it is the politically easy way out. When I served in the State Senate, I voted against the state's first major bond issue, a proposal for two areas I strongly support, mental health and higher education. I pointed out that the expenditure would be made over more than a six-year period, and we could slightly increase taxes and save the state a huge amount of money. I lost 55-2, and those leading the fight assured me there would never again be a bond issue by the state. Since then, of course, there have been hundreds of bond issues, and the amount of money the state pays for interest—and for which it gets nothing in return—mounts each year.

There is no excuse for the federal government issuing bonds for capital projects. The biggest single capital item that we face in a federal budget is a nuclear aircraft carrier, and it is paid for over a six-year period. The most that will be required in any one year is $1 billion, or one-fifteenth of one percent of the total budget. It is worth noting that long-term federal investment has declined, not risen, as the deficit has grown. The biggest public works project in the history of humanity is the U. S. interstate highway system. To his great credit, President Dwight Eisenhower proposed it. But he also recommended that bonds be issued to pay for it. A Tennessee Senator, Albert Gore Sr., father of our Vice President, said that would be foolish. Let's raise the gas tax and build it on a pay-as-you-go basis, he argued. He prevailed and saved the nation hundreds of billions of dollars in interest.

The debt today would be $860 billion higher if his amendment had not passed.

The Wharton School in Philadelphia, highly regarded for its work in economics, studied the balanced budget amendment proposal and said there would be short-term restrictive results from it in some areas because of less government spending. They also predicted, however, that 30-year bonds would go from 6.5 percent (the rate then) to 2.5 percent by the time the budget achieved balance. Think what that interest drop alone would mean for housing construction and industrial investment—and for the major item, of interest, in the federal budget. Data Resources Inc., another major econometric think-tank, also predicted a drop in interest rates.

I recall when New York City suddenly faced huge financial problems brought on by borrowing and borrowing and borrowing. When the day of reckoning came, we constantly heard, "Why didn't someone warn us?" This letter is one of many warnings to the nation. Programs for poor people in New York City were cut by as much as 47 percent. New York City had the great advantage of having the umbrella of the United States, and we properly helped the city through difficult times. But there is no such umbrella for the United States. The World Bank and International Monetary Fund can help us through minor scrapes, but we are 20 percent of the world's economy. There is no umbrella big enough for us. We have to face our difficulties and the sooner, the better.

Professor David Calleo of Johns Hopkins University is one of a growing number of students of the world's economy who have become supporters of a constitutional amendment. Recently he wrote: "Financially, the United States is fast growing into a giant banana republic."[29] Nobel Prize-winning economist James Buchanan comments: "It is difficult to construct any plausible argument against a constitutional rule for budget balance once the elementary facts of the matter are acknowledged."[30]

Every other generation of Americans took care of themselves and invested in the future. We are the first generation of Americans to only partially take care of ourselves and borrow from the future.

Touching on the generational theme, former Senator Paul Tsongas of Massachusetts testified on behalf of the amendment:

> We have in this country six living Presidents and former Presidents. Not one of them has ever [had] a balanced budget. Two Democrats, four Republicans—not one.
>
> In the United States Senate, there are 100 Senators, 93 of whom [have never seen] a balanced budget. Only one, Strom Thurmond, [has seen] more than one. . . . Back in the 1970s there was a lot of discussion about tax and spend, and you can argue that both ways. But what we have done since is spend and borrow. . . . [To] spend and borrow is generationally immoral. . . . Ronald Reagan and George Bush alone added $3 trillion, and this administration in the first term will add something like $800 billion. All of that is now left to our children. And what is disturbing is there is no apparent remorse. We just do it. The difference between this kind of addiction and normal [drug] addiction is that [the] people who get hurt by a personal addiction are the people who are addicted . . . in this case, the people who get hurt are not those who vote for the deficits. . . . If you ask yourself why are these deficits always voted, the answer is very simple . . . there are a lot of votes in deficit spending. There are no votes in fiscal discipline. What you have here is a sad case of pursuit of self as opposed to pursuit of

what is in the national interest. The balanced budget amendment is simply a recognition of that human behavior. . . . I celebrated my 53rd birthday yesterday. Most people look at birthdays as an agony, but given what I have been through in my life, every birthday is a triumph. And 10 years ago, when I was diagnosed as I served here, with cancer, one of the great concerns I had—in fact the most troubling—was thinking of my two-year-old child and the prospect that she would never know who her father was. The reason that had such impact on me beyond the obvious is that, as a child, I had the same circumstance; my mother had tuberculosis and I never knew her. I have no remembrance whatsoever of my mother. . . . What we are doing is dooming our children, and the notion that you can love a child and still do this means it has not been thought through.[31]

Jonathan Rauch, the author of a popular book, *Demosclerosis*, writes:

Children don't organize and lobby. . . . One way to take from the young is to reduce spending on them [but] another way is to pile up debts that they'll have to pay. Imagine yourself in the shoes of a politician facing demands from a swarm of noisy lobbies. Every time you hand out a subsidy check or a tax break, some group says, "Thank you," and rewards you with votes or campaign contributions or both. To pay for the subsidy, you can raise taxes, but that's politically risky. Why not put it on credit? No group screams at you if you do that, because many of the people who will pay don't exist. . . . What does a budget deficit mean? Not economic collapse or calamity. Rather, incremental but inexorable diminution of future wealth.[32]

The arguments against the proposal are that the Constitution should not be trivialized, and I agree, but this is anything but a trivial matter; that the Constitution should not deal with financial matters, but of course it deals with many financial matters, including patents and weights and measures; and then there are some more substantial arguments.

"We Need Flexibility to Deal with Recessions"

Economist Fred Bergsten, who served as Assistant Secretary of the Treasury under Jimmy Carter and chairs the Competitiveness Policy Council, spoke strongly on behalf of the amendment, saying the savings that it would bring would add to our productivity. Then he dealt with the need for an antirecessionary response:

> Don't just move to balance, but try to move to a modest surplus as the steady state, and then in recession periods you can move back to balance and get some net stimulus to the economy. . . . Critics argue that it would take away the flexibility in fiscal policy. But the truth . . . is there is no flexibility in fiscal policy today. President Clinton came into office wanting to put forward a stimulus for the economy. He could only put forward a tiny stimulus, one that was so small that you and the Congress rightly agreed that it would not make sense and voted it down. . . . To those who say the balanced budget amendment would preclude fiscal stimulus, I ask, "Compared to what?" Certainly not compared with today.[33]

Several other economists have called for developing modest surpluses, rather than deficits, including President Carter's key economic adviser, Charles Schultze.

"You will Hurt Our Social Programs."

Limiting deficits does mean that we will have to make some difficult decisions. No one in the Senate has fought harder for programs for those in great need than I have. Other cosponsors of the constitutional amendment, including House sponsors like Congressmen Joe Kennedy and Steny Hoyer, have also been strong supporters of these programs. But nothing could do greater harm to social programs than the path we are on now. As the June 1992 GAO report points out, interest payments are gradually squeezing out our response to social needs. What will change if this amendment is adopted is that my friends who advocate social programs, education, and similarly needed efforts will not be able to lobby simply for spending; they will also have to lobby for the revenue to pay for the programs—or to cut other programs. In the long run social programs will be major beneficiaries of a balanced budget amendment.

"The Secretary of Defense Says that a Balanced Budget Constitutional Amendment will Hurt Defense."

First, once you made the decision, Mr. President, to oppose the amendment, all your troops in lockstep said "the right thing." I understand and respect that. If your decision had been in the other direction, which much of your staff wanted, the secretary of defense and all the other cabinet officers would have had a different line, saying that the amendment was the greatest thing since sliced bread.

The nation cannot ultimately be strong militarily if it is weak economically. If we sensed a great military weakness, we would galvanize our resources and do what was necessary to maintain our necessary military strength. That we are faltering economically and have to make similar sacrifices to restore our economic health is not fully understood by the public and by public officials.

The GAO report cited earlier says that unless the budget is balanced eventually, interest will make substantial inroads in defense, causing as much as a two-thirds reduction. Former Secretary of Defense Dick Cheney and Senator Sam Nunn would not have supported the amendment if they believed it would hurt defense.

"The American Association of Retired Persons Says it Will Hurt Social Security."

No way!

We will all have to be pinched a little, but no group stands to benefit more than those on Social Security and those who will be on Social Security. Robert Myers, chief actuary for Social Security for twenty-three years, testified that the only way to prevent monetizing the debt and devastating the Social Security funds is through the balanced budget amendment. He wrote: "Regaining control of our fiscal affairs is the most important step that we can take to protect the soundness of the Social Security trust funds. I urge the Congress to make that goal a reality—and to pass the Balanced Budget Amendment without delay."[34]

"Labor Unions Oppose It"

One labor union is strongly opposed to it, and because of its voice the AFL-CIO went on record against it. The American Federation of State, County and Municipal Employees (AFSCME) is militant in their opposition, and they have one of the finest unions and some of the best leaders in the nation. Short-term, they are one of the few unions that could suffer under the amendment because there may be curtailment in the employment of government workers. Long-term, AF-SCME will benefit, as will everyone. But the construction unions and the industrial unions lose without the amendment, both short-term and long-term. Of the two million-plus jobs that we have lost because of the deficit, many have been steelworkers, auto workers, machinists, and people in the construction trades. They have suffered in a significant way.

"It will Become Meaningless—Congress will Find Some Way Around It"

If it were meaningless, my friend Senator Robert Byrd would not have expended so much effort to defeat it!

There are two significant reasons that the amendment will be effective.

The first is that we have a provision that requires that any increase in the national debt must have a 60 percent vote. That has muscle. That means that neither Congress nor an administration can play games by having some things on budget and others off budget.

Second, for all its flaws, Congress does revere the Constitution. When I am sworn into office as a senator, I take only one oath: to uphold the Constitution. And laws are not ignored by Congress either. The Gramm-Rudman-Hollings Act set up certain goals to move us to a balanced budget. When it started to pinch, no one stood on the floor of the Senate and said, "Let's just ignore the law." Because it was statutory, we simply got around it by amending the law. We cannot do that with the Constitution. Some say the 60 percent provision will give us an out and be abused. That is possible but not likely. It is at least a better gamble than following our present path to disaster.

I liked Maine Representative Olympia Snowe's response when asked if this "is not just a congressional gimmick?" She told the reporter, "If it were a gimmick, Congress would have passed it a long time ago."

"Congress can Pass a Balanced Budget Without a Constitutional Amendment—All it Takes is Courage."

That is correct, but incomplete. That argument helped to defeat the proposal this year. We fell four votes shy of having the necessary two-thirds to pass it. That same argument was used in 1986, when the amendment failed to pass the Senate by one vote. That year the federal debt stood at $2 trillion, and we heard the argument echoing through the chamber, "We Don't Need a Constitutional Amendment. We Can Do It Without One."

But we didn't. And now the deficit is $4.6 trillion.

What an amendment does is give us political cover and no place to duck. My friends from Texas tell me this old saw is historically inaccurate, but it illustrates the point: "There were so many heroes at the Alamo because there was no back door." We need something without a back door to force us to make the difficult decisions.

Senator Larry Craig, Republican of Idaho, is more conservative than I am but deeply believes in the need for the amendment. He has said that if it passes, he understands that some taxes may be necessary to bring the budget into balance. He is willing to increase some taxes but not without a constitutional amendment that assures him that the taxes will be used for deficit reduction. Those less conscientious than Senator Craig can go back home and say to their people, "I really didn't want to cut your program, but we had no choice under the constitutional amendment." Or, "I really didn't want to vote for that tax increase, but. . . . "

"The Amendment Does Away with Majority Rule—It Permits 40 Percent of the Senate or House to Block a Deficit."

There are eight different provisions in the Constitution that call for something more than majority rule—including the one for a constitutional amendment, which requires a two-thirds vote. Majority rule will hold if Congress plans for a small surplus or, at least, balances the budget. The Constitution requires more than simple majorities where the majority may do harm to the nation, and in fiscal matters we have done great harm to the nation.

"Those who Favor a Balanced Budget Amendment should Come Up with a Plan."

Several plans are being proposed, the most substantial being the one offered by the Concord Coalition. What we lack is the discipline that forces us to hammer out a politically acceptable plan. Senator Orrin Hatch and I will not agree on how a budget should be balanced, but we agree that it must be, and we are willing to commit ourselves to that. Our opponents, who say that we can balance the budget without a constitutional amendment, offer no program. The clear plan of the opposition is to do nothing more, to believe we can simply drift and be successful as a nation. When Senators James Exon of Nebraska and Charles Grassley of Iowa proposed an amendment in the Budget Committee that cut the budget $26 billion in five years—an average of one-third of 1 percent a year—the same people who said we can balance the budget without a constitutional amendment went apoplectic, saying that the $26 billion would devastate the country. They cannot have it both ways.

"Two Criticisms: The Courts will End Up Making Decisions for the Executive and Legislative Branches and The Amendment Precludes the Courts from Acting."

The criticisms cancel each other fairly well. Courts should not make political decisions, and they have shown great restraint in generally not doing that. The amendment provides that the courts can enter this field under guidelines set down by Congress in the law. The courts should not be making decisions about which budget should be cut and whether taxes should be raised but should retain the power to tell the other two branches of government to follow the Constitution.

What is discouraging is to read editorials in newspapers I respect, like the *New York Times* and the *Washington Post*, which trot out the old arguments and which have obviously not reexamined the issue. No mention is made about the dangers of hyperinflation; these realities have been totally ignored in their editorials. The editorials were written as they might have been in 1938, when FDR created small deficits to revive the economy. The economic threat posed by a course that will lead to monetizing the debt apparently receives no consideration. The history of nations has been ignored. The editorial pages have been set on automatic pilot, and they apparently will stay there, no matter what the economic weather. That is a bad way to run either an airplane or an editorial page.

In his testimony Paul Tsongas commented on how discouraged he would get with newspaper editorials defending deficit spending and reminding him of Dr. Strangelove and nuclear weaponry. He tells of going to a board meeting, mentioning to a fellow board member his disheartenment at the editorials and columns. His colleague responded, "Think about who writes these articles. They are all from academia, from politics, from the media, and from the bureaucracy. No one who is out there trying to compete in the world trade markets would even conceive of arguing in favor of deficit spending."[35]

Let me pay tribute to those who have shown the courage to reverse course or to reexamine the issue fairly: the *Philadelphia Inquirer*, the *Chicago Tribune* and columnists George Will and Michael Kinsley. Others could be mentioned, along with members of the Senate and House who have recognized the dimensions of the problem and now support the amendment, despite great pressure to oppose it.

One other criticism is summarized in the heading on a *Wall Street Journal* editorial, "Simon's Tax Increase." I have never pretended that this could be done without pain, and the pain must come on both the spending side and on the revenue side. Most analysts agree. No politician likes to vote for taxes—I'm no exception—but we have to acknowledge, at least privately, that both spending cuts and taxes are needed to control deficits.

However, to those who write that "America is clearly in danger of being taxed to death," a dose of reality is in order. Western European nations and Japan have a value-added tax; we have none. The average citizen in western Europe and Japan pays higher income taxes than does the average American, and the wealthy western European or Japanese pays appreciably higher income taxes. Twenty-two nations have higher cigarette taxes than we. Almost all nations have higher gasoline taxes than the United States. As far as I can determine, we are the only nation that permits deducting interest on a home mortgage from income for tax purposes. The Organization for European Cooperation and Development (OECD) 1991 listing of the effective total tax rate imposed on its citizens among the twenty-four major industrial nations found the United States dead last, with Sweden topping the list. Our taxes, relative to our national income, have dropped, though most people would have a hard time believing it. Listen to these words from a *Newsweek* article:

> Americans pay far less than they think. Of the 112 million federal income-tax returns filed for 1989, 23 million showed no tax liability at all. More than two-thirds of the rest faced the minimum rate, 15 percent—and after exemptions and deductions, the average federal income-tax bill for those 65 million taxpayers was a scant 7.8 percent of their reported income. Even folks in upper brackets often forget that the 28 and 33 percent tax rates apply only on the margin: the 13 million payers with incomes of $50,000 to $100,000 had most of their income taxes at 15 percent.[36]

Written in April, 1993 the article said that "it's hard to talk straight" about taxes.

However, without something to stop the deficit hemorrhaging, tax rates in the United States will eventually exceed those of most of our friends in western Europe and Japan because of debt service.

During the 1992 presidential race, Ross Perot spoke more candidly about the deficit and what needed to be done, including a tax increase, than either you, Mr. President, or former President Bush. It was his most significant contribution. He helped the American people understand the dimensions of the problem and that there are no painless solutions.

I fully understand the politics of all this, Mr. President. It is not easy to tell people the truth sometimes, particularly about taxes. Two years before our Revolution, Edmund Burke wrote: "To tax and to please, no more than to love and to be wise, is not given to men."[37]

The other side of the coin is that no developed nation except Israel spends as much of its budget on the combination of defense and loan interest as the United States—in other words, spends as little of it on things that matter in the life of the average citizen. If we adopt a balanced budget amendment, interest spending will automatically drop and in a few years the drop will be significant. I also favor limited additional cuts in defense spending, but that is one of the priority debates we must have. My observation is that we are much better situated to meet a potential military threat anywhere in the world than we are to meet some existing domestic threats at home and that greater balance is in order.

The Danger of Indexing

A quicksand we have entered is indexing, putting the inflationary factor into a variety of measures. I have been able to stop it occasionally, but it is one of those things that we do without much thinking and, once started, is difficult to stop. Indexing accommodates inflation. Social Security, for example, is indexed, though before indexation began, Congress would, year after year, vote to raise the amount recipients would receive. That is a preferable way to handle it. We indexed tax rates without holding a hearing on the matter. If the indexation on tax rates were stopped for just one year, the federal government would gain $36 billion in revenue in five years. Both Arthur Burns and Paul Volcker warned against indexing, saying it is in and of itself inflationary. We paid no attention to them and have harmed our economy.

Our failure to deal with the deficit has caused failure to fully use taxes collected for designated purposes, such as the Aviation Trust Fund, the Highway Trust Fund, the Land and Water Conservation Fund and other trust funds. We use these and other trust funds (primarily Social Security) to mask the real size of the deficit and don't spend the money for the purposes for which lawmakers intended it.

When Carl Curtis of Nebraska served in the Senate, he advocated a surtax to be automatically invoked by the President any time there was a deficit, arguing that such a penalty would restrain both branches of government and get us out of our fiscal mess, which is much worse now then when Senator Curtis served. He compared it to going to the dentist, painful but necessary. He wrote these prophetic words in his autobiography: "The alternative to balancing the budget . . . painful though any such process must be politically, is galloping inflation . . . and virtual collapse of the nation's economy."[38]

We Must Make Sacrifices

When asked at the House Budget Committee where your administration is going in future fiscal years, Dr. Alice Rivlin responded: "We don't have an administration policy on long-run fiscal policy at the moment."[39] That devastating comment came not from a Republican critic but from a member of your administration. There is no Clinton plan, Mr. President, to eliminate the deficit; there is no Clinton plan to consider the long-term fiscal situation, to build a better future for our grandchildren. There should be.

Early in this letter, Mr. President, I mentioned that you have one great plus and one great minus in your fiscal record. The great minus was your opposition to the balanced budget amendment. As you agonized on how to come down on this, you had a visit from Senator Robert Byrd, chairman of the Appropriations Committee, and his ranking Republican on that committee, Senator Mark Hatfield. I have a high regard for both of them. Their visit may have been decisive. They won out.

But Chelsea did not. My grandchildren did not.

I face a choice of sacrificing a little so that my grandchildren can have a brighter future, or passing our debts on to them. I don't have a difficult time making a choice on that. I don't think the American people do either, if it is presented to them properly.

As a leader, you should not hesitate to confront the American people with what they might not like to hear. They yearn for solid leadership. Once again, you must ask more of us. Even Rush Limbaugh said: "We were never required to make the kind of sacrifice that the World War II generation was asked to make. Things came too easy for us. To put it bluntly, many of the baby-boom generation are spoiled brats."[40] In 1990 Congressman Dick Gephardt made an observation that is still true: "I see the sacrifices leaders from Mexico to Czechoslovakia are asking their people to make. They have so little and are daring so much. We have so much and are asking so little of ourselves."[41]

Unless we are told bluntly—to use Rush's word—about our needs and the revenue that is required to make ours a better society, yours will be a presidency of greater hopes than accomplishments.

We are willing to sacrifice if we understand the reasons. If the objective is to make ours a better nation and better world, and you spell out the details, we are not only willing to sacrifice, we will be proud to do so.

Sincerely,

Paul Simon

Nine

Rebuilding a Healthy Industrial Base

Dear Mr. President:

Before you became President, you said: "We must reject the zero-sum thinking of traditional labor-management relations in which two parties face each other as adversaries. In place of this 'them versus us' system, we must offer a new covenant for labor and management, based on participation, cooperation and teamwork. Such an approach to working smarter will have to be adopted if America is to regain its competitive edge."[1]

Your instincts for the basics are sound. You do not use the corporation-bashing rhetoric or the antiunion diatribes of some of our friends. You also recognize that our industrial base has deteriorated. You understand that we will have neither a growing economy nor a sound industrial base unless we have a healthy labor union movement. All economists also decry our miserable savings rate. The needs are fairly clear, but the path to meeting them is tortuous.

Is there a means of finding our way through the maze, or is the right economic course impossible politically?

No one who understands the complexity of the economics and the politics of it would suggest that it is easy, but the rewards are great for our nation if we have political leadership with the courage and insight to tackle this issue.

There is no secret to how we change our course: 1) increase private and corporate savings; 2) reduce government debt—discussed in an earlier letter; and 3) reshape corporate and consumer debt. If we do all of these, the result will be lower interest rates, reductions in our trade deficit, and increased investment in our industrial base and housing construction. With that will come increased productivity. Lester Thurow summarized it well: "In the long run productivity, or output per hour of work, is the central factor determining the ability of any society to generate a world-class standard of living. It is not possible to divide what isn't produced."[2]

How do we get there? Those of us in politics like painless answers. They get us elected or reelected. But there is no painless, successful solution. The relatively minor pain we should inflict on ourselves, however, will pay huge dividends if we have the courage to do it.

What Can We Do?

Here are a few steps toward achieving the goals of rebuilding our industrial base:

Improve the savings rate. The statistics are hardly news. The U.S. savings rate is dramatically lower than those in Japan, Germany and other industrial nations. Senator Daniel Patrick Moynihan wrote: "We are consuming too much and saving too little. We have a lower rate of investment than any of our competitors, save Great Britain. The average age of machinery in our factories is twice that of Japan. . . . We are now saving five percent of income. Saving six percent won't change a thing. It is time we set our minds on 20 percent. Let the Reagan administration give us that goal."[3] He wrote that in 1981. I am writing in 1994, and the 1991 figures are the latest international figures available. "Pat" Moynihan bemoaned a five percent net savings and said only Great Britain had a worse record. The 1991 figure is down to 2.3 percent—worse than Great Britain's very weak 2.7 percent. Japan is at 20.4 percent, Germany at 9.9 percent, France at 7.5 percent, and Italy at 6.7 percent. This lack of savings retards our economic growth.

Reduce the federal government deficit. This is by far the most important single ingredient, already stressed in one of my earlier letters, but it cannot be emphasized too much. The Wharton study suggesting that thirty-year bonds would gradually drop from 6.5 percent interest to 2.5 percent with a balanced budget amendment to the Constitution is a clear indication that this path will produce results, as well as long-range protection for the economy.

Encourage corporate equity financing rather than debt financing. Our debt problem is not only the $4.6 trillion owed by the federal government, but also the $4.3 trillion owed by U.S. corporations. Getting the latter figure down without discouraging industrial modernization is important to the economy. Reducing it will also reduce interest rates and encourage further industrial improvement. That, in turn would encourage corporations to save money for projects, lift the stock market, and help federal government revenue slightly.

If corporations of more than $1 million in gross income could deduct 80 percent of their interest expense rather than 100 percent and then deduct 50 percent of their spending for dividends, it would make no immediate change in federal government revenue and would encourage corporations to finance their expansion by saving money or issuing stock, rather than through debt. Alan Greenspan, chair of the

Federal Reserve Board, has responded favorably to the concept. A practice of permitting corporations to deduct half the cost of dividends would also put our tax laws more in line with other Western industrial democracies.

Corporations with less than $1 million in gross income could make a choice of the full interest deduction or the dividend deduction. For several years after the law is changed, any corporation that would be put in a deficit financial situation by the interest change could opt to continue the 100 percent deduction, but there would be few.

To critics who say this would discourage corporations from modernizing their plants and equipment, the reality is that when purchases are made, they are made with the belief that they will add to income, not because of the deductibility of interest. When I was in the newspaper and printing business and faced the possibility of buying a new (or sometimes used) piece of printing machinery, I either bought it or not depending on whether it would or would not make money for us. Yes, I knew that interest could be deducted on the income tax form, but that played only a minor part in my decision-making.

In the future, when one corporation buys another, only half the interest from debt acquired for that purpose should be deductible. This should apply prospectively so that the rules are not changed on acquisitions already consummated.

We should discourage debt for nonproductive purposes. Not all corporate acquisitions are bad, but many are, and where they take place, let stock be issued. Too many corporations have shaken their foundations with unnecessary and undesirable debt. And even when the corporation remains solid, no national purpose has been served by using huge amounts of capital for one corporation simply to gobble up another. For example, U.S. Steel (now USX) bought

Marathon Oil for $6 billion and borrowed $4 billion of that. What did that do to modernize the outmoded steel plants in this nation? Nothing. How many new jobs did it create in the steel industry? None. How many new oil wells did it dig? None. What did it do to modernize Marathon facilities? Nothing. How many new jobs did it create in the oil industry? None. Who picks up the tab for the interest on the $4 billion borrowed and now deducted? You and I do. Has it benefited the nation in any way? Not that I can see. By making only half the interest deductible for acquisitions, corporations would be forced to carefully evaluate the move before one corporation consumes another, and where it is considered desirable, stock, rather than acquired debt, becomes an attractive alternative. Discouraging debt for acquisition purposes would not only be good for the nation's economy, it would be healthy for many of these corporations. Many companies have gone bankrupt because they painted an unrealistically rosy scenario of what would happen if they acquired another corporation, and the deal went sour. If an acquisition requires $500 million in debt, and there is a struggle to survive economically, heavy interest payments cloud the future. If $500 million in common stock is issued, there may be no dividends and there are no interest payments to make and no principle of $500 million to repay. There is no bankruptcy, and the future can still be bright for that company.

Stimulate consumer saving. We have made debt easy to acquire, savings difficult. Consumer debt now stands at $3.7 trillion. We pander to our weaknesses. One of the theories of the 1981 Reagan tax cut for wealthy citizens is that they would increase savings from their increased earnings. It fizzled. The savings rate went down instead of up. As a high Japanese financial official has observed: "The original intention of the Reagan fiscal policy was not that bad. The problem was that it did not work as intended. They expected that their policy would boost domestic savings, but it did precisely the opposite."[4] Lester Thurow writes: "To raise personal savings America must begin by eliminating the 'no down payment' society."[5] One of the reasons other nations have higher savings rates is that legal requirements for down payments on homes and cars and other large items are in great contrast to our loose practices. People save money in those nations because doing so is essential to acquire goods they want. In our country moves in this direction would have to be planned carefully and implemented gradually. We took a correct step when we made interest nondeductible for an individual except in the case of home mortgages. Additional actions that we could take:

☐ Remove the deduction for interest on vacation home mortgages. This would gain revenue for the federal government, reduce the deficit, and encourage savings to acquire a vacation home.

☐ Follow the German system of permitting interest earned on amounts deposited for at least seven years at thrift institutions to be tax free. That encourages savings and permits banks, savings and loans, and credit unions to plan more effectively.

☐ Create a new, revised individual retirement account (IRA). IRAs were cut back just when they were starting to have an impact. While the statistical measurement of the resultant savings from the IRAs suggests not much increase, my impression is that people started to see what savings could do when it is compounded.

Safeguard and stabilize pension funds. This is a complex area that deserves more than a few sentences, but in a few words, here are the basics:

☐ Pension funds should not be used for speculation. Any income from sales of stocks or bonds held less than one year should be taxable. That would permit movement but encourage greater stability.

☐ Private pension funds should be safeguarded so that employees, as well as corporations, have a voice in pension financial activities, and perhaps there should be a few mutually agreed-upon third parties for added protection. These funds should not be available for use by any corporations for less than fiscally sound purposes, and the pension funds should be protected so that a takeover corporation is not able to take advantage of a pension fund.

☐ State and local governmental pension funds should be more carefully safeguarded. When facing financial problems, some of these governments are getting into the bad habit of borrowing from pension funds. Many of those funds are going to have serious problems a decade from now. Some type of federal monitoring— and perhaps a reward or penalty—should be created to safeguard these important funds. Doing it will also help the nation's savings rate.

We do save now through private, state, and local government pension funds, but we can do a much better job.

These measures will add to savings, lower interest rates, encourage investment, permit more research, and add to productivity. The huge trade deficits the nation has been running have to be paid either with a lower standard of living or increased productivity. So far our principle answer has been a lower standard of living. That can change, if we have the courage to change it.

While the steps toward greater savings outlined above are needed, other moves are also required to build a healthy industrial base. They should include the following.

Encourage the expansion of the labor union movement.
Membership in labor unions among working men and
women is sharply lower in the United States than in other
industrialized nations. In the mid 1950s both Canada and the
United States had approximately 33 percent of their work
force unionized. Today it is 36 percent in Canada and 16
percent in the United States. Even that is deceptive because
much of the U.S. figure is for government employees. In the
nongovernment sector, only 11.8 percent of U.S. workers are
organized. In western Europe, 33 to 90 percent of the workers are covered; in Japan, 28 percent.

George Shultz, secretary of state in the Reagan administration but an economist by background, told the National
Planning Association of his concerns "about the possible
harm to American industry and society stemming from the
declining American labor movement." He said that in "a
healthy workplace, it is very important that there be some
system of checks and balances." He told the group: "Free
societies and free trade unions go together. . . . It's not an
accident that a lot of the fire for what happened in Eastern
European countries came out of a trade union, Solidarity."[6]

A *Washington Post* article points out that the income of the
richest fifth of our population has grown over the decades
while that of the poorest fifth has dropped, and economists
don't seem to understand the reason. The article states:

> This intellectual cockfight . . . concerns the central
> economic question of the 1990s: Why income
> growth has slowed from a jog to a crawl while the
> gap between rich and poor gets wider and wider.
> "We've suffered a substantial decline in the living
> standard for the average American worker over the
> last two decades, and we can't really explain it," said
> George Johnson, an economist at the University of
> Michigan who has spent many years trying. "If you

think about it, this is a profound embarrassment for the economics profession." "Why did the economic magic go away?" asks [economist Paul] Krugman in *Peddling Prosperity.* "The real answer is that we don't know."

I think there are three major reasons: 1) diminished demand for unskilled labor; 2) the 1981 Reagan tax changes that brought income tax breaks to the wealthy and little or none to those of more limited income; and 3) the drop in labor union membership. Labor union programs serve to help the income distribution factor in the economy, and as union membership declines, so does the distribution factor.

The drop in U.S. union membership is significant for additional reasons. One is that the loss in union membership percentages parallels a U.S. drop in productivity. Loss of productivity growth is caused in part by a failure to achieve higher wages. The average union member made $33,345 in 1992, and the average nonunion worker, $27,613. Higher wages paid to union workers encourage the use of labor-saving machinery. As late as 1986 the average manufacturing wage in the United States exceeded that of any nation, but as of 1993, eleven countries have higher average manufacturing wages. Not too surprising, many of them outstripped the United States in productivity growth. Industries invested in machinery to save on labor costs.

Union workers average longer on a job, develop more of a sense of loyalty to the company, and encourage labor-saving efforts. This is generally but not consistently true. Where you have had a bad labor/management climate, as in the case of Caterpillar in Illinois, this would not be the case. A more typical example is the steel industry. A combination of unenlightened decisions by both management and government discouraged modernization, but the Steelworkers Union, under the presidency of Lynn Williams, recognized that modernization had to take place to save the industry, even though that would temporarily cost steelworkers jobs.

Studies also show that satisfied workers are more productive and that union workers tend to be more satisfied. Research is fairly uniform in showing higher productivity with union workers, particularly in the construction industry. Some studies suggest a slight tendency for businesses with unions to show smaller profit margins, though there is no consistency in that and many exceptions.

Both labor and management have made a series of mistakes. On the union side:

☐ Sometimes labor union leaders are too rigid in not permitting people to be transferred from one job to another. Foreign labor unions tend to be much more flexible on this. Union-supported work rules sometimes are inefficient and hinder productivity. In addition to harming the immediate industry, that tarnishes the public image of the labor movement.

☐ Sometimes bluster replaces calm negotiation and becomes a tool for self-promotion.

☐ As in any profession, there have been cases of corruption that have received great publicity, hurting all union leadership.

☐ Many unions were slow in bringing minorities and women into their ranks and into leadership.

On the management side:

☐ Antiunion propagandists in a few business organizations have caused the employment of antiunion law firms and consultants whose confrontational tactics have been a disservice to management, labor, and the nation.

☐ Firing of employees involved in union organizing, using every possible legal tactic to delay recognition of a union, and the use of legal threats ("We'll close our plant if it's organized") have combined with other extreme practices to discourage organizing efforts.

☐ Sometimes, when there have been cutbacks on the pay of hourly workers, there have been huge bonuses for the top-salaried people, even when the corporation in question had serious losses.

The most important step toward an improved labor/management climate is an improved attitude on both sides. But the major reason for the difference between the United States and Canada, for example, is the legal framework. Here are practical steps to rectify the balance and sensibly encourage more union membership, the stated aim of the Wagner Act passed in 1935:

☐ In Canada if a majority of workers sign cards saying they want to organize and pay one dollar with each card, it is automatically done. In the United States legal delays may mean there will be no organization for as long as seven years. We should adopt the Canadian system, with a quick appeal possible to the National Labor Relations Board (NLRB) if there is a charge of fraud or coercion, then an election within thirty days, followed by immediate recognition if the result is favorable.

☐ While it is technically illegal now to fire someone for advocating union affiliation, thousands are fired for that reason each year. Most of those discharged do not contest the matter legally because they don't have the finances to do so. The average fine for the employer who is found guilty of this violation is $2,000. Antiunion law firms tell corporations that it pays to violate the law. Fines should be much steeper. Paul Weiler of

Harvard has suggested that employees fired illegally should have the right to sue employers for punitive damages, a right denied them under the present law.

☐ A law firm or consulting firm that advises people to violate the law should be subject to heavy penalties. The National Labor Relations Board also should be encouraged to take blatant cases of attorneys doing this to state bar associations for discipline.

☐ A corporation that has a pattern and practice of violating civil rights laws is denied the right to have a federal contract. Rightfully so. The same should be true for a firm that has a pattern and practice of violating labor laws.

☐ The NLRB should be required to rule on the unfair discharge of an employee within thirty days.

☐ When an employer requires employees to sit through an anti-union lecture, discussion, or movie on company time, the unions should have an equal period of time during the work day to explain their case. Now there is no such requirement, and businesses can legally fire an employee who refuses to attend an anti-union session. There should be balance. In one incident in 1984 nursing home supervisors wore "Union No" buttons. Seventeen employees showed up the next day wearing buttons advocating union affiliation, and all seventeen were fired. The imbalance in the present law needs to be rectified.

☐ If after a union is recognized a contract is not signed between the employer and the union within sixty days, binding arbitration should be required. First contract negotiations often take more than a year, and sometimes contracts are never signed, another way to avoid recognizing the union.

There is one other issue already high on the agenda for labor unions: that strikers cannot be permanently replaced. I favor the legislation. A tool rarely used in our past, striker replacement is illegal in Canada and most jurisdictions, except for Great Britain, Hong Kong and Singapore. Our two big economic competitors, Japan and Germany, do not permit permanent striker replacement. Labor/management relations should not deteriorate to the point that it is even considered, and the prospect of that bitter pill adds a grimness to the process that is not good for either side.

Hoyt Wheeler, a professor in the College of Business Administration at the University of South Carolina, did a study of union organizing in the southeast part of the nation. He testified: "My personal response to our experience . . . is that I am amazed that unions are ever able to win a representation election. The conditions set up by our legal system are so unfavorable that each and every union victory is a triumph of courage and intense effort."[8]

Ray Marshall, former secretary of labor and an exceptional cabinet officer, joined former Senator William Brock, who once chaired the Republican National Committee, in a series of sensible recommendations to improve the effectiveness of the workplace. Marshall later wrote: "Stronger labor movements are clearly in the national interest. The U.S. should modernize its labor laws to make it easier for workers to organize and bargain collectively and more difficult for employers to thwart those rights by legal and illegal means."[9]

One of the many reasons for encouraging more union membership is that unions can be a voice for the dispossessed in our society. With money playing such a huge roll in political campaigns, those who are left out too often are voiceless. Labor unionism at its best has been a voice not only for its members but for those who are ignored. The minimum wage laws, for example, did not directly help union membership but represented a significant gain for many of the unorganized. Our society has to build constructive mechanisms to respond to the needs of the most disheartened among us, and labor unions are one way of assisting.

One significant area: Businesses that are organized have less sexual harassment of women, providing women an added degree of protection in addition to a higher average wage. In theory any woman who is harassed can file a complaint with a federal agency, but that is rarely done. Complaining to the business agent of a union, however, is easy and quickly done and frequently gets results.

Profit–Sharing Helps Businesses and Workers

Create incentives for profit-sharing. We have inched in that direction with the encouragement of employee stock option plans, but meaningful profit-sharing goes much further. Where it has been tried, it has been successful, even though both management and labor generally are not enthusiastic about the idea. Management does not like to share profits, though it will benefit in two ways:

☐ Employees will understand they have more of a stake in what happens in the business. It will be interesting to watch what happens with unions purchasing much of United Airlines, and my guess is that it will be a success. I have already noticed—and two passengers on one flight mentioned it to me—that since the employees purchased TWA they show more enthusiasm;

☐ If the bonuses from profits are distributed once every six months, as the Japanese do, there will be a tendency for people to accommodate their living standard to their weekly or semiweekly pay, and the larger bonus check is more likely to go into savings.

Usually, profit-sharing is available only after employees have worked for a company for a specified period of time, ordinarily one or two years. One of the advantages of profit-sharing is that it encourages longevity by employees. In some industries, such as construction, it is more difficult to arrange because of the seasonal nature of the work, but creative people can do it and are doing it.

For profit-sharing to be successful for a business and for the nation, it must be tied to productivity growth. Without productivity growth, most industries will not experience healthy profits. The assumption is too widely made that if unemployment is low, inflation will grow. That is true only if productivity per worker does not rise. One of the brightest economic periods in the history of our nation occurred during President Truman's administration, when we had simultaneously low unemployment and low inflation under the direction of a brilliant noneconomist, Leon Keyserling. From 1947 to 1953, postwar years when many nations experienced inflation, economic growth in the United States averaged 4.8 percent, and there was virtually no inflation. Unemployment averaged four percent and reached 2.9 percent in Truman's final year. During that period, we carried on the Korean War, and the total deficit for the Truman years, using today's measurement standards, was $640 million, or less than $100 million a year.

The standard definition of inflation is "too few goods chasing too much money." Because of shortsighted policies, we have had to rely much too heavily on monetary policy to control inflation. But if instead we encouraged productivity so that we have more goods, the impact is deflationary. We have had periods of high unemployment and high inflation because there was no productivity growth. One of the great advantages of profit-sharing is that it encourages the growth of productivity.

There is some concern in labor circles that profit-sharing will reduce complaints about unsafe machinery and working conditions. That may happen occasionally, but profit through unsafe conditions is short-term gain, if it is that. The wisest employers know that. Long-term safety is profitable and adds to productivity.

Profit and quality go together, as some of our automobile manufacturers found out the hard way some years ago. Employees who understand that will make an extra effort to produce quality products when they have such a clear stake in the profits.

A way to encourage profit-sharing would be to reduce the corporate tax on any business that meets minimum criteria. A reduction of three to five percent, for example, should be enough to encourage consideration. But the major incentive should be the increased productivity and the improved atmosphere of the workplace.

Combine profit-sharing with some decision-sharing. The German experiment with work committees composed of management and labor, where employee representatives are picked by a vote of the workers, has been a success. The Germans, by tradition, also have union representation on the board of the corporation. We have had a little—very little— of that. Douglas Fraser, former president of the United Automobile Workers, served on the board of Chrysler during his presidency. It marked the first time that a major U.S. corporation elected a labor leader as a director. He excused himself when collective bargaining matters were discussed. A bright, practical, compassionate leader, I am sure he served Chrysler, as well as his union, well. He summed up his attitude: "We recognize that growing productivity is the only reliable basis for real progress in living standards. . . . However, higher productivity is not without its penalties in the form of job downgrading or, more frequently, outright job loss. Workers cannot be enlisted in wholehearted efforts to increase productivity unless protection against unemployment is assured."[10] That is where work committees (whatever they are called) and profit-sharing help to bridge the gap. People working together can find answers to difficult questions. Answers imposed on them without consultation create antagonism. A General Motors executive sounds a note similar to Doug Fraser's: "We must find innovative ways of utilizing people during economic downturns. . . . We cannot expect people to immerse themselves in the organization if the threat of layoff hangs over their heads."[11] Where teamwork is established, one not-so-minor advantage to both management and labor is that there is less contracting-out of work, making a plant less dependent on subcontractors who may or may not perform on time, or with quality. Keeping the work also diminishes job loss for labor.

Industrial Policy

Carefully plan for a prudent industrial policy. Other nations do it, usually with success. We also do it, but we don't give it a name, and we don't do it well. We do it because certain industries have political clout, but there is no systematic assessment of our economy, where we are going and what we should be doing. The oil depletion allowance created special tax benefits for developing the nation's oil reserves. The ethanol tax break is designed to encourage development of that fuel alternative. We subsidize irrigation and water projects in the West so farmers can grow more, and we pay farmers in the Midwest to grow less. Tax incentives for building commercial real estate took us too far, and in many areas we have more commercial real estate than we need. Amitai Etzioni of George Washington University observes:

> Innovative policy options are not even considered because it is widely expected that, given our inter-est-driven political system, they will be readily per-verted.[12]

Mancur Olson of the University of Maryland:

> It should be obvious from observations of the American government . . . that existing organized interests will greatly influence the selection of the members of any board or agency that implements an industrial policy. . . . A vast amount of evidence indicates that it is precisely in areas of high uncer-tainty and risk that governmental bureaucracies are least useful.[13]

Pete Peterson writes:

> We don't need or want an "industrial policy" that puts government in the business of micromanaging our private sector. If we create the right kind of overall economic climate for investment, private lenders and borrowers will allocate our savings more efficiently than any congressman or bureau-crat can.[14]

Charles Schultze, chair of the Council of Economic Advis-ers under President Carter, called the idea of the creation of an industrial policy "misguided."[15] That's one side of it. However, Martin and Sue Tolchin, journalists who study our economic scene, write: "Today, the question is not whether to support critical industries, but how to support them. Even the Japanese would like to see the United States adopt a consistent industrial strategy, if only to stem the ongoing criticism of Japan."[16] Our successful airplane production and sales are clearly the target of two nations, maybe more. They're planning for airplane production and encouraging it financially. We should be looking at what the coming breakthrough industries will be and encouraging research and development there. But industrial policy should be handled with extreme care. Those of us in politics are not necessarily good at making business decisions. A presidentially appointed committee of business leaders and economists like Lester Thurow, Fred Bergsten and Paul Volcker should give the concept a six-month study and make recommendations to the President and the Congress on what we should do. We can do better, but we should proceed with some caution.

Turn on our creative juices. The percentage of U.S. citizens securing patents from our Patent Office has been declining. Over a 14-year period the percentage of patents issued to U.S. citizens went from 67 percent to 53 percent and is still going down. Patents issued to Japanese citizens by the U.S. Patent Office during the same period increased from eight percent to 21 percent. Not only are applications by individual U.S. citizens declining, the corporate applications that U.S. firms once dominated have shifted to other countries, particularly Japan. When I visit college campuses, I occasionally ask, "How many of you have ever seriously thought about inventing something and patenting it?" Rarely are hands raised. Our attitude appears to be similar to the U.S. Commissioner of Patents who assured the nation in 1899 that all significant breakthroughs in inventions for humanity had already been achieved.

Much of the research in our nation now takes place at institutions, like Bell Labs, that often simply bypass the patent process because it is so cumbersome. Even acknowledging that, however, we are doing too little to encourage our creative people. I once worked with state legislators to get an "inventor-in-residence" bill passed for the colleges and universities in my state, but the governor vetoed the measure. Maybe it is not the ideal approach to the problem, but it is better than no approach. Academicians, business leaders, and the scientific community should get together to come up with answers.

Then when we have patents, we have to use them. The original patents on the video recorder were to an American firm. All video recorders are now produced outside the United States. There are other examples, unfortunately. We need to do more creative work within our country and take advantage of what we create.

Our Infrastructure

Build and rebuild our infrastructure.

☐ The interstate highway system added to our nation's productivity. In too many places it is in disrepair.

☐ Sweden, Spain, France, Japan and other nations have high-speed rail, but the United States has none. We're nibbling at the idea now, moving slowly. Very slowly. Five corridors have been picked as priorities for possible action.

☐ We have never approached mass transit in urban areas with anything like the comprehensive plans and dreams we had for the interstate highway system. Our cities and suburbs need this.

These are three of many illustrations of special opportunities that we have, each of which would add to our productivity and create jobs. What could we do to get this done? Each cent of a gasoline tax brings in $1.2 billion. If we increased the gasoline tax by seven cents and devoted two cents to interstate highways, two cents to state and local roads and bridges, two cents to urban mass transit, and one cent to high-speed rail, we would change the map of America for the better.

The information superhighway is part of our future, and the need is not resources by the federal government, but expediting where needless government regulations get in the way, monitoring to make sure that antitrust laws are not violated as we encourage this development, and facilitating the cooperation of federal research with private sector and university-based research efforts.

A host of other infrastructure needs should be addressed: We still have many rural areas without safe drinking water and/or a water system and sewer systems in older cities need repair. The list goes on and on. As we rebuild, repair, and modernize the nation, we add to our productive capacity and create good jobs for our people.

That agenda, Mr. President, is not an easy one, but you knew when you were elected President that it would not be easy. But what a great opportunity for you and the nation!

Sincerely,

Paul Simon

Ten

Health Care: Four Stars for Bill Clinton

Dear Mr. President:

This nation has needed a universal health care plan for decades, and now we have a President who may get us there. Unlike Social Security, which received not a single Republican vote when it passed, this time some Republicans also see the need, and the final vote in the Senate is likely to be 75-25 or better. That's good. I'm proud of my Republican colleague Senator Jim Jeffords for being the lone Republican cosponsor of your proposal, but more will vote for its final passage. Seeing that all Americans have quality health care should not be a partisan issue. However, there is a serious question if your proposal will be seriously weakened before it passes.

There have been bumps along the road, and there will be more before we get a bill to your desk. One problem has been that the legislation—both as it was being drafted and since then—has moved more slowly than it should. Delay has permitted enemies of the legislation to organize more effectively and focus on minutiae, distorting what you have proposed.

The star on this issue, outside of yourself, Mr. President, has been your wife. I have seen Hillary in 15 or 20 different health-related situations, and she always handles the issues and people superbly. She knows the details and comes across as dedicated, determined, and wanting to give people the protection they should have. There may be a member of the Senate or House who has not been impressed by her performance, but I haven't met the person. Praise is universal, and it is deserved.

Like any Senator who keeps in reasonably close touch with his or her constituency, I have heard too many stories that tear at my heart. Citizens come to me, crying as they tell their stories of desperation. I have to tell them there is nothing I can do—basically that their government doesn't care enough to help. I see too many letters from people who don't know where to turn—like the one in front of me now from a woman whose husband has a serious heart problem and can no longer work. They have been married 29 years and have health coverage through her job. But she is worried about losing her job. She does not mention her age, but my guess is that she is in her mid-fifties, with limited skills. If she loses her job, where can she go? Our answer for her now is that before we will help her, she and her husband must become paupers, then Medicaid will help. Does that make sense? If she works for a small business, her employer may be told by the insurance carrier, after they discover her husband's health condition, that the employer will either have to pay dramatically higher premiums or drop coverage for her.

What can the owner of a small business do? I shall always remember the visit I had early in my political career from a father of three young children. He had a serious renal disease and no insurance to cover it. He faced the choice of prolonging his life for a few years and losing the family home, or not going through the life-prolonging treatments and leaving his family their home after his death. "I've decided to die," he told me. And he did.

(I became the State Senate sponsor of the program to set up renal disease assistance in Illinois so other families would not have to go through that. It passed.)

The present system makes no sense. Fifty-eight million Americans will be out of coverage at some point this year; 38 million do not have coverage right now, two million more than last year at this time. Twelve million of those not covered by health insurance are children and, if no program is enacted, by the end of the century the majority of children will not be protected. Approximately half a million pregnant women have no health insurance coverage, and of the uninsured children, 58 percent are dependents of full-time workers. The unevenness of access to basic care is illustrated by an infant mortality rate almost twice as high for African Americans as for their white counterparts. Yale's Paul Kennedy quotes someone as saying:

> The U.S. occupies last place among the major industrialized countries . . . in child mortality, life expectancy, and visits to the doctor, although it probably leads the world in politicians who talk about family values.[1]

We have to do more than talk about family values.

I am strongly in your corner.

There are two fundamental questions before we get to final passage. First, what changes will be imposed by special interests? Second, what changes should be made to bring about the best possible plan?

This letter is being written before some committees act on the measure and at least two months before final passage. I serve on one of the two Senate committees of jurisdiction, the Committee on Labor and Human Resources, chaired by Senator Edward "Ted" Kennedy. Our committee members held weeks of informal sessions to discuss details, and then in a series of meetings from eight in the morning until well into the evening, we debated, adopted amendments, and produced a measure that I believe is a good one for the public. But each committee reporting in the House and Senate will produce differing versions and the compromises will come on the floor of the two bodies and in the House-Senate conference.

Here is part of what I see ahead, though the scene may have changed between the time of my writing this and your reading it:

Universal coverage. We should win on this, but it may be close. "Universal access" is a weak alternative and basically is what we have now. It's a nice-sounding phrase that does not protect people. You are right to make universal coverage an essential feature of the health care bill or you will veto it. And 95 percent is not enough! That leaves twelve and one-half million Americans abandoned. If some in the insurance industry, tobacco industry and a minority of business interests should prevail on this, take this issue to the people and they will elect more sympathetic lawmakers. The pressures that come from those who play a major role in financing our campaigns illustrate both the need for changing the campaign financing system and the reason it will take an extra effort to achieve what should not be a major struggle: all Americans covered by health insurance.

Choice of health provider: As you have pointed out many times, your proposal gives people choice, more than many have today. That will stay. But having a choice remains a problem in some rural areas of Arkansas, Illinois, and other states under both your proposal and the present system. If there is only one physician in a poor rural county, choice is more a theory than a reality. How we more adequately protect these areas and encourage greater options and improved quality remains a matter of concern. Your health plan will not solve all of our problems.

Employer mandate. This will be a hard-fought battle, and I hope common sense can prevail. If we were to start with a blank slate and suggest a system where employers could voluntarily pay for their employees' health care and were also responsible for helping pick up the tab for those employers who chose not to do so, people would laugh at the idea. Yet that is precisely the system that has emerged.

Most small businesses—62 percent of them have coverage—will benefit from the employer mandate in your bill because they will get reductions in the insurance they now pay and there will be at least some cost control factors in play for future years. The measure reported out of the Kennedy committee calls for small businesses—from whom we hear many of the objections—paying one percent of payroll for health care coverage if they employ one to six people; that's five cents an hour for someone being paid $5 an hour. For a business employing six to eleven people there would be a two percent charge, and the rate would ascend gradually from there. Compare that with the last increase in the minimum wage, which increased costs for many employers 40 cents an hour!

I read with interest the transcript of the meeting you had with small-business people on this issue. One pointed out that sometimes businesses cannot recruit people they would like to employ because they are unable to offer health insurance because of the cost. But under the incentives your plan provides, they will be able to offer health insurance, and it will be a helpful tool for recruiting. I like the comment of the New England businessperson:

> Every Vermont teddy bear [we make] comes with a
> lifetime health plan. We operate America's only
> teddy bear hospital, and should any Vermont teddy
> bear need rehabilitation, we do it free of charge.
> There is only one insurance company. There is no
> paperwork. If it looks like our teddy bear, we will
> replace limbs, replace eyes—doesn't matter how old
> you are. We truly have universal access for teddy
> bears. And it's frustrating that we have difficulty
> providing that for our employees.[2]

That company went from four employees to 200, and their
most difficult problem is providing health insurance, which
they cannot afford now but would be able to afford under
the Clinton plan. There are businesses who will pay more,
who do not want to offer coverage for their employees. The
owner of such a business has a price to pay, but a fair price.
Small businesses that offer insurance already find they have
less turnover of personnel, and those who do not now offer
it will find the same. Our committee voted to increase the
tax on a package of cigarettes by $1.50, but the reality is that
we cannot create a health system for the nation by calling on
only the cigarette smokers to sacrifice.

Crain's Chicago Business, a mini-*Wall Street Journal* for the
Chicago area, surprised a few of its readers with an editorial:

> Guaranteed health [care] coverage for every U.S.
> citizen is an essential part of any health reform
> measure. . . . The inability to meet medical bills has
> been a financial drain on both families and health
> providers. In Chicago alone, fifteen hospitals have
> been forced to close their doors over the past decade
> because of the high cost of providing indigent care.
> Business executives must keep in mind that univer-
> sal care is good economics.[3]

Health Care

The employer mandate takes advantage of the system we now have; it builds on that experience and should pass—after a tough fight. If it does, current estimates are that a decade from now the savings to business in one year will be $117 billion and the savings to individual households will be $69 billion.

Cost control. This is one of two areas where I have some uneasiness. Here the public interest in cost control runs into direct conflict with those who profit most from the present system. The basic concept of achieving savings through competition has been shown to work on a limited scale.

The proposed use of caps on premiums moves us into an untried area, where a standard benefit package will be complicated by enlarged demand. While the experience of several states and many corporations in using competition to keep prices down is positive, no one can know with certainty that prices will not escalate with nationally increased utilization of health delivery services. That is the reason for authorizing the National Health Board, created under the legislation, to set premium caps if premiums start getting too high. However, the insurance industry strongly opposes premium caps, and caps remained in the Kennedy committee bill by only a 9-8 vote; this suggests a major battle on the floor, which may be won by the insurance companies rather than the public.

Further emphasizing cost control, our committee, by a unanimous 17-0 vote, authorized the National Health Board to reduce benefits, if necessary, and to recommend to Congress tax increases that Congress would have to vote up or down within 60 days. Without effective cost control, the entire plan ultimately will be in serious trouble.

The difficulty with cost control is that it will collide with both spending habits and special interests that profit from the present system. We spend far more on health care as a percentage of our national income than people in any other nation, and changing those spending and consumer habits will not be easy. For example, physicians in the United States make 6.7 times the average person's wage compared to four times the average wage in Germany. Also we are addicted to having machines look at us whether necessary or unnecessary. Comparing total health care costs of the United States, Germany, France and Japan, the Organization for Economic Cooperation and Development's 1984 figures show that a home visit in the United States costs 2.1 times the average in other nations, an appendectomy is 7.6 times as much ($1,135 in the U.S., $237 in Japan, $114 in France, $95 in Germany), a hysterectomy is 6.7 times as much, and the list goes on. All of this will not change abruptly when we pass health care reform legislation. Cost control will not be easily achieved. The cost control mechanism will be strengthened if we give the National Health Board stand-by price controls on premiums. That is a little like giving a gun to a police officer: I hope he or she does not have to use it, but the presence of the gun does keep some people in line.

Revenue. This is the other area where I have some uneasiness. I will vote for an increased tax on a pack of cigarettes. It will bring in substantial revenue and discourage price-sensitive teenagers from smoking. But I also believe that despite the savings that are likely from managed competition and a great emphasis on preventive care, there is a reasonably good chance that there will be such a surge of new users of health services that both our delivery system and funding will fall short. When we guarantee coverage to 38 million Americans who have no coverage or extremely limited coverage, we will save money in a few years. During the interim, my intuition tells me that the sudden spurt of demand will be costly—perhaps more costly than has been contemplated. People with health insurance visit a physician twice as often on average as those without it. Increase the numbers of people who are covered by the 38 million not now covered, and it probably will lead to a temporary surge in demand. The Kennedy committee proposal for additional revenue includes a one percent payroll tax on all businesses employing more than 1,000 people. That, plus the cigarette tax, plus the ability of the National Health Board to reduce benefits, may be enough to pay for the program. Somewhat greater utilization of hospitals should lead to reduced per-patient overhead costs. But Congress and the public should enter this much-needed improvement with the realization that some type of revenue increment may be necessary. The original national health insurance proposal by Harry Truman called for payroll deductions to meet its cost. In shaping and paying for health care reform, we should strive to underpromise and overdeliver, not the reverse.

Long-term care. Your proposal is good but limited. It provides help for people at home rather than in nursing homes, and this should be encouraged. But there are people who will still need to be placed in nursing homes. Nursing home care is a mammoth financial drag on family resources, on state governments, and on the federal government. Full coverage for custodial care, when needed, would require big expenditures quickly. Senators Kennedy and Wofford have introduced a measure that in the Kennedy committee became an amendment to your proposal. It provides some protection and does it prudently by establishing a voluntary, government-managed insurance program to cover extended nursing home stays. People would be given the option of purchasing coverage at age 35, 45, 55 and 65, much as seniors can elect to participate in Medicare Part B today. Participants would pay a fee, depending on their age, when they become a plan participant. Premiums would start as low as $16 a month. Participants would choose a plan offering one of three benefit levels: $30,000, $60,000 or $90,000 of nursing home coverage. Each level would be combined with an equivalent level of asset protection. For example, if a person chooses a plan offering $30,000 worth of nursing home coverage, he or she would also be eligible for $30,000 in asset protection, meaning that the person or his or her estate could be forced to use assets to pay for bills above the protected amount. The federal government would pay for up to $30,000, or whatever the chosen policy amount is. The program would be self-financed, so there would be no additional cost to the government. It provides a way to plan for one worry we all have as we get older: being able to afford long-term nursing home care if we need it. In some way we must address the long-term residential need and we can't do it with a plan that will take effect in 30 years. In six years there may be as many as one million more Americans in nursing homes than there are today. Your proposal will cut that figure by encouraging at-home care. But we should not ignore the need for residential care as we deal with health care related reform.

Mental health. It is expensive to cover mental health care and more expensive not to cover it. My guess is that we will expand your proposal. Leading this effort are Senator Pete Domenici of New Mexico, Senator Paul Wellstone of Minnesota and Senator Alan Simpson of Wyoming. I applaud all three for their efforts. They are also a good illustration of the influence of wives, for Nancy Domenici, Sheila Wellstone and Ann Simpson are playing leadership roles, as is "Tipper" Gore, the wife of the Vice President. The three senators have all seen personal tragedy in the life of a relative, and that is a motivating factor, a proper motivating factor. The success rate for treatment of severe problems of mental illness is better than it is for cardiovascular surgery. No one would consider excluding the latter from a health bill, but some want to exclude the more successful mental health treatments. We need sensible limitations, but that is true in every area. Mental health also must include an adequate addiction program, residential and non-residential, for promptly dealing with drug and alcohol abusers.

Research. We must not diminish our biomedical research efforts. We can achieve immense savings for the United States and all humanity from research on cancer, AIDS, diabetes, arthritis, heart defects, and many other disabling diseases. Senator Tom Harkin developed an amendment that will at least maintain our present research effort, and that is included in the Kennedy committee bill. Research is important to our health—and is also important to our economic well-being. We want to continue to pioneer, and we can make money doing it. I confess to some pride when I read about foreign leaders coming to one of our preeminent medical centers for advanced treatment. We should keep our research lead but also work cooperatively with other countries.

Alliances. The idea of a purchasing cooperative to ensure citizens' insurance coverage at reasonable prices is drawing a great deal of fire. While alliances can be modified and the name will be changed, we need a mechanism for governance. The charge by the insurance industry that an alliance will result in a huge bureaucracy is simply not factual. An alliance in California handles insurance for 930,000 people at an administrative cost of one-half of one percent, with 97 people employed to run the program. That is hardly an administrative monster!

People as varied in their approach as Senator Kennedy and Senator Don Nickles of Oklahoma, one of the more conservative Republicans, have suggested the possibility of the alliance, plus the ability of citizens to purchase insurance from the same companies that the federal government employees can use. As a senator, I use one of these companies, which I chose from among the 19 health insurance plans available in the Washington, D.C., area. Other federal employees around the nation have similar choices in their areas. And, not so incidentally, under this system, which is in use right now, private insurance companies provide the health coverage, paid for by those of us who work for the federal government at a charge for administrative costs of approximately one-eighth of one percent of the payroll covered. In other words, administrative costs equal just $125 for every $100,000 in wages earned by covered employees. Presumably most of the nineteen qualified health insurance companies would be eligible for the purchasing cooperative, or alliance.

Prevention. When HMOs were first created, many of us felt they would stress prevention because of their total health responsibility. It didn't happen. They simply built on our culture, which is primarily crisis oriented rather than prevention oriented. Now some HMOs are doing better. Your proposal, Mr. President, to offer free physical examinations, free mammograms for women, and free dental care for children up to the age of 18 should encourage prevention. This may be controversial, with some Senators demanding a co-payment. However, we should not discourage people from getting regular physicals and taking other prevention steps. In Illinois more than 20 percent of pregnant women do not get early prenatal care, and the national figure is probably higher. Half the uninsured did not see a physician during the past year, while only one-quarter of those insured did not. The Kaiser Family Foundation, which has pioneered health care, concludes: "When the uninsured finally see a doctor, their health problems are likely to be worse and more difficult to treat."[4] Our present system reimburses procedures such as an appendectomy but does not reimburse a physician who talks to patients about what they eat, how much exercise they get, and what their family problems are that may be putting a strain on mental and physical health. Health education, whether from a physician, in a school, in a newspaper or magazine, or on a radio or television program, is important because we can prevent many medical problems.

For non-preventive measures, we should have a co-payment. Our Canadian friends say they made a significant mistake in not requiring a co-payment, that there is overutilization of the system by some who would be discouraged by a modest co-payment for the medical services they receive.

There are many of us who believe that we should gradually move to a single-payer system similar to the Canadian program, and your proposal permits states to do that. That will also be a fight. There will be attempts to eliminate that option. The Canadian single-payer system is really not a Canadian system, meaning a national one—the provinces adopted it one by one. The same is likely to happen in our nation. States closest to Canada will be first because they know of the system's popularity there. And if it works in individual states, it will gradually spread. The Congressional Budget Office reports that a single-payer model similar to Canada's would save the nation $114 billion by the year 2003. Administrative costs under our present system are double those in Canada.

Rural coverage. There are major problems of health delivery in rural areas, particularly poor rural regions, even worse than the access problems faced by people in the inner city. Twenty-eight percent of the U.S. population lives in areas called rural by our statisticians, but only 14 percent of the physicians are there. And, as a fine Illinois rural physician testified:

> Even more alarming is . . . that 25% of rural physicians may retire during the next five years and 45% of all family physicians are over 55 years old. . . . Last spring only 12% of graduating medical students elected a career in family practice.[5]

My guess is that health reform will not significantly improve the situation in rural areas. It can't do everything. But some of us will propose initiatives to encourage schools of medicine to be more aggressive in exposing all medical students to the advantages of a rural practice.

Calendar. Under your proposal, Mr. President, full coverage for all Americans will not take place until January 1, 1998, with gradual improvements before then. Some of my colleagues believe that is moving too quickly. I believe the opposite. Every month we delay implementing this program means agony for thousands of American families. I recognize that it cannot be done overnight, but I also believe that your plan should be enacted with a sense of urgency. Proposals to have the program take full effect in the year 2000 or 2005 or 2010 do not understand how costly that delay will be in both humanitarian and economic ways.

There are many issues I have not covered in this brief letter, Mr. President—matters that are important. What I know, however, is that we are on the verge of a great, historic step for our nation, thanks to your leadership. But being "on the verge" is not the same as being assured of the measure's passage. Your opponents are doing everything they can to confuse the issue, and they have been at least partially successful. In a Kaiser Family Foundation poll asking who would benefit most from your health care plan, people thought that 44 percent of the beneficiaries would be the poor. The reality is that only 29 percent would be. The public thought 36 percent of those benefiting from a health care plan would be the unemployed, but the actual figure is 10 percent. The *Wall Street Journal/NBC* poll of March 10, 1994, shows uncertainty and confusion about your overall plan, but when people are polled on the specifics of your proposal, they overwhelmingly favor it. That's the good news upon which we have to build.

Sincerely,

Paul Simon

Eleven

Environmental Choices

Dear Mr. President:

All of the issues I have discussed in these letters are interrelated with others, but nowhere is this more relevant than in the environmental field. Foreign policy must deal with desert problems and rain forests and population; education must train us to be sensitive to the fragile planet on which we live; crime is not only burglarizing a home, but also pouring toxic substances into a lake or stream; nuclear bombs and land mines are environmental problems as well as defense and foreign policy issues; whether we encourage the use of mass transit rather than automobiles is not only a transportation consideration, but it also makes a difference in air pollution; and the list goes on.

President Theodore Roosevelt led the charge to create our national park system and preserve unusual plots of nature, but generally the environment as a public concern is only decades old. Even phrases like "air pollution" are relatively recent additions to our language; we used to talk about "smoke abatement," but only halfheartedly, believing that steel mills had to emit huge quantities of smoke and dirt into the air, that utilities that burned coal had to darken the landscape with soot, and that the smoke and odors from oil refineries were simply part of progress, even though they damaged our health.

This is a different day. We have not applied all our knowledge, but we know much more. We have not fully accepted what needs to be done to protect our health and our planet, but the public attitude is improved, with most officials seriously discussing actions that their predecessors a few decades ago could not have imagined—despite the regular drumbeat of opposition from those who resist all change. Opponent Rush Limbaugh talks about "these watermelons (Environmental Wackos who are green on the outside but red on the inside)."[1] In a 1982 speech in the Midwest, President Ronald Reagan said: "If the federal government had been around when the Creator was putting His hand to this state, Indiana wouldn't be here. It'd still be waiting for an environmental impact statement."[2] But Limbaugh and Reagan are exceptions, at least in public statements.

The Importance of Water

There are many environmental concerns that require action, and your administration is moving in the proper direction on most of these, assisted by superior appointments such as Bruce Babbitt as secretary of the interior and your selection of Al Gore as vice president. But a difficulty of major international dimensions that will emerge is a shortage of water. It is not in the headlines now and will not be in the headlines until it is too late. Our aim should be to conduct policy in such a way that it does not emerge as the focal point of an international crisis.

Within the last few months, in separate interviews, both King Hussein of Jordan and Prime Minister Rabin of Israel have said that if there is another war in the Middle East, it will not be about land, it will be about water. A few days after signing the historic peace agreement with Israel, President Anwar Sadat said, "The only matter that could take

Egypt to war again is water."[3] Gaza's water soon will be unusable. Syria has serious water problems that include low supplies in the capital city of Damascus. That is only one critical area of the world for water. Mark Twain's comment contains some historic truth: "Whiskey is for drinking, but water is for fighting over." (Mark Twain, Winston Churchill, and W. C. Fields were not the only people to make light of water drinkers. Before the birth of Christ, the Roman poet Horace wrote: "No poems can please for long, or live, that are written by water-drinkers.")[4]

Population Pressures

The world population now stands at approximately 5.5 billion and it is rising. In numbers, the world's population grows each year by an amount equal to half of the current U.S. population. By the year 2050, population experts project a world with ten billion people. While population is rising, water resources are not. You do not need to be an Einstein to recognize that within ten or 20 years that will spell serious trouble. Two years ago I stood at the edge of what had been a port city on the Aral Sea, once the fourth-largest body of fresh water in the world. I looked down 50 to 75 feet to dry land. Soviet "experts" had assured Nikita Khrushchev that he could divert some of the water going into the Aral Sea for irrigation purposes and that the runoff and other sources would eventually replenish the temporary water loss. Shipowners were told not to worry. Now you can see ships stranded on dry land, literally fifty miles from the new shores of the shrunken Aral Sea.

We see other glimpses of the future in our relatively minor (compared to other nations) water shortages in California and Florida. In a few years Nevada may face a more serious problem. The Cape Verde Islands in the Atlantic off the coast of Africa are preoccupied with discussions about their long-term future, dependent as they are on severely limited water supplies. Nearby Mauritania, on the coast of Africa, grows only eight percent of its own food because of water shortages, and the desert is creeping into everything, including the capital city of Nouakchott. Algeria, Morocco, Tunisia, and Ethiopia will all soon face critical problems. The United Nations Children's Fund (UNICEF) has warned "that 35,000 children worldwide—a majority of them on the African continent—are dying daily from hunger or disease caused by lack of water or contaminated water. At the turn of this century, almost forty percent of the African population will be at risk of death or disease from water scarcity or contaminations."[5] At least 8,000 villages in India face critical water problems. Mexico has major water difficulties. Namibia is a United Nations success story with its new independence, multiparty government, and many indications of building the right type of base for future growth, but it faces one major shortage: water. There are many other examples.

What all of these places (except Nevada) have in common is that there is a huge amount of water at their doorstep, but it is saltwater. People can use only one percent of the world's available water for drinking, industrial, or agricultural purposes.

Desalinization

Nations can do a much better job of protection and utilization of water. We are making progress. Two decades ago my colleague Senator "Ted" Kennedy wrote: "It strains belief to know that Neil Armstrong can walk on the moon, 250,000 miles away, but that he cannot swim in Lake Erie, a few miles from his Ohio home."[6] Now he can. I remember when there were no fish in the Illinois River, and now people fish there again and safely eat what they catch. These pollution control measures are important, and they buy us a little time, but the eventual breakthrough for world stability has to be finding a less expensive way of converting saltwater to fresh water.

Desalinated water is used now in the United States and a number of countries for drinking, but it is too expensive to be used for agricultural and industrial purposes. That is the growing need: 69 percent of the world's fresh water is used for agriculture. There are more than 7,000 desalination plants in 120 countries, mostly in the Persian Gulf region, and 750 in the United States. Water from conventional sources is gradually becoming more costly, and desalinated water is gradually becoming less costly, but the huge gap that remains poses difficulties for individuals and for nations.

At a press conference in 1961 a reporter asked President John F. Kennedy: "Mr. President, this question might better be asked at a history class than at a news conference, but here it is, anyway. The Communists seem to be putting us on the defensive on a number of fronts—now, again in space. Wars aside, do you think that there is any danger that their system is going to prove more durable than ours?" President Kennedy replied:

> We have made some exceptional scientific advances in the last decade . . . they are not as spectacular as the man-in-space, or as the first sputnik, but they are important. I have said that I thought if we could ever competitively, at a cheap rate, get fresh water from salt water, that it would be in the long-range interests of humanity which would really dwarf any other scientific accomplishment. I am hopeful that we will intensify our efforts in that area.[7]

Two months after that press conference, President Kennedy spoke by radio to people gathered in Freeport, Texas, for the dedication of a saline water conversion plant. He told them:

> I can think of no cause and no work which is more important, not only to the people of this country but to people all around the globe, especially those who live in deserts or on the edge of oceans. I am hopeful that the United States will continue to exert great leadership in this field, and I want to assure the people of the world that we will make all the information that we have available to all people. We want to join them, with the scientists and engineers of other countries, in their efforts to achieve one of the great scientific breakthroughs of history. . . . Before this decade is out we will see more and more evidence of man's ability at an economic rate to secure fresh water from salt water, and when that day comes then we will literally see the deserts bloom. This is a work. . . more important than any other scientific enterprise in which this country is now engaged. It serves the interests of men and women every place. It can do more to raise men and women from lives of poverty than any other scientific advance.[8]

Five days later he sent legislation to Congress. Under his leadership our government invested $100 million in a single year in this research, and we achieved progress, but interest lagged after his death, and now we invest little. Congressman George Miller of California has a measure in the House and I have one in the Senate that would get us into research in this field once again. Senator Harry Reid of Nevada has been particularly helpful to me in the Senate. The legislation passed the Senate in 1993 but died in the House. I am hopeful we can enact legislation this year, Mr. President, and I appreciate your interest.

Egypt, with a rapidly growing population, lives on two percent of its land, with expansion limited by water. Right on the Mediterranean, Egypt's desert could bloom as much as Israel's has, if Egypt could convert seawater inexpensively to fresh water. Nearby Greece and Cyprus face similar problems, as do all the nations in the northern one-third of Africa, which border saltwater seas or oceans.

When Prime Minister Rabin paid his first visit to the United States after taking that office, he met with some of us on the Foreign Relations Committee. My colleagues asked him about relations with Syria and the Palestinians and similar areas of concern. I told him about my bill on desalination research and asked him about water. The normally low-key leader responded with enthusiasm and earnestness and added, "You probably did not know that before I entered the military, I was a water engineer." I did not.

Technologies used today for desalination are largely based on research conducted before 1982. By that time, in this country, federal research initiatives had all but died. Now the Israelis are doing research, the Saudis are doing some, as are the Japanese, and there is a modest amount taking place in the private sector here, but this is an effort that needs immediate, much more serious efforts by the United States and other nations. If we devoted five percent of the money we now have earmarked for the space station to the desalination research effort, progress would be made on something infinitely more important to the future of humanity.

There are more than financial difficulties. Conversion of saltwater to fresh water requires a great deal of energy. Research is needed. Use of energy can cause air pollution problems, and this is a particular problem in coastal regions. Most areas with a desperate need for water are places where solar energy would be a natural source. Is it practical now?

No. Are we far from the point where it is practical? No. Hydroelectric power is another energy source that has had limited research but needs much more: We know precisely when the ocean tides go in and out and the power they have, and yet we have only dabbled at research to harness this huge energy resource—right where desalination plants must be located. France has undertaken research on this, which we should follow closely, joining in the research if either human or financial resources are needed. Or what about research on burning salt as a source of energy? The cynics smile knowingly. They always do. But the cynics aren't going to build a better world. Two-thirds of the world's surface is covered by water that is high in salt content. The other third of the planet faces a water shortage. It takes no great mind to recognize that we must bring those two parts of our world together to help each other.

Respecting the Oceans

We must have greater respect for the potential source of so much badly needed water—the ocean. I recall visiting El Salvador more than 20 years ago. I watched a garbage truck back up to the edge of a cliff at the ocean's edge and simply dump all the garbage in the ocean. Those horrible-looking vultures that Central America has in abundance massed in nearby trees, ready for what they could salvage in food from a regular place for feeding. I am sure fish also awaited the truck. But bottles, cans and pieces of plastic were part if it, too, and I assume that any industry with toxic waste disposed of it in the same way. More recently I visited Luanda, the capital city of Angola in Africa. It has a population of three million—roughly the size of Chicago--and its raw sewage is dumped directly into the bay leading to the ocean. There I saw homeless children playing and bathing, as well as people fishing for much-needed food.

Using the ocean for untreated sewage disposal and other abuses not only does harm to the fishing industry and our ability to eat uncontaminated fish, it also fails to recognize that eventually we must make greater use of the ocean for food. We now use the ocean for food the way we used to use the land, by hunting. For "hunting" in the ocean we have devised a different word—fishing. On land humanity gradually learned that if people planted seeds, they could grow their food and not be dependent on the wild fruit that they and animals had to gather each year. Eventually, what we intentionally planted in the ground became our major source of sustenance.

Today we primarily "hunt" in the ocean, but we have learned how to "plant" ropes so that mussels will grow on them, large numbers of them in only a small piece of the ocean—food that is high in protein, a major deficiency in the diet of many of the world's people. That type of "planting" will increase over the coming decades in ways you and I cannot imagine, but that growth will be hampered if we do not learn respect for the ocean, just as planting on land is hampered when we do not have proper respect for the soil.

Population. If we do everything correctly to control environmental damage—and we will not—major harm will still occur from unbridled population growth. From the beginning of time until the year 1830, the world's population gradually grew to one billion people. Then in one century population doubled to two billion, and the time for adding a billion keeps shrinking. I was born in 1928, about the time we hit the two billion figure. If I live a normal lifespan, I will see the world's population more than triple, and if I am fortunate enough to live a longer-than-normal lifespan, I will see the world's population multiply by a factor of four.

Mr. President, you have reversed the population stabilization decisions of President Reagan, which George Bush retained, and I applaud you for doing so. Our refusal to support United Nations efforts to provide contraceptive information to poor women around the world and our frequent refusal to help groups like Planned Parenthood, which work on this issue domestically and internationally, were designed to please a politically potent domestic crowd but did not serve anyone's long-term interest. I have noticed in conversations with Secretary of State Warren Christopher, who is careful with his words and even with the modulation of his voice, that this is one subject that causes him to show emotion. He understands how devastating uncontrolled growth will be to our environment and to our chances for world peace and stability.

Mexico is an example of the problem. Mexico today has a population of approximately ninety million and a high but declining birth rate. If by the year 2000 Mexico reaches a birth rate that is only self-sustaining, eventually the country will have 175 million people. If the zero population growth rate is not achieved until the year 2020, Mexico will eventually peak at a population of 270 million. That is one of the reasons your support of the North American Free Trade Agreement (NAFTA) was so important. A significant factor in stabilizing population growth is a gradually increasing standard of living. Each year of action or inaction on population-related matters in Mexico and other nations (including our own) has an impact. Without curtailment of population growth and a rise in Mexico's standard of living, you can imagine the illegal alien problems we will have. With a population of ninety million next to us, we have difficulties. Think what it could be with 270 million neighbors to the south.

Africa is the only continent that is not experiencing a gradual rise in standard of living for its citizens. Not surprisingly, Africa is also the continent with the most serious population growth difficulties. At the present rate of growth, Africa's population will double in the next twenty-five years, and some experts believe it will be much higher. Results of polls among African women about "desired family size" range from five to nine children, far higher than other areas of the world.[9] The reason undoubtedly relates to deteriorating economies. Three decades ago a poll result in India would have been similar, with parents hoping to have enough children to survive and help them in their declining years, a form of social security. We should be dealing with Africa less on a crisis-to-crisis basis and, instead, place greater emphasis in our aid programs on the many basic economic needs of that continent, including family planning.

The good news is that family planning is no longer resisted. All nations recognize its importance, but it is something that benefits a nation long-term, and many African nations live from emergency to emergency and have little opportunity for long-term planning and action. There are still domestic critics who say that we should not push family planning in a specific country because of its Catholic or Moslem culture. Some of those critics might be surprised to know that the first U.S. President to lead internationally on the population question was Lyndon Johnson, who as Vice President had been persuaded by a Moslem leader, Pakistan's Ayub Khan, of the importance of population control for the developing nations. One of the most impressive population stabilization programs in any nation is in Tunisia, also a Moslem country, and leaders there are understandably proud of what they are achieving.

One of the most important tools in controlling population is promoting gender equity. When girls are educated as well as boys—and that does not happen in many nations—the female half of the population has an expanded vision of their opportunities, how too much child-bearing can restrict those opportunities and that having child after child after child until late middle age is not the automatic lot of women. Educating women and getting information to them about effective means of birth control should be a policy aim.

In the United States as many as half of all pregnancies are unintended. Our birth rate is higher than Western Europe's or Japan's, and that has environmental consequences because we consume and waste much more per citizen than people in any other nation. For example, we have only 4.5 percent of the world's population, but we consume 36 percent of the world's electricity. Unwanted pregnancies also lead to more abortions per 100,000 people than in Western Europe and Japan. We do not know all of the reasons for the differences, but sex education is generally more available and more explicit in those countries, and contraceptives are usually less expensive and more available to young adults.

Other Action

There is an almost endless list of additional steps that we should take, or take more vigorously, to improve our environment. My list would include:

Recycling of garbage. Some communities are doing it now. In Champaign and Urbana, Illinois, the sister cities work together, and people put out their garbage, separated by food, glass, cans, and plastic. Those communities not only are willing to do it, they take great pride in doing it. Recycling employs several people at the separation center. Branches of trees that either fall on the street or are placed there are collected, and the cities hire unemployed people and sometimes homeless people to cut the wood; then it is sold as firewood, paying for those employed. Everyone emerges a winner, including our environment.

International cooperation. Many problems—the threat to the ozone is an example—cannot be solved unilaterally by the United States. We must work with others. Our foreign aid programs should reflect our environmental concerns. We must understand that if we in the United States occasionally have a difficult time making the correction needed to protect nature, it is even harder to do for a nation of much more limited means, a nation that may see no way of solving an immediate problem, even though it recognizes the long-term gain. Working with the International Monetary Fund and other international organizations, the United States can help. We should lead in sensible endeavors and not drag our feet, and too often we have been foot-draggers. We still have not ratified the Law of the Sea Treaty, for example, fashioned in part to meet our original objections. We should also work to encourage developing nations to spend less of their scarce dollars on the military. Since we are the world's largest arms merchant, sensible leadership by us is meaningful. One significant step that you took, Mr. President, is moving away from nuclear tests. We are grateful for that.

Recognizing the importance of trees. Internationally that means designing programs that can save rain forests and encourage trees where the desert is encroaching. The desert problem is compounded by the desperation of the people who live there. It is easy for me to say we should save the trees, but visiting with a few people living in tents on the edge of the desert in Senegal, I noted that the goats were eating—and probably killing—the bushes that partially held back the desert. A man with whom I spoke through an interpreter knew that he threatened the future by his actions, but faced with the choice of survival or thinking about the future, he understandably chose survival. We need to give that man and his family better options. Simply to demand that they pay attention to our environmental ideals is unrealistic, and that conflict is leading, in the words of former President Jimmy Carter, to "the increasing disharmony and lack of understanding between the rich and the poor nations."[10]

Lester Thurow tells of visiting an area in northern Pakistan where there were few trees. He returned seventeen years later to discover forests and trees everywhere. He writes:

> This change did not occur spontaneously. It occurred because the Dutch used their foreign-aid money to expand the areas that could be irrigated so that farmers could plant forests without having to cut back on the area that they devoted to food production. Using their foreign-aid money, the Dutch made it profitable to plant trees. Illiterate peasants quickly learned that there was money to be made in planting trees. The Dutch can take pride on money well spent. [Pakistan] is clearly better off, and in a small way the Dutch are also better off. Every tree helps make our atmosphere better.[11]

What those goats did in Senegal, bulldozers and housing developers, farmers and others are doing here, though the long-term damage is less visible. When houses, parking lots, shopping centers, and soybean fields replace trees, our air becomes worse because of the air purification work that leaves do; and instead of absorbing water, the paved parking lot sends the water downstream, and soon one of us in the House or Senate will be calling on the Corps of Engineers to commence flood control measures.

Decaying leaves renew our overused topsoil. We have lost approximately one-fifth of our topsoil since 1950. A 1975 General Accounting Office report suggested that we should cut down fewer trees to preserve the nation's topsoil. Even better would be to plant more trees. A great idea for one of your Saturday broadcasts would be to ask Americans to plant 20 million trees a year—one for each twelve of us—and to ask those who cut trees to plant one for each tree removed. We would respond favorably to this voluntary effort and request.

Clear-cutting of trees in national forests should be prohibited. Selective cutting of trees not only does no harm if properly done, but can be good for the forests. Clear-cutting is both undesirable and unnecessary.

Bike trails. Some years ago, Senator Mark Hatfield of Oregon suggested that one percent of our highway funds be earmarked for bicycle trails. Representative Martin Sabo of Minnesota is a booster of bike paths in the House. I still like the idea. Other nations do better than we do on this—and are probably healthier as a result. Ideally a bike trail should not be a line marked on a highway, but literally a separate path paralleling the highway or using an abandoned railroad bed. States and communities that pioneer this idea will find appreciative users. There should be federal encouragement of this.

Mass transit and automobiles. How Los Angeles wishes that long ago someone had had the good sense to develop an underground mass transit system! I've been stuck on those LA freeways, breathing the fumes and getting more and more irritated, and I know that people I am to address at some meeting are also becoming concerned, if not irritated. If every four-lane highway tomorrow were to be six lanes, they would be almost immediately filled. Urban America needs help on mass transit, and the air all of us breathe will be better. A two-cent per gallon increase in the gas tax would bring in more than $2 billion for mass transit in our cities and be of great help to them.

Automobile manufacturers also have to be pushed to continue to make progress on emissions from cars. They resist. They also resisted when we mandated lead-free gas, saying it would make driving much more expensive, but it has not. They resisted having air bags, and now they're reluctantly coming aboard. My hat is off to legislators in California who have broken new ground in automobile air pollution control. A breakthrough that we will have one of these years is practical, usable electric cars. The "big three" of car manufacturing do not like the idea, and the oil companies detest it, but it should come, and it will come. If we don't take the lead in this, the Japanese or the French or someone else will, and then our manufacturers will be complaining about lost sales and lost jobs.

Planning. It's not a bad word. It is a way to preserve what is important. Daniel Burnham was a dreamer and a planner, and he decided to save the lakefront of Chicago for the people. He got it done, and I am grateful to him every time I visit the city. We need to do it at the federal level, also, for our parks, forests, wetlands, topsoil, and other treasures.

Energy. Here's a good example of the need for planning. Hazel O'Leary is an excellent energy secretary, but the nation still has no energy plan. We are now more dependent on foreign oil than we were in the 1973 crisis. We are guilty of what a former Nixon commerce secretary calls "energy gluttony."[12] We need to stress conservation much more, as we started to do after 1973. We can work with the utilities, devising plans to provide greater insulation for homes and taking the savings out of future utility bills to pay for it. Alternative forms of fuel, such as ethanol, need to be examined carefully and used where it is clear that the environment and taxpayers benefit. Giving tax breaks to utilities that put on scrubbers or fluidized beds to remove the carbon dioxide emissions from their coal would help everyone. Solar energy is not given as much attention as when we faced the energy crisis, but it still makes sense. Former Senator Charles "Mac" Mathias of Maryland and I visited refugee housing in Nicosia, Cyprus, built 55 percent with American funds. Each house had a solar heating unit on it for hot water. If American taxpayers can help provide solar heating in Cyprus, why not in Carbondale, Illinois, and Bakersfield, California? In 1981 my wife and I built a house and made it passive solar. In below-zero weather, we have the experience of a warm house during the daytime, with the furnace kicking on when the sun goes down. We could do much more to encourage that. While I have not been a nuclear energy enthusiast, I know that source of power will not go away. We need research on projects that will look at ways of solving the waste problem, other than dumping it on our friends in Nevada. We need creativity and common sense in the energy field. Listen to this commentary:

> From 1979 to 1986 there was more net increase in U.S. energy supplies from solar energy, wind, water and wood than from oil, gas, coal, and uranium. . . . A study by five national laboratories recently concluded that increasing R and D budgets by the cost of building one nuclear power plant ($160 million a year for twenty years) could, by the year 2030, enable renewable energy to provide about half the total energy and all the electricity used in the United States in 1989.[13]

Common sense. Much of the difficulty in the efforts to improve the environment comes when people do not use common sense. At one point a suburban director of the Illinois Environmental Protection Agency issued a directive, which, to implement, would have required hogs and cattle in Illinois to wear diapers. Well-intentioned, it was slightly impractical! We got the order changed. In deep southern Illinois there is a wetlands area around the Cache River that became a point of major controversy between farmers and environmentalists. When they came together to discuss it, they soon found that they agreed on almost everything, and they worked out a compromise that satisfied 95 percent of the farmers and environmentalists. A few on both sides remain unhappy, but there always will be a few who cannot be satisfied. Common sense also requires that when regulations are issued, they should have been studied carefully in advance in cooperation with the people affected, then assurances given that they will not be changed overnight. One Illinois industry with which I worked declined to make an investment that would have reduced a toxic water effluent because a representative of the EPA told them they were not sure how long the order would last before it would be changed. They were being asked to invest well over a million dollars and, understandably, they declined to do it. Everyone lost.

Jobs. There are those who claim that environmental improvements will mean loss of jobs. It is true that industries that have not been environmentally sensitive or energy sensitive have to make sometimes costly initial investments, and industries will have to adjust as new information about water or air effluents becomes available. But aside from the loss to some businesses initially, there should not be long-term losses from sound environmental practices. A man who heads a group called Christian Financial Concepts writes that we have a "fascist economy," and he attacks environmental endeavors by the government, saying that these are "downright harmful to our children's economic futures."[14] Mistakes can and will be made in any endeavor, and sometimes they are made in the name of environmentalism, but sensible measures to protect the environment will help our children immensely—not harm them—and also help those in business. While some businesses will lose, others will profit; and, particularly if we try to continue being one of the nations on the cutting edge of this field of technology, the net result should be a plus for the United States. And this does not even count the billions of dollars that we will save because of improved health and prevention of productivity losses.

When visiting Taiwan, a nation with roughly one-sixteenth our population, I learned of a $360 billion, six-year infrastructure program they were going to initiate. That would be the equivalent of our launching a $5.7 trillion project. The financial markets would go berserk if we tried that, but Taiwan has been much more prudent than we have been in fiscal matters, holding more foreign reserves than any other nation. Much of Taiwan's program deals with air pollution. When I returned from Taiwan, I discussed the idea of U.S. businesses taking advantage of this opportunity. Nancy Chen, a Chinese American who runs my Chicago office, suggested a gathering of U.S. business firms that work in the environmental field, together with Taiwanese officials. It turned out to be a successful endeavor, with several U.S. firms getting contracts. U.S. expertise and competence in the environmental field brought jobs to our country. Making lead-free gasoline did not cost us any jobs and created a car more saleable in other nations. To suggest that the choice is between jobs and the environment is like suggesting that we have to choose between good food and good water. We can have both. And a better quality of life.

The late Richard Nixon left a little-mentioned but remarkable record on the environment. He established the Environmental Protection Agency and the National Oceanic and Atmospheric Administration. He advocated using the Highway Trust Fund for mass transit and led the way for expanding the nation's parks. After Nixon's death, Jim Maddy, president of the League of Conservation Voters, said that the Nixon Administration "set a high-water mark that subsequent administrations have yet to match."[15] But your administration can achieve more, Mr. President.

Writing a half century ago, historian Arnold Toynbee, after a survey of nations and civilizations, came to the conclusion that "loss of command over physical environment is not the [cause] of the breakdown of civilizations."[16] He finds three examples of states that may have prospered because of their environmental handicaps: Holland, Venice, and Switzerland. All three were so preoccupied with differing environmental problems that they got into fewer wars than their neighbors and, therefore, prospered. He does not suggest, however, that environmental problems are a good thing. He cites Ceylon (now Sri Lanka) as a highly civilized place that was destroyed because after wars, the people were too weary to repair their partially destroyed irrigation system. As a result of that unwillingness, mosquitoes bred and spread malaria in Ceylon, causing its downfall. Had Ceylon repaired its irrigation system—taken care of its environmental needs—Toynbee concludes, its ancient civilization would have survived.

The League of Conservation Voters gave you a C-plus in their report card. I would grade you better than that, but I did notice that they gave you marks appreciably better than your predecessor's. That's not the comparison you are looking for, I am certain. The test is whether we are doing what we should for future generations in environmental matters. I am sure your reaction is like mine: Overall, we have not done badly, but we must do better.

Sincerely,

Paul Simon

Twelve

Foreign Policy

Dear Mr. President:

The only major area where you get average rather than above-average marks as our leader is foreign policy. You are doing better than you did a year ago, and a year from now you will probably do still better. Your interest and knowledge have grown. It is difficult to move from being Governor of Arkansas to being the world's most influential leader on Bosnia, Somalia, and other places you did not deal with as governor.

It will be necessary for you to devote more time to foreign policy once health care reform is passed, and events may transpire to cause you to direct much more attention to the subject prior to that. When you ran for the presidency, you emphasized domestic policy, both because that is the primary interest of our people and because it is the area in which you have greater background. Things that now often occupy your attention are different. Our relationships with other nations will consume more and more of your time.

What makes foreign policy both intriguing and frustrating is the limited control you have of the personalities and events on which you must base policy decisions. That is somewhat true on the domestic scene, but you have an understanding of, for example, South Dakota and Georgia and Oregon. The governors of South Dakota, Georgia, and Oregon operate within the restraints of federal and state constitutions and laws. But when a problem builds in Zaire—and there is movement toward a major crisis there—President Mobutu is the law and the constitution and operates without the constraints of democracies. That gives you a much lower comfort level in sensing the situation and dealing with it. In addition, you've been to South Dakota, Georgia, and Oregon but never to Zaire. You have something of a sense for the population makeup of the three states and for their economies, of the presidential levers to use to change things, but you cannot get a similar feel from a staff memorandum, on which you must rely to a great extent on issues concerning Zaire. Getting on top of the Zaire situation—just using that country as an example—requires time and attention.

The problem is further complicated by your having an extremely able Secretary of State, Warren Christopher, who is by nature cautious, and a head of the National Security Council, Anthony Lake, who prefers—properly so—to work more behind the scenes. That duo, combined with your natural inclination to pay limited attention to foreign affairs, has created something of a vacuum in foreign policy, into which Congress and other nations are moving.

I taught at the college level for two years. I hope you will not think it too impertinent for a former teacher to assign evaluations to your foreign policy record:

On Bosnia. I give both the George Bush administration and your administration well below average marks. The Serbs should have been told quickly, in clear, unmistakable terms, that their conduct violated the spirit and law of the community of nations, and when the economic boycott didn't slow them down, some form of action (I favored air strikes) should have been undertaken. During the campaign, you properly criticized George Bush for his inaction, but then your inaction followed. On the 700th day of the siege of Sarajevo, NATO finally told the Serbs to stop and pull back their artillery or there would be air strikes. That should have happened on the second day or the seventh day. Since that warning—as I write this—that devastated city has known a ghostly peace, but a peace. When the Serbs moved some of their artillery from Sarajevo to Gorazde, declared by the United Nations one of six "safe areas" in Bosnia, and began intense shelling of civilians there, Secretary of Defense William Perry—new at the job, but highly regarded in the Senate—responded to a press question by saying that we would not use air power to protect the city. The Serbs took advantage of that invitation and escalated their bombardment. But the United Nations Security Council previously had resolved—with our vote—to protect the city with "all necessary means, including the use of force." We were all over the lot. Finally, National Security Council Director Tony Lake made a speech at Johns Hopkins University in Baltimore saying that we were considering the use of air power, obviously a message for the Serbs and not the Hopkins students. A few days later, our planes went into action.

A large majority of the Senate Foreign Relations Committee believes that our response in Bosnia has been weak. Most of us do not want ground troops there unless a workable peace agreement is reached, but there is a fear, which I share, that the signal from Bosnia to tyrants around the world is that if you move on neighboring territory, the United Nations and the United States will not do much. The great threat to the world now is instability, and we have not helped the cause of stability with our conduct in Bosnia.

I regret to say that former President Richard Nixon came uncomfortably close to the truth when he wrote:

The U.S., the U.N., and the European Community vacillated, equivocated, orated, condemned and ultimately did nothing to counter effectively the Serbian onslaught. The massacre of scores of shoppers and their children in Sarajevo in February 1994 would almost certainly not have occurred had the West acted sooner. It is an awkward but unavoidable truth that had the citizens of Sarajevo been predominantly Christian or Jewish, the civilized world would not have permitted the siege to reach the point it did.[1]

The Serbs moved into the vacuum we and our European friends created. Yes, the Serbs used the ancient defense of righting the wrongs of history. But Hitler did that too, and that reasoning would permit the American Indians to reclaim Manhattan. Nations have to give up those ideas, and we must tell them so. I have sat through endless emotional debates in various corners of the world, including the ethnic neighborhoods of Chicago, where people argue about who really should be in charge of some piece of land. No one will win those arguments other than the arms merchants. We have to start from where we are and peacefully come to terms with one another.

Africa

Somalia was George Bush's finest hour, and history will be good to this nation for what we did, even though the action has limited popularity today. Ambassador Robert Oakley followed U.S. troop presence with at least semisuccessful negotiation among the various factions in Somalia. Then he left the scene, and the person put in charge of the U.N. operation there was a retired U.S. naval officer, Admiral Jonathan Howe—probably a good officer, but one with an inclination toward clear-cut military solutions to problems rather than durable diplomatic solutions. I soon heard complaints from charitable organizations that were distributing food and medicine, as well as others, that we had the wrong person in charge. I conveyed that to our leaders, but about that time General Aideed, who is anything but a knight on a white horse and whom we had inadvertently built up with our military action, demanded that Admiral Howe be forced to step aside, which meant that changing command quietly became impossible. If Aideed had kept silent, he would have achieved his goal.

Our clumsy attempts to capture Aideed resulted in 19 American deaths, including the repulsive scene on our television sets of an American body being dragged around by a jubilant group of young people—an American who went over there to help bring them food.

Congress was irate. The American people were irate. Warren Christopher and then-Secretary of Defense Les Aspin held a briefing for members of the House and Senate, with at least two hundred showing up. That was the first mistake. When you brief that large a group, it's too easy for the noisemakers to take over. The second mistake was that it became clear that there were too many unanswered questions and that those who might answer them had not been invited. The briefing was a disaster. Everyone sensed the vacuum, and calls for immediate withdrawal of our troops echoed in both the House and Senate chambers.

You then called a meeting of about 30 of us. We met for at least an hour and a half—the longest White House meeting on an international issue I can remember—and it went better than the earlier briefing, but your briefers conveyed the impression of an administration unsure of itself.

As I recall, Warren Christopher didn't say a word during the entire meeting. A compromise was worked out between Congress and the administration: Announce the withdrawal of all American troops by the end of March. I supported it because it was better than an immediate pull-out, but it was flawed policy—terrorists could easily wait until March 31 to restart their operations. To the community of nations, the United States looked weak.

Shortly after this meeting, President Mubarak of Egypt visited Washington, and I urged him to keep his troops in Somalia after ours pulled out. Without quoting him directly, it is fair to say that our action did not impress him, and he thought it strange that we, who had initiated the Somalia action and are better equipped than any other nation, should leave so quickly and ask other nations to shoulder the burden. Our awkward withdrawal would have been unnecessary had Congress and the American public sensed that your administration was clearly in charge and had specific but limited goals.

Fifty years after the end of World War II, we are still in Europe, but in Somalia we have retreated hastily. It has not been our finest hour, and it would not have happened if there had not been a policy and administrative vacuum.

Africa feels neglected. The only continent in the world with a decreasing standard of living, it is at the same time a continent with many countries either adopting democracy or moving toward it. In 1991 the gross national product of Africa south of the Sahara, not counting South Africa, was the same as Belgium's. Belgium has ten million people, the African nations 600 million. Eighteen of the world's poorest 20 nations are in Africa.[2] Africa needs attention. Strobe Talbott, Deputy Secretary of State, is interested in Africa, as is Tony Lake, your director of the National Security Council. George Moose, Assistant Secretary of State for Africa, is excellent. Warren Christopher is knowledgeable. Vice President Al Gore and your wife went to South Africa for the inauguration of President Nelson Mandela, a strong show of interest, which I welcomed. I am impressed by your knowledge of South Africa, a nation that has captured your interest and the hopes and concerns of others around the world. I hope that before too long, you can make a trip to a few nations in Africa. You need it, and they need it.

The positive actions in Africa, however, are balanced by a fuzzy policy of hesitation. After the civil strife erupted in Rwanda, Senator James Jeffords and I called the Canadian general in charge of the small United Nations contingent in Rwanda's capital city of Kigali. (It still amazes me that you can reach someone by telephone in the midst of internal chaos.) Highly respected by everyone, he told us that if he could get 5,000 to 8,000 troops quickly he could stop the slaughter. Senator Jeffords and I immediately dispatched a letter to you, with copies to Secretary of State Warren Christopher and Assistant Secretary George Moose. Then, on May 17th, the Security Council authorized 5,500 U.N. troops to be sent to Rwanda. Weeks later—in the latter part of June—U.N. Secretary General Boutros-Ghali told the *New York Times* it would take three more months to get the authorized 5,500 troops to Rwanda.

The Secretary General of the Organization of African Unity, Salim Salim, told me a few days later that he had the commitment from African nations for the troops but lacked the means to get them there. Secretary Christopher assured me that we were prepared to transport a battalion of troops from Mali, but there was haggling over some of the details. If all of this sounds confusing, it is. What we lacked was some sense of urgency. We have been unwilling to even call the brutal ethnic slaying of thousands what it is: genocide. The French, to their credit, finally committed 2,000 troops to help stop the killings and got them there within seventy-two hours of their announcement. When it became clear on our living room television sets that hundreds of thousands of people were being killed, and that emergency measures would be needed, you and your administration did the right thing, and headed relief efforts that not other nation could have accomplished. But earlier action that could have averted the disaster did not occur.

In an interview with *Time* magazine (August 1, 1994), U.N. Secretary-General Boutros-Ghali observed:

> It was eviddent from the beginning that the situation in Rwanda was going wrong. But we have not bee accustomed to having preventive diplomacy. During the cold war, [the U.S. was] ready to have its bombers flying 24 hours a day, which cost you $1 billion a day. But [now] U.N. members will not agree to spend $50 million to send troops on a mission to avoid conflict. You will pay the price sooner or later if you don't intervene.

The overall record of your administration on Africa is mixed: above average on South Africa, but not on most of Africa.

The Middle East

The Middle East has a real opportunity for a breakthrough, and your administration has played a constructive role. That White House ceremony with Prime Minister Yitzhak Rabin and Chairman Yasser Arafat shaking hands is an event no one who saw it will forget. Your administration played a key role in bringing the Israeli Prime Minister and King Hussein of Jordan together, and your people are laboring on the Syrian-Israeli situation. This is one area of world affairs where you have become appreciably more knowledgeable and where Warren Christopher has given a yeoman's performance. On the Middle East, your administration deserves high marks—an A.

Latin America

Latin America has not been high on the visibility chart, but it should be. Our relationship with most of the nations there is good, and NAFTA sent a healthy message to South and Central America. Marring this are policies in Haiti and Cuba that you inherited. On Haiti, the CIA and State Department sent totally contradictory signals about the stability of deposed President Aristide. The Haitian situation is complicated, as you know, but changing the course of that nation will require stability, firmness, and interest on the part of our nation—with no assurance that our policies will work. Your appointment of former Congressman William Gray as a special envoy on the Haitian situation is an excellent move. He is doing a solid job for you. We cannot abandon people being brutalized not many miles from our shore. You are not a racist, and I refused to sign an advertisement criticizing your Haitian policy because it included the suggestion that the policy you have is overtly racist. But there is an element of racism in the result of the policy. If the people in Haiti were middle-income whites rather than poor blacks, would our nation be responding differently and more effectively? I believe we would. U.S. public opinion would have demanded it.

Cuba's Fidel Castro is the worst leader in this hemisphere on human rights, with the exception of Haiti's leadership. But his record is hardly worse than China's, and we grant China special trade benefits. Castro will not be in power too much longer, if for no other reason than because of his age. His nation is deteriorating economically. If the United States were to make even a small gesture of agreeing to sell food and medicine to Cuba, it would be of help to the people of Cuba and might open dialogue and an improvement in human rights there. Full normal trade relations would be even better. Certainly our present policy has not caused any favorable movement. If we do not permit steps that can improve the economy of Cuba, then, when Castro falls, we will have a neighbor that will suddenly require a great deal of foreign aid. In the meantime, a minimal step we should take is to permit U.S. citizens to travel legally to Cuba. Unless there is a question of safety, U.S. citizens should be permitted to travel anywhere.

Your Administration's record on Latin America is good, but for Haiti and Cuba.

Europe

Eastern and Central Europe will remain unstable for some time, and we have to do what we can to encourage sound policies. Your interest in Russia is proper, but many Central European nations and the newly independent states feel neglected. Worse than that, some feel endangered. They see their giant neighbor, Russia, as unstable and having a future course that might include military expansion. Our interest in Russia is proper, though we should fine-tune our policy and clarify what we can do and can't do. As one respected Russia expert told me, "We have too many programs and not enough strategy." We should extend the hand of friendship to Russia, encourage the development of a sound currency, which is essential for economic progress, and then have a few targeted programs that can help create the framework for a healthy democracy. But we have to recognize that most of the decisions and action will have to be taken by the Russians: We cannot micromanage Russia. The approach we took with Poland and Hungary in 1989, when I introduced and the Senate passed the SEED legislation (Support for East European Democracy) by a vote of 99-0, should serve as a model. We had targeted economic and political aims. We played a small but significant role in a

Poland that today looks dramatically better than it did five years ago, a nation that appears headed toward a much better future. International and U.S assistance to Russia in currency stabilization must be conditioned on progress made on economic reform and building a pluralist society. Economic and political backsliding cannot be rewarded. Our aid effort, unfortunately, is somewhat unfocused.

The United States, Western Europe, and Japan can't reform the former Soviet giant through aid, but aid can help. We can focus on the creation of free institutions, especially those that encourage the workings of a free market and a civil society. And we have to address the security concerns of others in Eastern and Central Europe, which sometimes means we'll have to make decisions that may be unpopular in Moscow.

In the meantime, you have to recognize that the military umbrella of NATO can help stabilize Eastern and Central Europe. Poland, Hungary, and the Czech Republic should be brought into NATO soon, so that no Russian adventurer who might emerge as a national leader would miscalculate and be tempted to expand. As the Baltic states and others establish sound democracies, they can be welcomed into NATO—and we should make clear to the Russians that once their democracy is firmly established, we would welcome their inclusion in NATO. In the long run, the only military power that could represent a threat to Russia is China, and Russian membership in NATO should at some point therefore become attractive to the Russians.

In the meantime, the other newly independent nations that once constituted parts of the Soviet Union need greater attention. Could increased interest on your part bring Azerbaijan and Armenia to work together peacefully? Could you bring Turkey into a peace settlement between Armenia and

Azerbaijan in a constructive way? I don't know the answers, but we will not find out unless we try harder.

You understand the importance of this area. Your administration has been above average in its Eastern European performance.

Asia

Asia is tough because of China's intransigence. There are no easy answers. Our policy in that area of the world has not been as good on human rights as it should be, in part because of a mistake made before you took office. We recognized the People's Republic of China and withdrew our recognition of Taiwan (Republic of China). I have long favored recognition of the PRC as the legitimate government of the mainland and the Taiwanese government for Taiwan. Neither government likes that.

But that is what we did with West Germany and East Germany. We recognized that there were two governments and, though they did not like our dual recognition, that did not stop the two from eventually unifying. Taiwan now has a multiparty system and a free press and, by every standard, it is much more sensitive to human rights than the government of China. The French, Norwegians, and others send cabinet members to Taiwan to visit with government leaders there. We refuse. Taiwan is one of the major trading nations, having more foreign reserves than any nation, and for us to fail to recognize Taiwan makes even less sense than the policy we have had on Vietnam. When President Lee of Taiwan had to refuel in Hawaii, we did not permit this freely-elected president to get our of his plane, and did not permit the general in charge of the air base at which he landed to greet him. When President Lee wanted to return to Cornell for his class reunion, we turned him down. One way for us to signal greater independence and courage to

China is to have a more open, cordial relationship with Taiwan. Even mainland China is moving in that direction. For us to recognize a brutal dictatorship and fail to recognize a nation that now shares our ideals and values is inconsistent with our criticism of China on human rights.

Vietnam has been a policy plus for you. Our previous policy toward Vietnam hurt the United States economically, barring Caterpillar, Amoco and many other companies from signing contracts with Vietnam, while Japan, Taiwan, France, Great Britain and others walked away with the business. Our aloofness did not improve Hanoi's poor record on human rights. But the government in Hanoi has been cooperating on the POW/MIA issue. Establishing diplomatic ties with Vietnam is a plus for the future of that area and a credit to your administration.

Myanmar, formerly Burma, remains stuck in its dictatorial system of government, and we should be doing more to nudge that country in the right direction. If it doesn't improve, Myanmar, which supplies the majority of the world's heroin, ought to feel an economic pinch. We owe a word of appreciation to Senator Moynihan and, more recently, to Congressman Bill Richardson of New Mexico, who have paid attention to that nation and brought about some dialogue within the country.

You have generally handled Japan's difficult situation well.

You are monitoring North Korea closely and that, along with working with South Korea and Japan on the issue, should continue. While North Korea's total military expenditure cannot compare to South Korea's, its nuclear potential is troubling, as is its tendency to sell weapons to terrorist states. North Korea today has as tight and repressive a dictatorship as any in the world, and that condition always has the potential for trouble.

Relationships between India and Pakistan will not improve appreciably, if at all, as long as both nations maintain nuclear weapons. To move away from the nuclear threat will require the participation of China and the leadership of the United States and Russia.

Overall, in Asia, I would give your administration a slightly above-average marks..

For now, I am leaving many areas of interest untouched, including Canada, western Europe, and Australia, among others.

Trade

Trade is part of foreign policy, and with NAFTA, GATT and other matters, your leadership has been strong. Sometimes there has been a little too much rhetoric that plays to the American audience politically—specifically Japan-bashing—but that's a minor and understandable deficiency. In trade your administration's policies and efforts are well above average.

Recomendations

In addition to the three specific policy recommendations that follow, I would reemphasize the need for your greater personal involvement. On foreign policy you should also make clearer that Warren Christopher is your chief spokesperson, not anyone else. Give the Secretary of State more rein. Tell him you have confidence in him and want him to lead with more strength. He will not abuse the power.

The world has shifted in a short time from one laboring under the great threat of a confrontation between the two superpowers, each with the ability to destroy civilization, to a world in which the great threat is instability. And there is now only one superpower. Nations must sense our interest and concern and also understand that to threaten stability in a region by moving militarily against neighbors will bring down the wrath of the community of nations in a meaningful, decisive way. We don't want to be, in the overworked phrase, "the policeman for the world," but if there is to be stability, we have to be the police chief. We will work with the United Nations and with NATO and other regional groups, but no other nation has close to our economic and military power. If we were to cut the defense budget in half—which I do not advocate—we would still be overwhelmingly the world's biggest military power. While a few other nations now make more per hour in wages and have higher average annual incomes, no other nation comes anywhere near to being one-fifth of the world's economy. All of this gives us added leverage and added responsibility.

Here are my three foreign policy suggestions.

First, our **foreign aid should be tilted more clearly toward reducing poverty and promoting democracy.**

In the past we had the excuse of the Cold War to justify aid to dictators, and we gave them far too much military aid. Military aid should diminish more markedly. And we should improve economic aid. Some years ago, when I served in the House, I got an amendment adopted requiring that half of all economic foreign aid go to the poorest within a nation, exempting the Middle East because of its special problems and exempting other nations where the President waived it in the national interest. The conference between the House and Senate reduced that to forty percent, and it remained there until a few years ago when, unknown to me, it was quietly dropped. It should be restored. Among the world's poor, we should pay particular attention to women. A 1980 United Nations report noted that, while half the world's population is composed of women, they did two-thirds of the work and got one-tenth of the income. Things have improved since 1980, but not dramatically. We should help the poor, and we should help democracy.

Nations like Namibia, in southern Africa, that are showing an amazing ability to develop healthy democracies should get priority in aid. Even friendly dictators are poor investments.

The popular perception of foreign aid differs dramatically from the reality, and you may want to challenge the perception. When people complain about foreign aid, I often ask them what percentage of the budget they believe nonmilitary foreign aid is. They frequently guess 15 to 20 percent. When I tell them it is less than one percent they are usually startled, particularly when I add that we provide less foreign aid as a percentage of our national income than any Western European country or Japan. Nor do they realize that a high percentage of foreign aid is spent purchasing U.S. products.

More than two decades ago the United States suggested that all wealthy nations should donate one percent of their national income to the poorer nations, about one-third of what we did under the Marshall Plan. A few nations are doing it, but our total is less than one-fifth of one percent. Ronald Reagan in 1988 described our reductions in foreign aid as "devastating. . . . We have neither adequate means nor enough flexibility to advance our purposes and meet our vital commitments."[3] Countries contributing at least twice what we do as a percentage of national income for foreign economic assistance include Canada, Belgium, Britain, France, Sweden, Denmark, Japan, the Netherlands, and Norway. Lester Thurow observed: "In a rather brief time, America has gone from being the most generous of countries to being the least generous of countries."[4]

The best summary of what foreign policy should be remains the words of George Marshall at Harvard, with which he outlined what became known as the Marshall Plan: "Our policy is directed not against any country or doctrine, but against hunger, poverty, desperation and chaos. Its purpose should be the revival of a working economy in the world so as to permit the emergence of political and social conditions in which free institutions can exist."[5]

Second, the UN's peace-making, as well as peace-keeping, efforts need to be strengthened.

Let me illustrate the point with a personal experience. I returned from Somalia late in 1992 on a Sunday evening. Monday morning, I called U.N. Secretary General Boutros-Ghali and described the desperate situation in Somalia, the chaos and starvation. Somalia had received little help from the United Nations. Six weeks earlier, the Security Council had authorized sending 3,500 troops, and the Pakistanis agreed to provide them. Now, five hundred Pakistani troops were holed up in Mogadishu, the capital. I urged the Secretary General to get the additional 3,000 troops to Somalia immediately. He said he would be sending them by ship. I told him they had to go by plane, that the situation was desperate. "Your country charges me a great deal when we use your planes," he told me. "We don't have the money." I asked if we could count such flights as payments against the U.S. arrearages to the United Nations. He replied in the affirmative. I called Secretary of State Larry Eagleburger and asked him to phone the Secretary General to see if we could get something worked out. I also indicated to both that more than 3,000 troops were needed. Without imposing too many details on you, after their phone conversation, Eagleburger reported to President Bush, and the President asked Eagleburger to go to the United Nations to discuss the situation with the Secretary General. That initiated a whole series of meetings, and that Thursday morning at a White House meeting attended by four of us from Congress and key executive branch people, the President made the courageous decision to send in the troops and save lives.

Without U.S. action, it would have been the largest single starvation in any nation since the Ukrainian famine of the 1930s or the Irish famine of the 1840s. It would have been unconscionable for the United States, as the world's only superpower, to have done nothing.

But the United Nations takes too long to act. Once the Security Council makes a decision, the Secretary General has to start appealing to nations for help, some of whom are receptive to the idea but have poorly trained and poorly equipped troops.

The United States and other major nations should agree to have a specific number of troops, available on 24 hours' notice for peace-making or peace-keeping purposes when the U.N. Security Council acts, to be available if the President and the other heads of state approve, in the numbers they approve. The major nations could each agree to perhaps 3,000 troops, and the smaller nations 600 to 1,000. These should be volunteers from within the armed forces, who will receive a pay increase for volunteering but who understand clearly that they are taking an added risk. It would, in a sense, be a version of the French Foreign Legion, an international fire brigade.

As I write this, the two sides in the Angolan civil war are close to an agreement, brought about by an excellent U.N. mediating team assisted by a U.S. diplomat, former Ambassador Paul Hare. If the peace agreement should be signed by the leaders of the two sides, the United Nations must immediately have 5,000 to 6,000 troops as peace-keepers who may have to become peace-makers. But will the United

Nation move quickly enough? Can it? Will the United States, with a none-too-sterling record in Angola, make this a priority and help? I don't know the answers to these questions. What I do know is that we aided one side in the civil war (not with my vote) and Angola now has more land mines than any country—between 9 million and 20 million scattered across the countryside, some built in the United States, more financed by us. Because of the land mines, it undoubtedly also has more amputees than any other nation. We should sense special responsibilities there. Somehow the United Nations must be structured to move quickly so that thousands more do not die needlessly in that ravaged country and in other places.

The United Nations then has to set up tighter administrative machinery to deal with this reality. The respected Brussels-based organization, Doctors Without Borders, which works in trouble spots around the world, recently charged that the U.N. troops lack the discipline on occasion to conduct themselves properly:

> With nobody to investigate, judge and punish its own abuses of power, the U.N. is displaying legal and operational irresponsibility. . . . Steps have been taken to impress on the U.N. that it is required to observe the laws of war and the rules set out in the Geneva Conventions for the use of force. The U.N. must also set up the bodies and create the system needed to ensure compliance with these laws.[6]

The United Nations should move not simply for disciplinary reasons but to make sure it has a good structure for leading and monitoring its far-flung responsibilities.

Having nations committed to assisting U.N. peace-making with troops would give the United Nations more muscle, give it the ability to respond quickly to world emergencies, and develop a force for stability in a world that desperately needs stability.

Peace-keeping is another matter, where we must do our share but where the risks are significantly reduced. We cannot refuse to work with other nations and, at the same time, keep complaining that everyone wants us to be "the policeman of the world." The only way to avoid that is cooperation. And the United States should be careful when we ask others to put troops into Bosnia, Rwanda, Cambodia, Cyprus, and other troubled areas, that we don't somehow think it is beneath us to do so ourselves. Even small numbers of technicians to assist would make our pronouncements appear a little less elitist.

That should include a willingness to have our troops serve under foreign commanders—we did it as far back as the days when George Washington had some of our troops fighting under French leadership. NATO is a good example. It is an anachronism to insist that the military leader of NATO be an American. As we downsize our troop force there, we should welcome a commander from Britain, Germany, Italy, or some other nation. If we don't want to play a dominant military role, we have to work with others more.

Third, at some point, Mr. President, **you should talk candidly to the American people about the role and place of our armed forces and say that enlisting in them does involve risk.**

When people enlist in the Chicago police force, they know they are taking risks. When there are casualties, no one suggests that we should pull the police out of Chicago.

When I hear someone say, "All the people in Somalia are not worth one drop of American blood," that shows a flaw in the understanding of the world we share with everyone; also a flaw in the understanding that when people enlist in our armed forces, they should know that they may be taking risks and that we are proud of them and will back them.

Tragic and unnecessary as some of the casualties in Somalia were, the total number killed there (36) was fewer than the number of cab drivers killed in New York City last year (42). We cannot assume a burden somewhere and then send the message to terrorists that if they just kill a few American soldiers, Congress and the American people will demand that our troops come back. That invites more terrorism and casualties. We should use our troops only when necessary—Grenada was an example of inappropriate use of force. But when we do use force, there should be firmness. I once heard someone described as "tough as a two-dollar steak." There should be those around the world who sense that about the American President. That will not happen if, any time there are casualties, we immediately turn tail and run. Your critics at home and abroad say that we are not following a steady course on our foreign policy. There can be no cost-free, risk-free foreign policy that is steady. Both the world and our nation need the stability that can come only with a firm, clear, steady United States foreign policy.

You have not spoken plainly to the American people about this.

There is a little-noticed plus you have achieved in foreign policy that deserves mention. You have been sensitive to other nations, and you have toned down the bragging rhetoric. If we have been good, let others say it. Your two predecessors had a tendency to boast in speeches about our country and our conduct. Our friends in other nations know that boasting is for domestic political consumption. It receives a chuckle at best and sometimes disdain. A good example not to follow came on the floor of the Senate at the turn of the century, after the United States put down the

Filipino rebellion. Senator Albert Beveridge said: "We will not renounce our part in the mission of our race, trustee, under God, of the civilization of the world. . . . It has been charged that our conduct of the war has been cruel. Senators, it has been the reverse. . . . Senators must remember that we are not dealing with Americans or Europeans. We are dealing with Orientals."[7]

We have usually not been that crude but often we are not as sensitive as we should be. I appreciate your sensitivity. A new-born infant is concerned only with itself, but as life goes on, he or she becomes more and more sensitive to others. There are people who do not mature emotionally and psychologically, who remain too self-centered for their own good and society's. The same is true for a nation. In its infancy its concerns are with itself, but as it matures, it also should develop a sensitivity to others.

Every president is gradually drawn more and more into foreign policy. Some, like George Bush and John Kennedy, had an intense interest before their presidencies. Your interest is more recent and of less intensity. It would be good for you to lead events more, rather than be captured by events. Yes, there's grumbling when you pay more attention to Russia than to North Dakota.

But we do a certain amount of grumbling no matter what the President does—you've discovered that! The world needs a leader, not a vacuum, and your growing interest and concern will help fill the vacuum.

Sincerely,

Paul Simon

Thirteen

A Final Word

Dear Mr. President:

Woodrow Wilson once wrote: "We grow great by dreams."[1] You had a dream of becoming President of the United States, and you have achieved that dream. Now, when you get a chance to relax for a moment, late at night or at Camp David, or even as you jog, I am sure you dream about doing the best job possible for the nation and for the world.

Your advisers come and tell you, as you weigh a decision, "This may hurt you politically." Don't offend anyone needlessly, but don't be too sensitive. *Newsweek* says of you: "Clinton tends to shun the bolder options."[2] Prove that comment wrong! Sam Rosenman, who befriended both Franklin Roosevelt and Harry Truman, reflected that Truman "paid much less attention to what his actions were doing towards his chances for reelection. . . . Truman did a great many things that Roosevelt, because he knew the effect it would have, never would have done."[3] We as a nation want that hallmark of Harry Truman to be a strong part of your presidency. You have to be able to follow your instincts, tell people the truth, and, above all, show courage. History will judge you kindly if you will do that.

With that in mind, a word about Whitewater: It's easy for me to say, but you can't worry about it too much. Be open, admit your mistakes, and go on being the best president you can be. The same is true of appointments: My colleagues say that you should move more rapidly on them; there is some frustration with the delays. But this too is a minor issue in the big scheme of things. And you have to know that some of this criticism comes with the territory. Even Thomas Jefferson was not immune. When he became a candidate for president, the *Hartford Courant* warned of the results of a Jefferson Administration:

> Neighbors will become enemies of neighbors, brothers of brothers, fathers of their sons, and sons of their fathers. Murder, robbery, rape, adultery and incest will be openly taught and practiced, the air will be rent with the cries of distress, the soil soaked with blood, and the nation black with crimes.[4]

Lincoln had even worse things said about him.

You also have a great quality that we sense: You genuinely like people and respect them. You care. You want to heal the wounds that divide this nation. And you are capable of bringing us together. You and I both know many good, well-intentioned, racially sensitive white politicians who simply don't feel at home walking down the street in an African American neighborhood. Because of our backgrounds, you and I do. That ability to feel at ease with people in a variety of situations is a great asset to the nation and it can become an even greater one. Journalist Haynes Johnson was correct when, after spending two years interviewing people across the nation, he said that as a people we are "terribly disturbed about the future."[5] And Stephen Carter also captures where we are with the title of his book, *The Culture of Disbelief.* But we don't like our disbelief. We yearn for firm, call-it-as-you-see-it, dedicated leadership. You have the ability to provide that. Bringing this nation together will take more than gestures, however, more than an appearance at a church or a neighborhood or a town meeting. Your legacy should be more than health care reform, important as that is. You may be president only four years. Don't put anything off for your second term. You do not want some historian to write that you sensed what needed to be done, but after checking with your pollster and your staff, you decided it would be too risky politically, so you played at the edges of our problems rather than providing leadership in solving them. We want to be challenged. You have to ask more of us, tell us candidly what our problems are, and explain what we must do to solve them. That's leadership. I want your daughter Chelsea and my granddaughters Reilly and CJ to read this about you in a history book some day:

"Here was a President of uncommon vision and compassion and courage."

Sincerely,

Paul Simon

Notes

Chapter Two

1. Edward Gibbon, *Decline and Fall of the Roman Empire, Great Books of the Western World,* Mortimer Adler, ed., (Chicago: Encyclopedia Britannica, 1952), p. 393.

2. *Congressional Record,* Senate, May 27, 1993, p. 6664.

3. *Ibid.,* p. 6665.

4. "Democratically Financed Elections," by Ellen Miller and Philip Stern in *Changing America,* edited by Mark Green, (New York: Newmarket Press, 1992), p. 760.

5. *Ibid.,* pp. 760-761.

6. John Stuart Mill, *Representative Government, Great Books of the Western World,* Mortimer Adler, ed., (Chicago: Encyclopedia Britannica, 1952), p. 369.

7. Ronald Reagan, quoted in "Of Many Things," by George W. Hunt, *America,* November 7, 1992.

8. Quoted in "The Leader of the Opposition," by James Bowman, *National Review,* September 6, 1993.

9. "Democratically Financed Elections," by Ellen Miller and Philip Stern in *Changing America,* edited by Mark Green, (New York: Newmarket Press, 1992), p. 761.

Chapter Three

1. "Are the Media out of Control?", a symposium, *New York Times Magazine,* June 26, 1994.

2. "How Do Tobacco Executives Live With Themselves," by Roger Rosenblatt, *New York Times Magazine,* March 20, 1994.

3. 1 *Corinthians* 14:8.

4. *The Game,* by Michael Kelly, *New York Times Magazine,* October 31, 1993.

5. "A Cold Eye on Russia," by Rowland Evans and Robert Novak, *Washington Post,* March 28, 1994.

6. Senator Paul Simon, *The Once and Future Democrats,* (New York: Continuum, 1982), pp. 7-8.

7. Plutarch, *The Lives of Noble Grecians and Romans,* Dryden translation, *Great Books of the Western World,* Vol. 14, (Chicago: Encyclopedia Britannica, 1952), pp. 648-49.

8. Quoted in "How Former Presidents Have Used the Polls," *National Journal,* August 19, 1978, p. 1314. No author indicated.

9. Attributed to Alexander Ledru-Rollin as well as others, including Gandhi.

10. John Adams, *The Adams Family,* (Boston: Little, Brown: 1930), p. 95.

11. "The President Didn't Really Mean that," by Daniel Schorr, *Los Angeles Times,* February 14, 1994.

Chapter Four

1. Quoted in "The Leader of the Opposition," by James Bowman, *National Review,* September 6,1993.

2. Limbaugh, *See, I Told You So,* p. 243.

3. "Talent on Loan from the GOP," by James Fallows, *Atlantic Monthly,* May 1994.

4. Rush Limbaugh, *The Way Things Ought To Be,* (New York: Pocket Star Books, 1992).

5. Limbaugh, *See, I Told You So,* (New York: Pocket Books, 1993), p. 262.

6. Limbaugh, *The Way Things Ought To Be,* (New York: Pocket Star Books, 1992), p. xiv.

7. *Ibid.*

8. Limbaugh, *See I Told You So,* (New York: Pocket Books, 1993), p. 112.

9. Limbaugh, *The Way Things Ought To Be,* (New York: Pocket Star Books, 1992), p. 241.

10. *Ibid,* p. 41.

11. Limbaugh, *The Way Things Ought To Be,* pp. 41-43.

12. Limbaugh, *See, I Told You So,* p. 54.

13. "Day of the Dittohead," by David Remnick, *Washington Post, February 20, 1994.*

14. D. Keith Mano, interview with Rush Limbaugh, *Playboy,* December 1993.

15. Peter G. Peterson, *Facing Up,* (New York: Simon and Schuster, 1993), p. 31.

16. Peterson, pp. 34-35.

17. Limbaugh, *See, I Told You So,* (New York: Pocket Star Books, 1993), p. xiv.

18. *Ibid.,* p. 100.

19. "Talent on Loan from the GOP," by James Fallows, *Atlantic Monthly,* May 1994.

20. Limbaugh, *See, I Told You So,* p. 151.

21. *Ibid.*

22. Limbaugh, *The Way Things Ought to Be,* p. 146.

23. *Ibid.,* p. 140.

Chapter Five

1. Herodotus, Melpomene, Vol. 6, *Great Books of the Western World,* (Chicago: Encyclopedia Britannica, 1952), p. 164.

2. This instance and others from England are taken from *Hanging in Judgment,* by Harry Potter, (New York: Continuum, 1993), p. 6 forward.

3. *Ezekiel* 7:23.

4. Lisbeth Schorr, *Within Our Reach,* (New York: Doubleday, 1988), pp. 5-6.

5. St. Augustine, *Confessions, Great Books of the Western World,* Mortimer Adler, ed., (Chicago: Encyclopedia Britannica, 1952), p. 8.

6. "A Governor's Perspective on Sentencing," by Pete duPont, *Crime and Punishment in Modern America,* Patrick McGuigan and Jon Pascale, editors, (Washington: Institute for Government and Politics, 1986), pp. 314-315.

7. Quoted from a folder, "Judges Speak Against Mandatory Minimum Sentences," distributed by the Federal Judicial Center, no author indicated, p. 2.

8. *Ibid,* p. 3.

9. *Ibid,* p. 5.

10. Testimony before the Subcommittee on Crime and Criminal Justice, House of Representatives, July 28, 1993.

11. *United States vs. Kwok Ching Yu,* 90 Cr. 47, 1993 U.S. Dist. LEXIS 16839, at 1, CS.D.N.Y. Nov. 30, 1993).

12. "...And Throw Away the Key," by Jill Smolowe, *Time,* February 7, 1994.

13. Quoted in "Truth and Justice," by Charles E. Silberman, *New York Times,* January 30, 1994.

14. Gerald Ford, *State of the Union Address,* January 19, 1976.

15. Ronald Reagan, *State of the Union Address,* January 27, 1987.

16. William Bennett Turner, quoted in *Life Sentences,* by Wilbert Rideau and Ron Wikberg, (New York: Times Books, 1992), p. 257.

17 Charles Colson quoted in ". . . And Throw Away the Key," by Jill Smolowe, *Time,* February 7, 1994.

18. Joe Wallach, quoted in "Prisons in Turmoil," by Nicholas Horrack, *Newsweek,* September 14, 1970.

19. Kathleen Hustad, quoted in *Voices from the Future,* edited by Susan Goodwillie, (New York: Crown, 1993), p. 232.

20. C. Paul Phelps in *Life Sentences,* edited by Wilbert Rideau and Ron Wikberg, (New York: Times Books, 1992), p. 190.

21. John Dunne, letter to Governor "Buddy" Roemer, May 13, 1991, quoted in Rideau and Wikberg, p. 256.

22. "Why Prisons Don't Work," by Wilbert Rideau, *Time,* March 21, 1994.

23. James Bennett, *I Chose Prison,* (New York: Knopf, 1970), pp. 13-14.

24. Institute of Medicine, *Treating Drug Problems,* Dean Gersten and Henrick Harwood, eds., (Washington: National Academy Press, 1990), p. 191.

25. Jimmy Hoffa, *Hoffa: The Real Story,* (New York: Stein and Day, 1975), p. 188.

26. Bruce Jackson, "Our Prisons Are Criminal," N*ew York Times Magazine,* September 22, 1968.

27. Lisbeth Schorr, *Within Our Reach,* (New York: Doubleday, 1988), p. 263.

28. "A Mother Jones Pullout," by Julie Petersen and Ariel Sabar, *Mother Jones,* January/February, 1994.

29. "Take It From Insiders: Get Smarter, Not Tougher," by Gregory J. Boyle, *Los Angeles Times,* November 10, 1993.

30. Marc Mauer, Assistant Director, The Sentencing Project, testimony before the U.S. House Subcommittee on Crime and Criminal Justice, February 22, 1994.

31. William Bradford Reynolds' Agenda," no author indicated, *Chicago Lawyer,* May 1988.

32. "Prevention and Punishment," editorial, *New York Times,* January 20, 1994.

33. Deborah Prothrow-Stith, *Deadly Consequences,* (New York: Harper Perennial, 1993), p. 5.

34. Quoted in *Voices from the Future,* Susan Goodwillie, ed., (New York: Crown, 1993), p. 157.

35. James Bennett, *I Chose Prison,* (New York: Knopf, 1970), pp. 14-15.

36 "Reflections on...Violence and Crime," editorial by Michael Lerner, *Tikkun,* Vol. 9, No. 1 (no date).

37. Henry George, *Social Problems,* (New York: Schalkenbach Foundation, 1934), p. 82.

38. Marc Mauer, Assistant Director, The Sentencing Project, testimony before the U.S. House Subcommittee on Crime and Criminal Justice, February 22, 1994.

39. Marian Wright Edelman, testimony, Senate Subcommittee on the Constitution, 23 March 1994.

40 Plato, *Laws,* Book IX, (Chicago: *Encyclopedia Britannica,* 1952), *Great Books of the Western World,* Volume 7, p. 754.

41. "Wild Pitch," by Jerome Skolnick, *American Prospect,* Spring 1994.

42. Abraham Lincoln, First Inaugural Address, 4 March 1861. *Inaugural Addresses of the Presidents*, (Washington: Government Printing Office, 1989), p. 141.

Chapter Six

1. From a collection of illustrations of James G. Pyrros, Detroit, Michigan. *James G. Pyrros Journal*, 1961. Unpublished.

2. Rev. James Harvey, quoted in Within Our Reach, by Lisbeth Schorr, (New York: Doubleday, 1988), p. 140.

3. Chapter 2, "Understanding Welfare Dynamics," in Welfare Realities by Mary Jo Bane and David Ellwood (Cambridge: Harvard University Press, 1994).

4. Sen. Paul Wellstone, conversation with Paul Simon, April 27, 1994.

5. "The New Dialectic" by John Kenneth Galbraith, *American Prospect*, Summer 1994.

6. "Racial Stereotypes Pervade All Cultures," by Raymond Coffey, *Chicago Sun-Times*, March 3, 1994.

7. Roger Wilkins, quoted in "Wilkins to Prez: Need Jobs, Not Sermons," *Southwestern*, February, 1994.

8. "U.S. Adds Programs with Little Review of Local Burdens," *New York Times*, March 24, 1992, by Michael de Courcy Hinds.

9. Robert N. Bellah, in the *Financial Times*, quoted in *Boiling Point*, by Kevin Phillips, (New York: Random House, 1993), p. 53.

10. "Out of Wedlock, Out of Luck," by William Raspberry, *Washington Post*, February 25, 1994.

11. Memo from Frances Fox Piven and Richard Cloward to Senator Paul Wellstone, March 19, 1994. Several other statistics in this chapter are taken from that memorandum.

12. Quoted in *Voices from the Future*, (New York: Crown, 1993), Susan Goodwillie, ed., p. 187.

13. Harry A. Scarr, acting director, Bureau of the Census, letter to Paul Simon, February 25, 1994.

14. "The Holiness Option," by William Sloane Coffin, *New York Times Book Review*, February 18, 1990.

15. Limbaugh, *See, I Told You So*, (New York: Pocket Books, 1993), pp. 63-64.

16. Felix Rohaytn quoted in "How to Create a Million New Jobs," by Hobart Rowen, *Washington Post*, November 26, 1993.

17. Elliott Currie, *Reckoning: Drugs, the Cities, and the American Future*, (New York: Hill and Wang, 1993), pp. 254-256.

18. Speech of Senator Robert Byrd, *Congressional Record,* June 29, 1993, p. S8159.

19. "To Solve a Problem, We Must Face It," by Ellen Warren, *Chicago Tribune,* May 26, 1994.

20. Sen. Daniel Moynihan, statement at Democratic Senators retreat, April 16, 1994.

21. "Reducing Poverty," by Robert Greenstein in *Changing America,* edited by Mark Green, (New York: Newmarket Press, 1992), p. 428.

22. February 2, 1990 *Atlanta Constitution,* quoted in *The Closing Door,* by Gary Orfield and Carole Ashkinaze, (*University Chicago Press,* 1994), p. 74.

23. *Deuteronomy,* 15:11.

Chapter Seven

1. Aristotle, quoted by Diogenes Laertius, Lives of the Philosophers, trans. A. Robert Caponargi, (Chicago: Henry Regnery, 1969), p. 189.

2. Plato, *Timaeus, Great Books of the Western World,* Robert Hutchins, editor, (Chicago: Encyclopedia Britannica, 1952), Vol. 7, p. 474.

3. Plato, *Laws I, Great Books of the Western World,* Vol. 7, p. 648.

4. Augustine, *Confessions I, Great Books of the Western World,* Vol. 18, p. 5.

5. Edward Gibbon, *Decline and Fall of the Roman Empire, Great Books of the Western World,* Vol. 40, p. 88.

6. Alfred North Whitehead, *The Organization of Thought* , 1917), p. 28.

7. Abraham Lincoln, Address to the Wisconsin State Agricultural Society, September 30, 1859, Abraham Lincoln, Speeches and Writings, 1859-1865, (New York: Library of America, 1989), p. 99.

8. John D. Rockefeller III, *The Second American Revolution,* (New York, Harper and Row, 1973), pp. 131-132.

9. "Amid Some Grumbling, Clinton Wins Praise for His Reforms of Arkansas Education," by Goldie Blumenstyk, *Chronicle of Higher Education,* April 29, 1992.

10. Carl Albert, *Little Giant,* (Norman: University of Oklahoma Press, 1990), p. 293.

11. Kevin Phillips, *Boiling Point,* (New York: Random House, 1992), p. 174.

12. H. G. Wells, *The Outline of History,* (get data—chapter 40).

13. Andrew Young, foreword to *The Closing Door,* by Gary Orfield and Carole Ashkinaze, (University of Chicago Press, 1991), p. ix.

14. Lester Thurow, *Head to Head,* (New York: Morrow, 1992), p. 52.

15. Charles Schultze, *Memos to the President*, (Washington: Brookings Institution, 1992), p. 230.

16. Gary Orfield and Carole Ashkinaze, *The Closing Door*, (University of Chicago Press, 1991), p. 190.

17. Lester Thurow, *Head to Head*, (New York: Morrow, 1992), p. 278.

18. *Boston Sunday Globe*, Oct. 7, 1990, Quoted in Deadly Consequences, by Deborah Prothrow-Stith, (New York: Harper Perennial, 1991), p. 162.

19. Quoted in *Within Our Reach*, by Lisbeth Schorr, (New York: Doubleday, 1988), p. xxvii.

20. *Proverbs* 22:6.

21. Michael Forter, *The Competitive Advantage of Nations*, (New York: Free Press, 1990), p. 629.

22. Gary Orfield and Carole Ashkinaze, *The Closing Door*, (University of Chicago Press: 1994), p. 69.

23. Richard Riley, interview with Elizabeth Shogren, *Los Angeles Times*, February 18, 1994.

24. 1987 study, quoted in *The Closing Door*, by Gary Orfield and Carole Ashkinaze, (University of Chicago Press: 1991), p. 127.

25. Patricia Graham, *Sustain Our Schools*, (New York: Hill and Wang, 1992), p. 102.

26. Quoted by Daniel Boorstin in *Hidden History*, (New York; Harper and Row: 1987), p. 195.

27. Walter Lippmann, *American Inquisitors*, (New Brunswick: Transaction, 1953), p. 92.

28. "New Directions in Economic Policy," by Lawrence Summers, in *Knowledge, Power and the Congress*, William Robinson and Clay Wellborn, editors, (Washington: Congressional Quarterly, 1994), p. 189.

29. "Analysis Links Achievement and Spending," by Lonnie Harpl, *Education Week*, March 23, 1994. See also "Does Money Matter?" by Larry Hedges, Richard Laine and Rob Greenwald, *Educational Researcher*, April 1994.

30. Daniel Boorstin, *Hidden History*, (New York: Harper and Row, 1987), p. 72.

31. "The Eternal Question of Suffering and Evil," by Elie Wiesel, 1988 lecture, College of St. Thomas, Minnesota.

Chapter Eight

1. George Bernard Shaw, *Everybody's Political What's What*, (London: Constable, 1944), p. 256.

2. "Challenges to American Policy," by Gerald Ford, *Thinking About America*, Annelise Anderson, Dennis Bark, editors, (Stanford: Hoover Press, 1988), p. 537.

3. John Altgeld, *The Cost of Something for Nothing*, (Chicago: Hammersmark, 1904), pp. 14-15.

4. "Thinking About Cities in the 1990s," by Andrew Young, *Thinking About America*, Annelise Anderson and Dennis Bark, editors, (Stanford: Hoover Press, 1988), pp. 420-421.

5. *Investing in Children and Youth*, (Washington: Milton Eisenhower Foundation, 1992), p. 240.

6. Paul Samuelson, "The Deficit: Danger But Not Doomsday," *New York Newsday*, 18 August 1985.

7. "America's Budget Deficits . . . They Redistribute Income to the Rich," by Richard Koo, International Economy, May/June 1991.

8. *Budget of the United States, Analytical Perspectives*, Fiscal Year 1995, (Washington: Government Printing Office, 1994), p. 25.

9. Warren Buffett letter to Paul Simon, September 27, 1993.

10. Kevin Phillips, *Boiling Point*, (New York: Random House, 1993), p. 256.

11. "Clinton's Big Opportunity," by Benjamin Friedman, *New York Review*, 3 December 1992.

12. "The Decline in U.S. Saving and Its Implications for Economic Growth," by Ethan Harris and Charles Steindel, *NYFRB Quarterly Review*, Winter 1991.

13. *World Economic Outlook*, (Washington: IMF, 1993), p. 99, 102.

14. "The U.S. Trade Deficit: Implications for U.S. Living Standards," by Craig Elwell, paper published by Congressional Research Service, Washington, D.C., 1991.

15. "The Decline in U.S. Saving and Its Implications for Economic Growth," by Ethan S. Harris and Charles Steindel, NYFRB *Quarterly Review*, Winter 1991.

16. Lester Thurow, *Head to Head*, (New York: Morrow, 1992), pp. 234-235.

17. *Ibid.*, p. 233.

18. Martin and Sue Tolchin, *Selling Our Security*, (New York: Knopf, 1992), p. 21.

19. Alice Rivlin, *Reviving The American Dream*, (Washington: Brookings, 1992), p. 41. 2

20. David Calleo, *Beyond American Hegemony*, (New York: Basic Books, 1987), p. 102.

21. Thomas Jefferson, letter to J. W. Eppes, Sept. 1813, The *Jefferson Cyclopedia,* Editor, John Foley, (New York: Funk and Wagnalls, 1900), pp. 226-227.

22. Thomas Jefferson, letter to Samuel Kercheval, July 12, 1816, *Writings of Thomas Jefferson,* Paul Ford, editor, (New York: Putnam, 1899), Vol. 10, p. 41.

23. "Hamilton the Hero," by Thomas K. McCaw, *New York Times,* May 2, 1993.

24. *Ibid.*

25. Testimony, Senator Budget Committee, June 4, 1992.

26. *National Party Platform,* Donald Johnsen, editor, (Urbana: University of Illinois Press, 1978), Vol. 1, p. 98.

27. Andrew Jackson, letter to Dr. L. H. Coleman, 26 April 1824, University of Virginia Library.

28. *MacMillan Book of Business and Economic Quotations,* Paul Blair, editor, (New York: MacMillan, 1984), p. 77.

29. David Calleo, unpublished manuscript, 1993.

30. "Constitutional Imperatives for the 1990s," by James Buchanan, *Thinking About America,* (Stanford: Hoover Press, 1988), pp. 257-258.

31. Paul Tsongas, testimony, Senate Subcommittee on the Constitution, February 15, 1994.

32. Jonathon Rauch, *Demosclerosis* (New York: Times Books, 1994) p. 153.

33. Fred Bergsten, testimony, Senate Subcommittee on the Constitution, February 15, 1994.

34. Robert Myers letter to Paul Simon, February 15, 1994.

35. Paul Tsongas, testimony, Senate Subcommittee on the Constitution, February 15, 1994.

36. "Once Again, Tiptoeing Around the Word," by Marc Levinson, *Newsweek,* April 26, 1993.

37. Edmund Burke, first speech on "Conciliation with America: American Taxation," April 19, 1774, *Dictionary of Quotations,* (New York, Columbia University Press, 1993) p. 893.

38. Carl Curtis, *Forty Years Against the Tide,* (Chicago: Regnery, 1986), p. 159.

39. Alice Rivlin, testimony, House Budget Committee, 8 February 1994.

40. Quoted in "Day of the Dittohead," by David Remnick, *Washington Post,* February 20, 1994.

41. Quoted in "Defeatist Democrats," by David Broder, *Washington Post,* March 7, 1990.

Chapter Nine

1. Quoted in hearing, *Senate Subcommittee on Employment and Productivity*, December 9, 1992, p. 2.

2. Lester Thurow, *Head to Head*, (New York: Morrow, 1992),pp. 164-165.

3. Daniel Moynihan, *Came the Revolution*, (New York: Harcourt Brace Jovanovich, 1988), pp. 21-25.

4. Toyoo Gyohten in *Changing Fortunes*, by Gyohten and Paul Volcker, (New York: Times Books, 1992), p. 185.

5. Lester Thurow, *Zero-Sum Solution*, (New York: Simon and Schuster, 1985), p. 218.

6. "Worrying Over Weakened Unions," by Leonard Silk, *New York Times*, December 13, 1991.

7. "Trading Shots With a Wunderkind," by Steven Pearlstein, *Washington Post*, 3 April 1994.

8. Hoyt Wheeler, testimony before the Commission on the Future of Worker Management Relations, Atlanta, GA., January 11, 1994.

9. "Work Organization, Unions, and Economic Performance," by Ray Marshall, *Unions and Economic Competitiveness*, Lawrence Mishel and Paula Voss, editors, (Armonk, New York: Sharpe, 1992), p. 313.

10. Douglas Fraser, "Employee Participation for Productivity: A Labor View," *Productivity: Prospects for Growth*, Jerome Rosow, editor, (New York: Van Nostrand Reinhold, 1981), p. 310.

11. Stephen Fuller, "Employee Participation for Productivity: A Management View," *Productivity: Prospects for Growth*, Jerome Rosow, editor, (New York: Van Nostrand Reinhold, 1981), p. 308.

12. Amitai Etzioni, *The Spirit of Community*, (New York: Crown, 1993), p. 215.

13. Mancur Olson, "Rational Ignorance, Professional Research, and Politicians' Dilemma," *Knowledge, Power and the Congress*, (Washington: Congressional Quarterly, 1991), pp. 151-152.

14. Peter Peterson, *Facing Up*, (New York: Simon and Schuster, 1993), pp. 241-242.

15. Charles Schultze, *Memos to the President*, (Washington: Brookings, 1992), p. 320.

16. Martin and Sue Tolchin, *Selling Our Security*, (New York: Knopf, 1992), p. 302.

Chapter Ten

1. Paul Kennedy, *Preparing for the Twenty-First Century*, (New York: Random House, 1993), p. 303.

2. Person not identified, transcript, White House press office, 22 March 1994.

3. Editorial, "The Case for Universal Coverage," *Crain's Chicago Business,* February 11, 1994.

4. "Uninsured in America," policy report by the Henry J. Kaiser Family Foundation, January 1994.

5. Dr. James Turner, testimony before hearing conducted by Senator Carol Moseley-Braun and Senator Paul Simon, October 16, 1993.

Chapter Eleven

1. Limbaugh, *See, I Told You So,* (New York: Pocket Books, 1993), p. 105.

2. Ronald Reagan, February 9, 1982 from *Speaking My Mind,* (New York: Simon and Schuster, 1989), p. 427.

3. Quoted in "Water Wars," by Joyce Staff, *Foreign Policy,* Spring 1991.

4. Horace, *Epistles,* Book 1, Epistle 19, trans. and ed. Jacob Fuchs, (New York: Norton, 1977), p. 72.

5. Quoted in "Water Wars," by Joyce Starr, *Foreign Policy,* Spring 1991. The figure used in the original article was 40,000, but UNICEF now uses a 35,000 figure.

6. Edward Kennedy, 22 April 1970, *A People of Compassion: the Concerns of Edward Kennedy,* edited by Thomas P. Collins and Louis M. Savary, (New York: Regina, 1972), p. 69.

7. April 12, 1961, *Public Papers of the President,* John F. Kennedy, (Washington: Government Printing Office, 1962), p. 261.

8. June 21, 1961, *Public Papers of the Presidents,* John F. Kennedy, (Washington: Government Printing Office, 1962), p. 467.

9. Paul Kennedy, *Preparing for the Twenty-First Century,* (New York: Random House, 1993), p. 213.

10. Jimmy Carter, "Challenges Old and New," *Thinking About America,* edited by Annelise Anderson and Dennis Bark, (Stanford: Hoover Institution, 1988), p. 547.

11. Lester Thurow, *Head to Head,* (New York: Morrow, 1992), p. 223.

12. Peter Peterson, *Facing Up,* (New York: Simon and Schuster, 1993), p. 166.

13. Hunter Lovins, Amory Lovins and Richard Heede, "Energy Policy," *Changing America,* edited by Mark Green, (New York: Newmarket Press, 1992), p. 678.

14. Larry Burkett, *Whatever Happened to the American Dream,* (Chicago: Moody Press, 1993), pp. 56-57.

15. Press release of the League of Conservation Voters, May 5, 1994.

16. Arnold Toynbee, *A Study of History*, (New York: Oxford University Press, 1946), p. 255.

Chapter Twelve

1. "His Final Words," by Richard Nixon, *Time, May 2, 1994, excerpted from his book,* Beyond Peace.

2. "In Decolonized, Destitute Africa Bankers Are the New Overlords," by John Darnton, *New York Times,* June 20, 1994.

3. Ronald Reagan, "The United States and the World in the 1990s," *Thinking About America,* Annelise Anderson and Dennis Bark, editors, (Stanford Hoover Press, 1988), p. 564.

4. Lester Thurow, *Head to Head,* (New York: Morrow, 1992), p. 224.

5. George Marshall, speech at Harvard, 5 June 1947.

6. *Life, Death and Aid,* Francois Jean, editor, (New York: Routledge, 1993), p. 107.

7. Albert Beveridge, speech in the Senate, January 9, 1900.

Chapter Thirteen

1. Woodrow Wilson, quoted in "Thoughts on the Business Life," *Forbes,* March 30, 1981.

2. "Courting Rituals," by Eleanor Clift, *Newsweek,* May 23, 1994.

3. Sam Rosenman, quoted in *Truman,* by David McCullough, (New York: Simon and Schuster, 1992), p. 476.

4. "Burleigh," in *Hartford Courant,* September 15, 1800, quoted by John Gardner, *On Leadership,* (New York: Free Press, 1990), p. 160.

5. Haynes Johnson, interview, *Chicago Tribune Magazine,* April 10, 1994.

Hustad, Kathleen, 75
Hyde, Henry, 124

I

I Have a Dream Foundation, 147
IBM, 114
Illinois River, 238
illiteracy, 79, 84, 135
India, 238
industrial policy, 213
inflation, 211
infrastructure, 216
Internal Revenue Service, 156
International Monetary Fund, 171, 181
Investing in Children and Youth, 165
Iran, 41, 68
Iraq, 68
Irving, J. Lawrence, 72
Israel, 175, 193, 241
Italy, 199

J

Jackson, Andrew, 179
Japan, 68, 132, 138, 141, 149, 173, 174, 191, 192, 198, 201, 210, 214, 216, 226, 241
Jefferson, Thomas, 178
Jeffords, James, 153
Jews, 42, 101
Job Opportunities and Basic Skills Program, 125
Johnson, Lyndon, 96
Johnston, Bennett, 34
Jones, Nathaniel, 71

K

Kaiser Family Foundation, 231, 233
Keating, Charles, 19
Kemp, Jack, 62, 123
Kennedy, Edward, 221, 223, 227, 229, 238
Kennedy, Joe, 185
Kennedy, John F., 239
Kennedy, Paul, 221
Kerrey, Robert, 162
Kerry, John, 25, 26
Keyserling, Leon, 211
Khrushchev, Nikita, 237

King, Martin Luther, 95
Kinsley, Michael, 191

L

Lake Erie, 238
Land and Water Conservation Fund, 194
Lang, Eugene, 147
Larry King Show, 38
Limbaugh, Rush, 32, 53, 54, 55, 58, 59, 60, 62, 64, 195
Lincoln, Abraham, 91, 128
long-term health care, 227
Louisville, Ky., 54
LTV Corporation, 26

M

Madison, James, 177
Makanda, Il., 54, 137
mandatory sentencing, 69, 71, 72, 73, 89
Marathon Oil, 201
Marshall Plan, 125
Marshall, George, 38
Marshall, Ray, 209
Martin, Lynn, 25
mass transit, 216, 235
Mauer, Marc, 86
Mauritania, 238
Medicaid, 113, 220
Medicare, 12, 227
Mediterranean Sea, 241
Meese, Edwin, 83
mental health, 228
Mexico, 68, 195, 238
Mill, John Stuart, 32
Miller, Arthur, 110
Miller, Ellen, 31
Miller, George, 240
Milton Eisenhower Foundation, 165
minimum wage, 62
Mitsubishi, 149
Morocco, 238
Moslem religion, 42
Mountains of Debt, 169
Moynihan, Daniel P., 103, 120, 125, 199
Muslims, 100
Myers, Robert, 186